The Contradictions of Neoliberal Agri-Food

VOLUME FOUR

Rural Studies Series
Sponsored by the Rural Sociological Society

The Contradictions of Neoliberal Agri-Food

Corporations, Resistance, and Disasters in Japan

Kae Sekine and Alessandro Bonanno

WEST VIRGINIA UNIVERSITY PRESS

MORGANTOWN 2016

Copyright 2016 West Virginia University Press
All rights reserved
First edition published 2016 by West Virginia University Press
Printed in the United States of America

24 23 22 21 20 19 18 17 16   1 2 3 4 5 6 7 8 9

ISBN:
pb   978-1-943665-19-8
epub   978-1-943665-20-4
pdf   978-1-943665-21-1

Library of Congress Cataloging-in-Publication Data
is available from the Library of Congress

Cover design by Than Saffel
Book design by Than Saffel
Cover image by Kae Sekine

CONTENTS

ACKNOWLEDGMENTS

This book is the result of a long-standing conversation among ourselves and between us and members of the agri-food intellectual community. Arguably, among the intellectual communities that identify themselves with the term *rural studies*, the agri-food community is one of the most prolific and critical of dominant socioeconomic arrangements. It is first and foremost to the authors who belong to this intellectual community and who write about the limits of Neoliberalism in Japan, in the United States, and in other parts of the world that we owe a debt of gratitude. Their insights into the conditions of the Neoliberalization of agriculture and food, their various readings of its contradictions, and their proposed solutions to existing problems inspired our thinking and writing. We would also like to thank all the people who participated in the interviews employed in the writing of this book. Their observations, comments, criticisms, and hopes provided us with invaluable information. A number of individuals specifically contributed to the completion of this book. We express our gratitude to all of them. In particular, however, we thank Billy R. Brocato. His first-hand knowledge of Japan, its culture, economy, and politics made his comments and suggestions invaluable. Thank you, Bill, for all your support. We also acknowledge the contribution of Debbra Vogel, who through her editorial suggestions greatly improved the readability of this volume. Mary Emery provided valuable comments at various stages of this project and effectively supported our effort. Last but not least, we thank Ray Jussaume for his penetrating and always accurate comments. His understanding of Japanese agri-food and Japan helped us tremendously. While we are grateful to all those who directly and indirectly assisted us in the writing of this book, we remain fully responsible for its content and possible errors.

Kae Sekine and Alessandro Bonanno
Nagoya, Aichi,
September 2015

Introduction

This book is about the neoliberalization of the Japanese agri-food sector. More specifically, it is about the consequences of the introduction of measures and policies that are based on the theory of Neoliberalism. This is the theory that, in recent years, has guided the restructuring of the Japanese economy and society and, within it, the agri-food sector. The investigation into the implementation of neoliberal measures in Japanese agri-food is complemented by analyses of three additional and interrelated themes. The first refers to the impact of the March 2011 triple disaster (earthquake, tsunami, and the meltdown of the Fukushima Daiichi nuclear reactor) that garnered worldwide shock. The devastation generated by this multiple event and the manner in which it was used to further liberalize farming and fishing are relevant reasons to include it in this volume. Second, one of the most decisive dimensions of the neoliberalization of the Japanese economy is the government design to expand the presence of corporations in agri-food. Accompanied by corporate plans to invest in the sector, the corporatization of agri-food is a defining dimension of contemporary Japan. Importantly, this book reveals how a major departure from the established policies enacted after War World II promoting the ownership of farmland and fishing rights by family-based operations led to current neoliberal policies that undermined Japan's traditional agri-food sector. Finally, we focus on resistance to the neoliberalization and corporatization of agri-food. While Neoliberalism is dominant in Japan, as in many other parts of the world, and political groups that support it were successful in recent elections, the opposition that it engenders is significant. This is also the case for the events illustrated throughout the book. Accordingly, an analysis of the neoliberalization of Japanese agri-food could not be effectively carried out without a review of the opposition that it creates among farmers, fishermen, consumers, and other relevant actors.

In pertinent literature, the concept of agri-food is employed to define the complex system that covers the production, distribution, and consumption of agricultural and food products. It is associated with analyses of the social relations, actors, and institutions that characterize this sector. In this book, we follow this general tradition. However, we focus almost exclusively on the production side of agriculture and food, paying particular attention to the evolution of farming and fishing, the major actors involved in these activities, and pertinent policies and actions of the state at various levels. The complexity of the topic and the intended size of the book motivated us to confine our analysis to these topics. In this book, we underscore the behavior of relevant groups. However, we also approach our study from a systemic point of view, stressing the position of agri-food in the overall context of the Japanese economy and society. This multifaceted approach is employed to avoid the perils associated with economistic renderings of the evolution of agri-food and, simultaneously, postures that stress the behavior of individual actors as the primary focus of analysis. In the case of the former, we try to transcend readings that look at agri-food mostly in terms of its economic performance and those of its components. In the case of the latter, we hope to go beyond the position that sees in the actions and rationality of farmers, fishermen, and relevant institutions explanations of the evolution of the sector.

There are at least four reasons that convinced us of the relevance of this project. First, Neoliberalism is one of the most discussed topics in scientific and political circles. However, and quite surprisingly, there are relatively few analyses of Neoliberalism in agri-food. Additionally, when discussed, it is treated in incomplete and rather distorted ways. In this book, we summarize—albeit succinctly—the basic tenets of Neoliberalism and discuss its implementation in, and consequences for, Japanese agri-food. Second, while Japan is one of the most important economies and societies in the world, its agri-food sector is a theme that has received limited attention by the international scientific community. Only a handful of works have been published in English, while contributions published in Japanese are rarely translated into major Western languages. By providing an updated analysis of the evolution of the sector and its status, we hope to contribute to the reduction of this gap. Moreover, the works published on this topic tend to examine agri-food in sectorial and economic terms, often downplaying the social and systemic dimensions that it entails. In this book, we contribute to the existing debate by stressing the social and systemic dimensions of Japanese agri-food and, in so doing, provide a novel explanation of its contradictions and problems.

Third, Japanese agri-food is, in itself, a unique case to study the neoliberalization and corporatization of social relations. Since the early post–World War II years, not only Japanese agri-food but also the entire economy have been regulated by a strong interventionist state. While this Fordist approach differed from the versions applied in Europe and North America, it created a sector that was heavily dependent on state support. Simultaneously, agri-food performed in ways that permitted the rapid and successful growth of manufacturing, and with it, of the entire Japanese economy and society. The introduction of Neoliberalism clashes with this tradition and proposes the alteration of embedded cultural, social, and economic behaviors. This situation, we believe, makes it a unique field of study. Finally, much of the literature introduced in the book has been available only in Japanese and circulated within Japanese scholarly circles. By discussing it in English, we provide a bridge between the Japanese and international audiences interested in these themes. In recent years, a sustained effort to open domestic debates to international audiences has characterized the activities of Japanese academia. We hope to contribute to this effort.

Neoliberalism

As mentioned above, central to this book is the theory and practices of Neoliberalism. Stressing the numerous readings of this theory that have emerged in recent years, the economic philosopher Philip Morowski defines Neoliberalism as a "thought collective." Also, and joining a large group of scholars (e.g., Brown 2015; Crouch 2011; Dumenil and Levy 2011; Harvey 2005a; Stedman Jones 2012; Stiglitz 2013), he underscores the fact that Neoliberalism is a political program that, however, contains conflicting calls and contrasting views (Mirowski 2013). In effect, it is virtually impossible to provide an all-encompassing and synthetic definition of Neoliberalism. It has too many variations and different applications to be reduced to such a definition (Wolf and Bonanno 2014). Yet, some of its tenets are recurrent elements that make up the policies and measures applied in Japanese agri-food and in other countries around the world. Among these characteristics pertinent to this study are the following.

First, Neoliberalism is different from classical Laissez-Faire Liberalism. Neoliberalism rejects the idea of the nonintervening state in favor of selective state intervention. The state is not required to implement measures that, ultimately, protect the lower and middle classes from the unwanted consequences of capitalism. Simultaneously, however, it is called on to intervene in favor of the creation of markets—that is, the marketization of society—and the maintenance of the conditions that allow these markets' undisturbed functioning. The state is also called on to intervene in support of large corporations during economic and political crises as the well-being of corporations is equated to the well-being of society. The role of the state is, therefore, to construct markets, protect corporations, and act in defense of the neoliberal view. The ultimate objective of

3

Neoliberalism is to create a system centered on the continuous existence and reproduction of unconstrained market relations.

Second, the control and regulation of the economy and society is transferred from the state to the private sector through the proliferation of third-party regulators.[1] In this context, the state does not shrink (this is mostly confined to its social services and welfare, as indicated above) but becomes the major actor in the marketization of society. Political decisions are transferred to the market, so that "what is good for the market is good for society," and the market is viewed as the desirable generator of policies. Accordingly, there is no separation between the market and the state. Additionally, the assumed impartiality of market outcomes disqualifies the notion of the desirability of politically discussed and agreed-on decisions and the democratic process that they entail. Politically agreed-on decisions are defined as always imperfect and the result of the actions of powerful groups. Sustaining this view is the assumption of the superiority of individual freedom over democracy. Individual freedom is the condition that allows the functioning of the free market, but it is also possible only through the free functioning of the market. Democracy always mandates a restriction of individual freedom as the majority rules over the minority and, therefore, it is an obstacle to the free functioning of the economy and the prospering of society.

Third, substantive freedom is not a goal. The only freedom sought is that of the market. In this context, inequality is accepted as a condition of and for the market, as it promotes efficiency (best allocation of resources) and progress (incentives to modernize and grow). The market is elevated to the ultimate indicator of desirable social arrangements, because it contains all the necessary pieces of information that no group of humans can ever match. In this context, the free functioning of the market creates objective and fair values through the establishment of prices for goods, services, and labor. Accordingly, the market is natural and impartial, and citizens should be treated as consumers to take advantage of the goodness of the market system. The separation between market outcomes that are impartial and political decisions that are partial must be maintained through the intervention of the state.

Finally, the distinction between humans and corporations is erased. Neoliberalism treats humans as capital that needs to be managed accordingly. People are seen as if they were enterprises. Individuality and individualization become paramount. The individual is placed at the center of society, and social organizations are transformed into agglomerates of individuals. As problems are reduced to the behavior of individuals, solutions are also left in the hands of individuals operating in the market. Accordingly, more markets must be created to address problems. Inequality, success, failure, and poverty, for instance, are all outcomes of individual actions and market processes.

Thesis of the Book

The book's primary thesis is that a fundamental socioeconomic and cultural incompatibility exists between the neoliberal proposal and the sociohistorical conditions of Japanese farming and fishing. This situation led to a progressive crisis of the sector, whose consequences are felt by many of the people who live off agri-food production and the rural areas that they call home. We contend that in the post–World War II socioeconomic development model adopted in Japan, agri-food played a secondary, yet not negligible, role. In that model, the expansion of the economy was successfully centered on the development of urban manufacturing and the export of its products. The structurally fragmented and economically inefficient agri-food sector was deemed to be inadequate for international competition and as a sector that could promote economic growth. However, a large portion of available workers resided in rural areas and worked in agriculture and fishing. Accordingly, the progressive release of this labor force through rural to urban migration represented a fundamental factor in the expansion of manufacturing and the economy as a whole. Simultaneously, the persistence of small family farms and fishing operations allowed the relative stability of rural communities, the production of local food, and the stewardship of the environment. The importance of these conditions explains the social and political relevance of protectionist measures that characterized agri-food for decades.

In macro socioeconomic terms, access to consumer good global markets was fundamental for the economic expansion of Japan. Accordingly, large Japanese corporations' ability to acquire a significant share of the industrial world market and maintain this position for a number of years became paramount. Simultaneously, the concomitant request from other world powers—chiefly the United States—to open the Japanese agri-food market to imports showed the economic weakness of the sector but also allowed a flow of much cheaper food imports. While low food prices hurt local production, they benefited the industrial sector, as the cost of maintaining the growing urban working class was contained.

The crisis of the Fordist regime in the United States and Europe found Japan at the height of its economic expansion. It could be argued that the lack of competiveness of North American and European multinational corporations and the fiscal crisis of the corresponding nation-states occurred at a time when pertinent global markets were largely under the control of Japanese corporations. Paradoxically, the existence in Japan of a much less developed and modernized agri-food industry and the roles that it played in the overall socioeconomic system were contributing factors in the achievement of this economically prominent position.

Forced to react to the post-Fordist global restructuring and the emerging requirements of Neoliberal globalization, Japan's postwar expansion model entered its final crisis. Following a phase of financial speculation and asset appreciation, in the late 1980s the country entered a long period of stagnation and deflation that continued into the second decade of the twenty-first century. The solution often advocated, but also partially resisted, was that of the neoliberalization of the economy. By the end of the first decade of the new century, agri-food, like the rest of the country, entered a period of market deregulation and liberalization in line with the basic tenets of Euro-American Neoliberalism. The point that we stress in this book is the incompatibility of the requirements of Neoliberalism with the structural and cultural conditions of Japanese farming and fishing.

Structurally, Japanese farms could not compete with world producers in terms of both basic commodities (such as rice) and specialized food items (such as fruits and vegetables, cheese and meat products). On the one hand, the gap with highly productive farming sectors worldwide was too large to be overcome even through the process of corporatization of productive units that characterized the neoliberalization of agriculture. On the other hand, the relatively limited dimension of niche markets for specialized products and the minor presence of geographical identification[2] policies and products prevented the emergence of relevant alternative growth patterns for family farms. Culturally, the emphasis on community collective decisionmaking and participation in the management of natural resources clashes with the focus on individualism and competitiveness advocated by Neoliberalism. Accordingly, Neoliberalism continues to remain a "foreign" entity in the culture of rural Japan. Faced with these two types of incompatibility, Neoliberalism is a difficult road to travel for Japanese farming and fishing and, to a similar extent, for the rest of society. Its anticrisis prescription of additional marketization of the economy contains all the requisites for the building of a legitimation crisis. Prime Minister Abe's insistence on the use of Neoliberalism and his success in the December 2014 political elections signal an uncertain future for the country.

Organization of the Book

The book is divided into nine chapters. Following this introduction, chapter 1 reviews salient literature published in English and Japanese. The first section reviews the literature on the neoliberalization of Japanese agri-food. This literature stresses the negative consequences of neoliberalization but also indicates the ability of rural residents to establish spaces of resistance. Contributions that analyze the consequences of the triple disaster of March 2011 are reviewed in the second section, while the third section analyzes works on the corporatization of agri-food. The concluding section of the chapter provides a review of the literature on the relatively understudied topic of resistance to the neoliberal restructuring of agri-food.

Chapter 2 presents a synthesis of the evolution of the Japanese agricultural and fishing sector from the post–World War II years to 2010. The goal is to provide the reader with a review of salient socioeconomic events that characterized this component of the Japanese economy and society. It opens with a review of the development of agriculture and fishing during the post–World War II era, including the postwar reconstruction process, the years of *Rapid Economic Growth*, and its end in the early 1970s. The chapter continues by covering changes that occurred from the mid-1970s to 2010. This section of the chapter illustrates the characteristics of the shift from Fordism to Neoliberalism and the growth of globalization. The chapter concludes by describing the expansion of the presence of transnational corporations and the establishment of a business-friendly procorporate environment.

Chapter 3 provides analyses of pertinent events that unfolded after the earthquake, tsunami, and meltdown of the Fukushima-Daiichi nuclear reactor of March 2011. This chapter stresses the acceleration of the introduction of neoliberal agri-food policies that characterized this period. The Japanese government approached reconstruction of affected agricultural and fishing areas through the implementation of measures that centered on the further strengthening of market deregulation, the promotion of the involvement of large private firms, and the reduction of wealth redistribution and social welfare measures. Accordingly and following neoliberal tenets, the case of Japan can be described as characterized by the subordination of state intervention to corporate plans. The chapter illustrates the severity and complexity of the consequences of the disasters and reviews salient postures and actions of major actors, such as corporations, the state, farmers, fishermen, and consumers. The contested and socially constructed dimensions of the triple disaster are highlighted.

Through an analysis of cases involving four corporations—Dole Japan, Kagome, IBM, and Sendai Suisan—the expansion of the corporate presence in agri-food production is explored in chapter 4. It is argued that the adoption of neoliberal policies promoted the corporatization of agri-food that was identified as the solution for the limited development of the sector. The first of the four cases presented illustrates this process through an analysis of the actions of Dole Japan. This is a subsidiary of the Dole Food Company, one of the largest global corporations in the fresh fruit and vegetable trading sector. The second case refers to Kagome. Kagome is a major tomato ketchup and juice maker with corporate roots in Japan; a worldwide market; and a global network of farms, contractors, and processing facilities. The third case involves the IBM subsidiary, IBM Japan, a corporation that is registered as a "non-agri-food" firm. Yet, like other information technology corporations, it has entered the agri-food market in search for new sources of profit. The fourth and final case is about Sendai Suisan, a seafood trading company. Sendai Suisan is a dominant corporation at the regional level in Tohoku and the first private corporation to obtain fishing rights. These rights were granted in one of the Special Zones for Reconstruction (SZRs) established after the 2011 disasters.

Chapter 5 continues the analysis of the corporatization of Japanese agri-food by further reviewing direct investment strategies carried out by Dole Japan. It investigates this corporation's industrial plans and actions but also the opposition that it has encountered from local farmers, farmers' cooperatives, authorities, and other local actors. The chapter opens with an analysis of the system of operation of Dole Japan's farms, its branding strategies, sales, and impact on local farming. It continues by reviewing the case of one of Dole Japan's farms, the I LOVE Nittan Farm located in the prefecture of Hokkaido in northern Japan. This narrative illustrates how the Nittan Farm successfully expanded its size, displayed significant power in negotiations with local government agencies, and established itself in the local farming sector. The case of the I LOVE Izumi Farm in the Prefecture of Kagoshima, in the Kyushu region is also presented. Following a pattern virtually opposite that of the Nittan Farm, the Izumi Farm failed to increase its size and could not consolidate available land. This outcome, we contend, is the result of the opposition from landowners that motivated Dole Japan to quickly close this farm. Dole eventually relocated it to the Prefecture of Nagasaki in the Kyushu region, responding to local leaders' invitations to move this operation to the area. The third and final case analyzed in this chapter involves the I LOVE Tome Farm located in Miyagi Prefecture in the Tohoku region. The Tome Farm is the only farm that produces paprika in greenhouses, as all other Dole Japan's farms grow vegetables in open fields.

Primarily, the case of the Tome Farm illustrates the discrepancy between expectations about corporate-induced socioeconomic growth harbored by local government officials and actual consequences of the establishment of this farm.

Chapter 6 investigates the corporate agri-food strategies implemented in the aftermath of the triple disaster. After the Great East Japan Earthquake, tsunami, and nuclear reactor meltdown of March 11, 2011, neoliberal-inspired reconstruction policies were quickly adopted centering on the establishment of SZRs, or areas endowed with special incentives to attract corporate investment. These policies followed the "Creative Reconstruction" approach that saw in the deregulation and reduced public oversight of private initiatives the necessary formula to reignite economic growth and social development. While state financial intervention was necessary to subsidize and trigger an inflow of private investment, it was seen as a move that would actually reduce state expenditures and provide a more robust economic expansion. In this chapter, the case of corporate-sponsored agri-food production for the fresh market of Sendai City in the Prefecture of Miyagi is presented. This initiative was originally conceived to promote a business-friendly environment in which local farmers and corporations, such as Kagome and IBM, would cooperate and, as a result, promote the growth of agriculture and the sustainability of local rural communities. Despite these plans, local farmers and residents became dissatisfied with, and eventually opposed, this project. The chapter illustrates the general conditions of agriculture in Sendai City, the local consequences of the Great East Japan Earthquake, and the associated recovery process. Following this section, the chapter reviews the Sendai City SZR program and the implantation of the Michisaki Farm. The latter is a production project involving local farmers and corporations that was opposed by farmers and local residents. Local resistance hampered corporate plans, which had to be scaled back. Reduced employment and land utilization resulted from this move. Simultaneously, the lack of tangible benefits for local farmers and residents and their limited involvement in the decisionmaking process were decisive factors in the emergence of dissatisfaction with, and opposition to, reconstruction plans. Resistance, the chapter contends, remained uncoordinated, as both grassroots mobilization and institutional support did not materialize. Finally, the chapter argues that this neoliberal theory–inspired process of reconstruction required strong state involvement despite pronouncements about the saliency of private initiatives, and it engendered consequences that did not satisfy local farmers and also created problems for corporations.

Chapter 7 examines the liberalization of fishing rights, the postdisaster reorganization of the fishing sector, and resistance triggered by these reconstruction plans in the Tohoku region, the coastal area adjacent to the epicenter of the 2011 earthquake. In this region, many fishermen lost their lives, boats, and homes, while fishing ports and grounds became unusable as structural damage, debris, and radioactivity affected operations. The national government as well as local administrations solicited corporate investment to reconstruct and restructure. Following this policy, Yoshihiro Murai, the governor of the Prefecture of Miyagi, established a SZR for one of the fishing communities of Ishinomaki City in the Prefecture of Miyagi. Promoting economic restructuring and profitability, reconstruction plans included the granting of fishing rights to corporations and the elimination of small fishing ports used by family-owned boats. Fishermen, cooperatives, and residents denounced this plan as a way to use public funds to promote private interests and eliminate small and family-owned fishing operations, fishing cooperatives, and, ultimately, to avoid addressing the economic and social needs of the local population. This chapter first reviews the conditions of fisheries in Ishinomaki City. Then it illustrates the process that led to the establishment of the SZR in this area along with the local resistance that it engendered. Finally, the case of an alternative reconstruction project that was carried out in the area is discussed.

Chapter 8 provides some specific conclusions about the four central themes of this book. In particular, it first offers some concluding observations on the characteristics of Neoliberalism and the consequences of its adoption in Japanese agri-food. It stresses the limits of this policy both in terms of the support of family farming and fishing and as a system of production and a way of life. Additionally, the chapter contends that limited understanding of the characteristics of Neoliberalism opens the door for the proposition of alternatives that do not actually transcend the parameters of this ideology. Second, the chapter comments on the use of Neoliberalism to address the consequences of disasters in farming and fishing communities. The local resistance that it engenders is widespread yet variable, resulting in the concomitant existence of organized and much stronger episodes of opposition and atomized and weaker forms of resistance. As the government insists on the corporatization of rural areas, the solutions to the problems created by the application of Neoliberalism are sought in the creation of more markets and further neoliberalization. Third, the chapter proposes some conclusions on the pro-market intervention of the government. The government sees corporatization of the sector as an effective strategy to address economic stagnation and structural weakness. This discourse is supported by claims that describe family farming and fishing as ineffective, inefficient, and run by aging operators who offer little hope for the growth of market competitiveness. The limits of the adoption of Neoliberalism are illustrated by an analysis of the gaps between neoliberal pronouncements and the actual conditions concerning labor relations, outcomes and quantity of investment, the mobility of capital, and the fiscal soundness of proposed policies.

Finally, this chapter probes the reasons, conditions, and forms of resistance that developed in opposition to neoliberal agri-food policies and corporate involvement in agri-food production. In this section, the differences between more successful forms of resistance in the fishing sector and instances of individualized and overall weaker resistance in farming are evaluated. It is argued that these differences can be explained through four points. First, the introduction of SZRs created a new and unprecedented context that allowed corporations to acquire fishing rights. Second, opposition occurred with the presence of some strong institutional leadership in the fishing cooperative structure. This situation did not materialize for the farming sector. Farmer organizations' loyalty to the government prevents them from mobilizing and coordinating opposition. Third, fishing sector opposition enjoyed external political support and significant press coverage. Finally, fishermen and their cooperatives enjoyed the powerful support of nongovernmental organizations, consumer cooperatives, residents, and intellectuals.

Chapter 9 provides a systemic view of the evolution of agri-food under Neoliberalism. It begins by stressing the relevance of agri-food in the overall post–World War II growth model. It is argued that it was because, rather than in spite of, the less "advanced" status of farming and fishing that the impressive success of the Japanese growth model was possible. In this context, the chapter offers a reading of the sector that emphasizes the totality of the socioeconomic evolution of the country and the conditions that made farming and fishing functional in the postwar growth period but contradictory in the following decades. By presenting a succinct review of the basic tenets of Neoliberalism, their incompatibility with the more collectivist, cooperative, communal-oriented practices and culture of rural Japan are illustrated. Dwelling on Habermas's (1975) concepts of crisis of legitimation, a reading of the current crisis of social integration and system integration is proposed. The incompatibility between the local culture and practices with the neoliberal approach, it is contended, creates contradictions that cannot be addressed through available instruments. Accordingly, the inadequacy of the implementation of neoliberal measures translated into a systemic crisis that could hardly be addressed through the introduction of a course of economic policy implemented by Prime Minister Shinzo Abe, or "Abenomics." In effect, the economic policy that Abenomics proposes for the agri-food sector is a continuation of the neoliberal path employed in recent years and offers market solutions to problems that have their origins in these very market mechanisms. It is concluded that, while evaluations of Abenomics are premature at best, its problematic nature leaves little optimism for a future in which the aspiration of farmers, fishermen, and their communities along with those who hope for the betterment of the systems of production and consumption of food are fulfilled.

NOTES

1. The agri-food sector is one of the most notable examples, as it is characterized by the significant growth of third-party certification schemes to ensure the quality of its products (Busch 2014).

2. The concept of geographical indication (or GI) refers to names employed to define specific products generated in specific geographical locations. These locations are historically recognized as the places of origin of the products in question. GI labels are used to certify that products possess qualities that other similar products do not have.

CHAPTER 1

Agri-Food in Japan

A Literature Review

Introduction

This chapter reviews the salient literature regarding the agri-food sector in Japan. We explore relevant contributions that address the four themes of the book: the implementation of neoliberal measures, the impact of disasters, the role and actions of corporations, and resistance to the neoliberalization and corporatization of agri-food. Accordingly, the chapter is divided into four sections. In the first section, we examine works that deal with the neoliberalization of Japanese agri-food and its consequences, along with contributions that discuss the role and position of social institutions and relevant actors in the sector. Further, we divide the literature into English-language and Japanese contributions, thus introducing the copious literature originally published in Japanese to an international audience. This group of works is dominated by analyses that examine the agri-food sector using a political economy approach. We also review some works that are exemplary of studies employing different theoretical perspectives. While most of the works reviewed tend to conflate Neoliberalism and globalization, the analyses of the liberalization of markets and its consequences provide a significant analytical basis for subsequent chapters in the volume.

The second section reviews the literature on the consequences for the agri-food and rural regions embedded in the triple disaster of March 2011. This literature is organized into three categories. The first includes works that focus on the Fukushima-Daiichi nuclear power plant meltdown and the consequent radioactive contamination of agri-food products. The second category includes studies that probe the damage that the triple disaster generated to local farming and food supply chains and that analyze the characteristics of the reconstruction process. Finally, authors included in the third category emphasize the role that the public sector and public policies played in the reconstruction process. Nearly all works in this literature are critical of the process of reconstruction that followed the 2011 disasters. The results demonstrate that the implementation of neoliberal measures becomes a tool that empowers large corporations and diminishes the well-being of family farm holders and local communities. However, some authors contend that the promotion of neoliberal measures by local and national governments opens up some of the democratic spaces available in the private sphere that are not available in the public sphere.

The third section reviews contributions on the corporatization of agri-food. We focus on the neoliberal-inspired expansion of corporations in the sector and its consequences. This literature is further divided into four areas. One area is formed by early studies that introduced international debates to a local audience and, consequently, ignited the growth of empirical and theoretical studies on the topic. The second portion of this group includes authors who investigate the expansion of transnational corporations (TNCs) in countries other than Japan, including the United States, while the third group includes analyses of Japanese food trading and food processing corporations and their global activities. The fourth and final portion of the literature review concerns the growing number of works studying foreign and Japanese agri-food corporations that promote capital investments in Japan.

The final section of this chapter reviews works associated with episodes and processes of resistance. It discusses the evolution of this literature, stressing the recent surge in research on opposition to the neoliberalization and corporatization of agri-food. Despite this recent spate of publications, it is concluded, the overall theme of resistance is poorly discussed in Japan as the theme of opposition to dominant actors in agri-food.

The review of works on the four themes of the book informs the analysis that we carry out in the rest of this volume.

Research into Japanese rural sociology is extensive. Yet the agri-food scholarship is at best in a state of "relative isolationism." The term "isolationism" refers to the fact that relevant debates are largely confined to works published in Japanese and circulated within Japan. The limited familiarity of international readers with Japanese agri-food and the concomitant limited publication of local works in English and other major Western languages contribute to this situation. Additionally, the cultural perception, once common among Japanese scholars, that Japanese life and social relations could not be accurately analyzed in languages other than Japanese is a fundamental contributing factor (see chapter 9). This situation is relatively fluid for two basic reasons. First, recently the Japanese scholarly community has begun to internationalize its research, which has led to the proliferation of publications in English and other languages. Second, works are being written in English by a small, yet very prolific, group of Western agri-food scholars who specialize in Japanese studies (e.g., Jussaume 1994a, 1994b, 1991, 1990; Jussaume and Higgins 1998; Jussaume, Hisano, and Taniguchi 2000) and by an equally small but prolific group of Japanese sociologists who are or were associated with Western academic institutions (e.g., Iba and Sakamoto 2014; Kimura 2013, 2010; Kimura and Katano 2014; Sakamoto, Choi, and Burmeister 2007; Tanaka 2008). These authors often employ the case of Japanese agri-food not only to discuss issues pertaining to Japan but also to participate in international debates. In essence, the increasing global interconnectedness of the sociological community is at work to alter this "relative isolationism."

The Neoliberalization of Agri-Food in Japan

The debate on Neoliberalism accelerated in the mid-2000s after the introduction of translated works, such as the popular essay on the history of Neoliberalism by the British social geographer David Harvey (2005a; see also Harvey 2005b). Since then, a significant number of works has populated the local literature focusing on the characteristics of Neoliberalism and its implementation in the country (e.g., Hamada, Kayshap, and Weinstein 2011; Hashimoto 2014; Hattori 2013). In the case of agri-food, numerous publications and related interpretations have fueled international debates on the hegemonic position of Neoliberalism, its consequences, and resistance to it (Wolf and Bonanno 2014). These publications had a relatively limited impact on local debates but were quite relevant to works about Japan published in English. In effect, this literature can be divided into two nearly parallel camps. The first is represented by analyses of Neoliberalism in agri-food in Japan published in English and the other refers to works covering the same topic but published in Japanese.

The Literature in English

In the case of works published in English, the size of the literature is quite limited, primarily because only a limited number of pertinent documents and scientific papers essential for these analyses are available in languages other than Japanese. This situation makes it difficult for non-Japanese speakers to study agri-food in Japan. Accordingly, and as indicated above, this production is the almost exclusive prerogative of a small groups of Japanese researchers working abroad and of non-Japanese scholars who specialize in Japanese studies. Among the latter, it is important to mention the seminal work of Raymond Jussaume

Jr. and his associates (e.g., Jussaume 1994a, 1994b, 1991, 1990; Jussaume and Higgins 1998; Jussaume, Hisano, and Taniguchi 2000; Jussaume and Judson 1992). For this discussion, the significance of Jussaume's work rests on his illustration of the first stages of the process of deregulation of Japanese agri-food and the implications that it had on relevant actors and, in particular, on family farmers and consumers. Because his sociological work appeared almost exclusively in the 1990s, documenting the early stages of the neoliberalization of Japanese agri-food, Jussaume is credited with introducing Japan to the international agri-food audience. As the contours of the neoliberal restructuring were not completely clear at the time, Jussaume's analysis elucidated the fundamental characteristics and consequences of the neoliberalization of Japanese agri-food, including the corporatization of the sector, the crisis of family farming, and the opposition that these processes engendered. Central to his thesis of crisis in the sector is the growing pro-food safety sensitivity of Japanese consumers that allowed him to forecast correctly the anticorporate mobilization in support of the production of quality food and the growing connection between interest in personal health and food safety.

Contributions that are more recent tackle the consequences of the full adoption of Neoliberalism in the country. Kiyohiko Sakamoto and his associates (Iba and Sakamoto 2014; Sakamoto, Choi, and Burmeister 2007) study the farming sector and rural regions, and they analyze Neoliberalism in terms of the construction of possible alternatives. The theme of alternatives to Neoliberalism is also addressed by Aya Kimura through various publications (Kimura 2013, 2010; Kimura and Katano 2014). Stressing the importance of feminist theory to the study and reorganization of agri-food, Kimura's work is relevant for this discussion because of her analyses of new forms of regulation and the consequences of the nuclear disaster (see chapter 3 and later in this chapter).

The contributions of these two authors are important, as they examine the shortcomings of neoliberal postures adopted to reorganize agri-food. Sakamoto and his associates point out that the neoliberalization of farming increases this sector's crisis as the important vital roles performed by farming in the past are compromised and the hoped-for increases in productivity and international competitiveness have proved difficult to achieve. They contend that high costs of labor and land hamper any real possibility of increasing productivity to competitive levels. For Kimura, the existence of alternative agri-food networks is a fundamental aspect of current conditions in Japan that needs serious evaluation to help build a better future.

However, they also share a common and relatively positive view of the effects of neoliberalization in agri-food and rural regions. In his work with Iba (Iba and Sakamoto 2014), Sakamoto stresses that the neoliberal deregulation and concomitant reduction of local services mobilize communities and generate new process of solidarity that ultimately lead to local groups' empowerment. Recognizing the dominant power of Neoliberalism, they also stress the availability of opportunities for resistance and the creation of alternatives. Kimura, who through her analysis of food certification schemes emphasizes the emancipatory dimension associated with this process, maintains a similar position. Arguably, both these convergent positions can be viewed as theorizations that underscore the dialectic of domination, whereby processes of domination also contain elements that contribute to the liberation of subordinate groups. As emphasized by Kimura, the development of critical subjectivities is central to emancipatory processes. At the same time, though, this reliance of subjectivity and processes of self-help brings to mind classical discussions of "artificial negativity,"[1] in which administered forms of control are interpreted as emancipatory. Additionally, the situations lauded by these authors do little to alter the processes of neoliberalization and corporatization. For example, discussed in the following chapters, the once politically controlled access to land and fishing rights has been deregulated to favor the increasing presence of corporations.

The Literature in Japanese

The camp containing works written in Japanese is significantly larger. Interestingly, and to different degrees, virtually all these contributions treat the neoliberalization of agri-food as part of the process of globalization[2] (e.g., Kagatsume 2007; Nakano and Sugiyama 2001; Taniguchi 2008). Regardless of this focus on globalization, this literature can be organized into two distinct groups. The first, and much larger, group contains works that employ a political economy approach. They study agri-food in terms of the economic interests and political influence (or lack of it) of salient actors and document the consequences that the implementation of neoliberal policies have had for the various social groups and the sector. The second, and much smaller, group includes contributions that approach the issue of the neoliberalization of agri-food from other theoretical perspectives. Given its size, the political economy group can be further divided into three subgroups. The first discusses the implementation of neoliberal measures in agri-food almost exclusively in terms of the consequences of globalization of the economy and society; the second offers an analysis that tackles Neoliberalism in a more direct manner; the third group focuses on future policies that could address Neoliberalism's consequences.

The political economy group: Neoliberalism as part of globalization. The first group of the political economy camp can be further divided into two types of analyses. The first focuses on market liberalization and the creation of institutions that promote it, such as the General Agreement on Tariffs and Trade (GATT), the World Trade Organization (WTO), and, more recently, the Trans-Pacific Partnership (TPP), while the second includes studies that take a closer look at the consequences of Neoliberalism for agri-food and rural areas. As part of the first subgroup, in separate works Chiba (2001) and Murata (2003) map out the gradual trade liberalization of agri-food and study the negotiation processes characterizing the creation and expansion of GATT, the WTO, the bilateral Free Trade Agreements (FTA), and the Economic Partnership Agreements (EPA). In Particular, Murata stresses the relevance of corporate agendas for shaping these negotiations and for related domestic policy reforms. Additionally, and as they focus on the international arena, both Murata and Chiba tend to explain market liberalization in terms of the interests of salient nation-states and their geopolitical interests. In a similar fashion, Tashiro (2011) provides a political economy analysis of the negotiations for the establishment of TPP, probing not only its economic aspects but also its geopolitical and military dimensions. While this author contends that farm-income support policies follow from Neoliberalism, he also equates Neoliberalism with market fundamentalism.

The second subgroup contains works that critically examine the impact of globalization on agri-food and rural areas (e.g., Fujii 2007; Okada 2007). Both Fujii (2007) and Okada (2007) identify in market liberalization and the consequent growth of agri-food imports two factors that promote the decline of local production, the deterioration of the living conditions of rural communities, the reduction of the rural population, and the abandonment of agricultural land. Moreover, Fujii (2007) documents the decline in agricultural land prices and profitability that followed the introduction of neoliberal measures in the mid-1980s. According to Fujii, this is one of the outcomes of the dominant roles that transnational corporations played in the promotion of trade liberalization. Tomohiro Okada (2007) denounces the government-led consolidation of municipalities that resulted from the fiscal crisis of the state and consequent change from deficit spending to subsidy reductions. He claims that the Japanese state played a key role in the establishment of this trend, as increased support to corporations and decreased spending on rural communities aggravate the conditions of the latter, which are already suffering from the negative consequences of other aspects of globalization.

The political economy group: Works more directly addressing neoliberalism. Although in the political economy camp, the analyses of Neoliberalism remain relatively underdeveloped and subordinated to the study of globalization, some recent publications have partially addressed this shortcoming. This segment of literature (e.g., Kase 2008; Yokoyama 2008) probes the evolution of the liberalization of the Japanese agri-food markets that was accelerated by the Plaza Accord of 1985. It illustrates the international conditions that led to market liberalization, documenting the pressure exerted by the United States to decrease protectionist policies in support of local agriculture and, in particular, of family farming. The United States, it is maintained, desired to counter the expansion of Japanese corporations into North American manufacturing markets through the augmentation of U.S. agri-food exports to Japan. These studies underscore the neoliberal character of the policy changes that characterized the agri-food sector and stress the resulting decline of price support programs, introduction of new income support schemes, land market deregulations, and harmonization of domestic policies. In particular, Kase (2008) focuses on the historical and structural factors that promoted global capitalism and the conditions that, beginning in the 1970s, led to the Great Recession and stagflation of the following decades. The core of his thesis rests on the argument that the implementation of neoliberal policies failed to reverse the Great Recession. Accordingly, he contends that it is desirable to adopt different types of policies to address the economic problems of Japan, including assigning a greater role to agriculture in the revitalization of the national economy.

Hidenobu Yokoyama (2008) studies the processes of deregulation and marketization introduced in Japan in the mid-1980s and the ambiguity that they entail for Japanese agri-food. The Japanese government, he maintains, has consistently promoted market liberalization for its industrial products. However, it has also sought a more moderate liberalization of the agri-food market. He maintains this ambiguity has been partially addressed by the reorganization of protectionist agri-food policies that remain partial in the context of an accelerated reliance on imported products. As this ambiguity continues, Japan may face the "coexistence of a diversified agriculture"—which is the basic position of both Japan and the European Union (EU) in negotiations within the WTO— that will encounter difficulties in contributing to the creation of sustainable forms of agri-food development and an increase in the country's food self-sufficiency. Alternatively, he sees structural reform policies as engendering an acceleration of market liberalization through Japan's enhanced presence in the WTO, the bilateral FTA, and the EPA. This is seen as an equally, if not greater, problematic outcome.

The political economy group: Emphasis on alternative policies. Analyzing the crisis of Japanese agri-food under globalization, Kawamura (2012) explains it in terms of the different levels of mobility (or liquidity, as he terms it) that exist between land as an important input of production and agri-food commodities as outputs of production. While the former has no mobility, the latter has great mobility and is easily circulated worldwide. Suggesting strategies that can overcome the problem caused by this disparate mobility, he recognizes the importance of civic agriculture projects that link producers, consumers, and rural communities to their urban counterparts. He also stresses the desirability of moving away from Fordist forms of production and competition based on low product differentiation in favor of niche production. Finally, he argues for greater input from rural sociologists in the development of alternative policies.

That globalization and Neoliberalism are interrelated processes is argued by Toshiko Masugata (2014). She concurs with many of the authors discussed above that market liberalization and the supporting ideology of Neoliberalism has characterized globalization and its evolution since the early 1990s. She adds, however, that early forms of production conceived as alternatives to Neoliberal globalization have fallen short of expectations. This is the case for organic farming, which has been coopted by the very corporations that supporters of alternative types of production oppose. Accordingly, she contends that it is necessary to introduce novel strategies that focus on the re-embedding of food and agriculture into local communities. Specifically, she supports the movement of *Teikei*, or Community Supported Agriculture, which adds local meanings that transcend those associated with the production of environmentally sound organic commodities. *Teikei*, she concludes, offers a tool to overcome the problems associated with mainstream agri-food by fostering processes of reconciliation between local consumption and local production and between people and nature.

Following Masugata and employing a feminist perspective, Rieko Tsuru (2014) contends that the neoliberal agri-food policies recently implemented favor producers who embrace this ideology and its associated administrative practices. This posture, she continues, benefits a small number of elites and hampers the well-being of the great majority of agricultural workers. Her solution to the current status quo rests in the promotion of collective management of local natural resources accompanied by the creation of food networks and direct links between producers and consumers. These alternatives provide contrasting practices to discourses based on an individualism that attributes to individual initiative successes as well as failures. She concludes by stressing that the increasing inequality faced by women should be addressed and that preferred solutions to extant problems should be sought outside Neoliberalism.

The differences between Neoliberalism and globalization are tackled by You, Lee, and Yoshida (2011), who define Neoliberalism in terms of the domination of financial capital (financialization). Under this new world economic order, financial capital controls productive capital and, accordingly, affects the organization of productive sectors, including agri-food. These authors further underscore the neoliberal character of government policies. In particular, they stress that the government design to "professionalize" farming by increasing farms' size, productivity, and production disproportionally shifts importance to the economic dimension of farming. This process occurs in a context in which other strategies and emphases are possible and, in fact, are desirable. Often local actors, they continue, reject this neoliberal view and mobilize to practice different approaches to natural resource use and agricultural production. Criticizing the individualistic and productivist tendencies of Neoliberalism, they underscore the importance of agricultural cooperatives in the revitalization of farming and the need to shield rural communities from the consequences of neoliberal agri-food policies.

Kyoji Takeda (2014) further continues this line of inquiry and provides a detailed account of the evolution of neoliberal agri-food policies. He divides it into four periods, beginning with the end of the Rapid Economic Growth era. He contends that the decades of the 1960s and 1970s were characterized by economic structural improvements featuring a shift toward Liberalism. The 1980s signaled the introduction of economic structural adjustments marked by an overt turn toward the adoption of Neoliberalism. The 1990s saw the deepening of Neoliberalism through measures that, he argues, constituted the economic structural reform period. Finally, a more advanced (or second) economic structural reform period began with the new century (2000s), and it is defined by the full adoption of Neoliberalism. He concludes by pointing out that the logic of Neoliberalism and the rationality of farmers are incompatible. Accordingly, in the case of farmers and their organizations, growth should be pursued through the production of relatively small quantities of a variety of products to be commercialized in niche markets. This strategy stands in sharp contrast to corporate industrial plans that contemplate mass production of selected commodities.

The wealth of research generated by the political economy camp indicates the fervor with which Neoliberalism in agri-food is debated. Compared with the equally large Western literature on this topic, the similarities are many. In particular, there is convergence on the consequences that the implementation of neoliberal measures create for agri-food communities and the sector. Additionally, both literatures demand the development of alternatives. Similar to many works produced abroad, the Japanese literature stresses the promotion of community-based networks of production and consumption based on local forms of civic agriculture. In terms of differences, however, Japanese authors appear to be less critical of current alternative proposals than their foreign counterparts. In the West, a growing number of authors think that projects like organic farming and civil agriculture, ultimately, share the same individualistic and market-oriented assumptions that power Neoliberalism (Wolf and Bonanno 2014).

Other theoretical approaches to neoliberalism in agri-food. The group of works that falls outside the political economy camp also contains noteworthy contributions (e.g., Kako 2006; Okuma 2011; Taniguchi 2006). Downplaying the differences between globalization and Neoliberalism, Toshiyuki Kako (2006) and Kenji Taniguchi (2006) recognize the expansion of trade liberalization and the increased influx of imported agri-food commodities in Japan as some of the relevant characteristics of globalization. They also point out that globalization engendered the deterioration of the rural economy and limited domestic agricultural production. Identifying these trends as problematic, they call for an alteration of current policies. In particular, Kako (2006) suggests that local product consumption should be increased, as it enhances food safety and food security. Additionally, he urges the development of an alliance among East Asian countries to strengthen food security and gain more influence in international trade negotiations. Taniguchi (2006) underscores the desirability of increasing the export of Japanese value-added agri-food products to East Asian countries. He argues that this move could be hampered by the limited productivity and production for export characterizing Japanese agri-food. In this regard, he suggests introducing measures that would strengthen organizations of agricultural producers and enhance their ability to market local products overseas. Simultaneously, he identifies some items that actually facilitate the growth of Japanese exports. He contends that the economic growth of many East Asian countries has increased the purchasing power of the local working and middle classes. Accordingly, these consumers can now direct a portion of their greater purchasing power to the acquisition of quality imported foods. Additionally, Japanese food retailers have increased their local presence and could invest in additional outlets. All these occurrences, he concludes, make this strategy preferable to the status quo.

Departing from the analyses presented above, Michiru Okuma (2011) contends that globalization and Neoliberalization are two separate and independent phenomena. He places the beginning of globalization in the 1990s and includes within it market liberalization and the international harmonization of agri-food policies. Considering this globalization politically neutral, he calls it a process independent of specific political powers or ideologies. In his view, treating globalization as a phenomenon dominated by Neoliberalism is already a value judgment that taints the impartiality of scholarly analyses, and as such, it is a posture that is inadmissible in scientific terms. He demonstrates this point by comparing Japan with the EU and the United States. Japan, he documents, suffers from problems that are largely absent in the United States and the EU. For instance, the rapid decline in the food self-sufficiency ratio that affects Japan is not recorded in North America and Europe. Accordingly, this and other Japan-specific issues cannot be attributed to globalization, as that would imply their common occurrence worldwide. Building on this analysis, he concludes that the problems affecting Japanese agriculture are the outcome of misguided and ineffective decisions made at the government level and concomitant inadequate responses generated by stakeholders.

The studies included in this group often complement those in the political economy camp. But they diverge in important ways, such as the frequent adoption of a "taken-for-granted" view of the historical and ideological reasons behind the growth of globalization and the implementation of neoliberal measures. As these phenomena are endogenous forces, solutions for problems are presented in frameworks that do not transcend the current status quo. Additionally, nearly all these studies focus on the economic performance of agri-food. Accordingly, this economistic approach prevents the adequate inclusion of social variables and perspectives in these studies, limits the understanding of the importance of ideological constructs and discourses, and tends to downplay the overall role that agri-food plays in the broader economy and society of Japan. It is this systemic dimension of agri-food that is stressed in our final analysis of Japanese agri-food (see chapter 9).

Disasters and Reconstruction Processes

The international literature on disasters and reconstruction processes has grown significantly since the beginning of the century. While studies typically focus on the consequences that disasters have on social and economic structures and relevant actors (e.g., Albala-Bertrand 2006; Tierney 2006), a wealth of more recent contributions stress the socially constructed nature of disasters and, in particular, the manner in which broader trends in capitalism and hegemonic socioeconomic regimes shape the creation and outcomes of disasters as well as the ways in which disasters are employed as powerful restructuring tools. In her pathbreaking work, Naomi Klein (2007) introduces the concept of "Shock Doctrine" to illustrate how the adoption of neoliberal policies in the aftermath of natural and human-made disasters affects the outcomes of these

23

disasters but also paves the way for pro-corporate restructuring processes. She contends that the introduction of these measures is also a tool to wipe out pre-existing obstacles to capital accumulation, such as public regulations and social redistributive policies. Her point is that through the Shock Doctrine approach, corporate groups and their political allies transform disasters into opportunities to further deregulate and reform the economy and society. Following this analysis, researchers have demonstrated the connection between Neoliberalism and exploitative disaster reconstruction processes (e.g., Gunewardena and Schuller 2008) and the negative consequences of short-term profit-oriented corporate moves and the public policies that support them (e.g., Freudenburg, Gramling, Laska, and Erikson 2009). Also documented is the connection between climate change caused by human economic activities and disasters, and the disparity with which the consequences of disasters are experienced by individuals, communities, regions, and countries (e.g., Jones and Murphy 2009; Lundahl 2013; Miller, Antonio, and Bonanno 2011; Okada 2012a, 2012b; Rodriguez, Quarantelli, and Dynes 2007). Adding to these contentions and discussing the consequences of Hurricane Katrina, Block and Somers (2014, 190–191) speak of "contractualization of citizenship" to indicate how the application of the ideology of market fundamentalism inexorably leaves people with limited means behind. They may retain their formal rights as citizens, but they have lost the ability to exercise them.

The consequences on agri-food of the March 2011 triple disaster and related reconstruction processes were widely discussed among Japanese scholars (e.g., Demura 2012, 2011; Furukawa 2014; Hamada 2013a, 2013b, 2012; Kawai 2011; Sakai 2012; Shimizu, Bannai, and Shigeno 2013; Tsunashima 2014, 2012; Tsunashima and Ogawa 2013; Yokoyama 2011; for English language accounts, see Allison 2013; Gill, Steger, and Slater 2013; Kingston 2012; Samuels 2013). This discussion also involves noted Western scholars, such as the late Ulrich Beck, who in a recent Japanese publication comments on these disasters. Following his theory of "World Risk Society" (Beck 2009), Beck and his Japanese associates point out that global level disasters, such as the nuclear power plant meltdown at Fukushima, the global financial crisis, and climate change have contradictory consequences as they empower states and civil society movements but also allow corporations to profit from these occurrences (Beck, Suzuki, and Ito 2011). In their theorization, the new world risk is more egalitarian in nature, for it affects people in ways that are largely independent of their class membership, nationality, and other socioeconomic variables. Accordingly, it differs from established forms of risk that emerged in previous eras of modernity, such as poverty and class inequality. Dwelling on these considerations, they expect that risk will foster the emergence of cross-class solidarity. While the individualization of risk (risk to be faced by and paid for by individuals) remains a constant peril, Beck and his associates conclude that the triple disaster could turn into an opportunity for Japan to rethink past domestic-centered practices and introduce a cosmopolitan—or a greater emphasis on the global dimension—approach to risk.

Along with this literature published in Japanese, relevant works also appeared in English (e.g., Hashimoto 2014; Kimura 2013; Maya-Ambia 2012). This literature can be organized into four categories. The first group includes works that focus on the Fukushima-Daiichi nuclear power plant meltdown and the consequent radioactive contamination of agri-food products (e.g., Hasegawa 2014; Kimura 2013; Maya-Ambia 2012; Ooki 2013; Shimizu 2011). A segment of this literature stresses the socially constructed and political nature of this disaster. Writing in English and Spanish, Carlos Maya-Ambia (2012) argues that the nuclear meltdown is the result of human error that involves the actions of politicians and officers of the Tokyo Electric Power Company (TEPCO). He makes clear that this is not a random occurrence but is the outcome of politically generated poor planning, resulting from the collusion between bureaucrats and energy (but also other sector) companies that prioritized their economic and political interests over safety and the well-being of local communities. Similarly, Shuji Shimizu (2011) stresses the intersection between the nuclear disaster, on one hand, and the inequality between rural and urban regions and the financial interests associated with nuclear plants on the other. He points out that, despite claims of local socioeconomic growth to justify the establishment of these plants, these communities did not develop either economically or socially. Shimizu concludes that the history of nuclear energy in Japan is a strong indication that reconstruction of disaster-affected communities should be organized along alternative lines.

A second segment of this component of the literature focuses on reconstruction and alternative paths to it. Koichi Hasegawa (2014) argues that the Fukushima-Daiichi disaster worked as a catalyst to mobilize an active, civil society-based antinuclear movement. Although small compared to those of other advanced countries, this movement gained momentum after the disaster. It received broad popular support and was able to involve some groups of citizens that previously had remained on the sidelines of the debate. Despite this activism, the antinuclear movement was not powerful enough to prevent pronuclear parties, such as the Liberal Democratic Party (LDP), from winning national elections in 2012 and 2013. This setback notwithstanding, Hasegawa recognizes this movement's achievements, such as the establishment of a new regulatory body and new regulations for nuclear power plants. Additionally, due to its actions, the former conservative Prime Minister Junichiro Koizumi and center-right political leader Morihiro Hosokawa abandoned their pronuclear stance and became active supporters of the antinuclear cause. Overall, the author concludes, this movement's impact on the domestic political arena is growing. Yet its future strength remains to be determined.

Aya Kimura (2013) and Shigeru Ooki (2013) both focus on the establishment of safety standards for the regulation of food contaminated by radiation. They probe the creation and implementation of standards by relevant actors, such as the government, food retailers, consumer cooperatives, and consumers. According to both authors, most food retailers and consumer cooperatives established standards that exceeded those of the government. Insisting on the superiority of private standards over government standards and employing the case of the consumer cooperative Seikatsu Club, Kimura contends that the private sphere not only guarantees better safety standards but also that the practice of involving private stakeholders offers meaningful opportunities for a democratic debate that are hampered in the case of government-sponsored regulations. Focusing on the issue, Ooki (2013) contends the Japanese Consumer Cooperative Union's policy on radioactive foods' contamination, inspection practices, and dissemination of information were inconsistent. In the immediate aftermath of the nuclear meltdown, this organization opposed the establishment of fresh standards by cooperatives and retailers, for it maintained that they could damage the interests of producers. Subsequently, however, it promoted the creation of its own, more stringent, standards and inspection procedures. Despite these differences, both authors recognize the important role that consumer cooperatives play in the opening of democratic spaces, not only for the creation of better food standards but also for fostering needed cooperation between producers and consumers.

The third category of works includes studies that probe the damage that the triple disaster inflicted on local farming and food supply chains. These works analyze the characteristics of the reconstruction process (e.g., Food System Research Association of Japan 2012; Shimizu, Bannai, and Shigeno 2013). For an area in the Prefecture of Iwate, Shimizu and his associates (2013) used pre- and post-disaster fieldwork to document the severity of the 2011 triple disaster. They contend that the socioeconomic conditions of the region will continue to decline as a result of the severity of the damage and of the characteristics of the local economy and labor force. They point out that the advanced average age of farmers, the concomitant lack of generation replacement, the less-than-desirable levels of farm productivity and market access remain obstacles to enhancing production. Simultaneously, however, they contend that production geared to alternative forms of energy, such as biomasses and hydroelectric power, may be an option to reinvigorate the local economy. Alternative patterns of reconstruction based on the partnership between consumers and producers are advocated by the Food System Research Association of Japan (2012). The authors involved in this project focus on the reorganization of the food supply chains that, they contend, require enhanced cooperation among all stakeholders. They conclude that it is important to create partnerships among actors in food systems. Discussing the issue from a theoretical point of view and expressing a more pessimistic opinion about the future than heralded by other authors, Hashimoto (2014) defines reconstruction policies in Japan as examples of "neoliberal totalitarianism," because they disregard the rights of farmers and fishermen to effectively determine their futures. Agreeing with analyses of the reconstruction process (see chapter 3), he equates the post–triple disaster reconstruction activities with neoliberal restructuring. In his view, differences between the conservative LDP and the more progressive Democratic Party of Japan (DPJ) are erased in the practice of promoting a reconstruction process that favors market relations and corporate actors. Both political parties, he insists, ultimately espouse Neoliberalism. He concludes that even though the debate on Neoliberalism continues, its impact on disaster reconstruction is clearly visible and highly undesirable.

The fourth and final category of works included in this group pays particular attention to the role that the public sector and public policies played in the reconstruction process (e.g., Okada 2012a, 2012b; Okada and Japan Institute of Local Government 2013; Tashiro 2012). One subgroup of authors contends that the concept of Shock Doctrine can best exemplify post–triple disaster reconstruction of the agri-food sector. Employing this concept, Yoichi Tashiro (2012) points out that the response to both the 2011 triple disasters and the TPP is part of a neoliberal plan to restructure agricultural production in Japan that favors corporations. As previous attempts to corporatize agriculture yielded poor results, reconstruction, he concludes, requires the prioritization of local residents' views and way of life as key considerations. Similarly, Okada (2012a; 2012b) and his associates (Okada and Japan Institute of Local Government 2013) point out that reconstruction policies are vigorously proposed by corporations and their allies in the political arena. This is not a new process, they continue, as the introduction of neoliberal policies to address post-disaster reconstruction has been employed on previous occasions. Accordingly, they conclude by pointing out that neoliberal reconstruction policies for corporations should be replaced by policies for the "reconstruction of humans," or the reconstruction and betterment of the living conditions and livelihood of local residents.

A second subgroup of papers reviews the establishment of the Special Zone for Reconstruction (SZR) program, focusing on the case of the liberalization of fishing rights in Ishinomaki City in the Prefecture of Miyagi (see chapter 7) (e.g., Demura 2012; Furukawa 2014; Hamada 2013a, 2013b, 2012; Kawai 2011; Sakai 2012; Tsunashima 2014, 2012; Tsunashima and Ogawa 2013; Yokoyama 2011). There is significant agreement among these authors that the creation of this SZR and the associated liberalization of fishing rights was a move against the well-being of local family fishermen and their cooperatives. Additionally, they contend that the pro-corporate norms that allow large enterprises to acquire the rights to fish in local waters lacked democratic procedures and unilaterally dismissed objections from the opposition. This opposition was voiced by a great number of stakeholders, including such professional groups as fishing cooperatives and the Area Fishery Adjustment Committee, such political entities as the Diet and local Council, such advisory groups as the National Reconstruction Design Council, and local fishermen and residents.

Similar studies document other cases of SZR program implementation, such as that of Sendai City, in the Prefecture of Miyagi (see chapter 6). For example, Fukushima (2013) and Sekine (2013) contend that the implemented reconstruction policies promote the consolidation of farmland and restructuring of production. Family farmers who see their independence, way of life, and social and economic well-being threatened by the corporatization of farming view both outcomes as worrisome. Sekine further documents the development of corporate investment in agri-food production and the financial support that corporations received from the local government. Fukushima concludes by stressing the inequity associated with the distribution of reconstruction public funds that disproportionally favors large farms and corporate initiatives. Sekine (2013) investigates the establishment of the Michisaki Farm: a corporate operation created by local large farm holders with technical support from corporations. After its formation, however, tension erupted between the Michisaki Farm and local small farmers and between the farm and corporations. This instability, she concludes, points to the importance of giving due space and voice to family farmers, small part-time farmers, and subsistence farmers in reconstruction processes.

The bulk of this literature is critical of the process of reconstruction that followed the 2011 disaster. It sees in the implementation of neoliberal measures a tool to empower large corporations and diminish the well-being of family farm holders and local communities. These themes will be central in the analysis and discussion presented in this volume. Note, however, that the promotion of neoliberal measures by local and national governments allows some of these authors to stress the importance of the democratic spaces available within the private sphere. This is an argument that, by being critical of governmental policies, complicates the simple state-market dichotomy and opens another front of discussion that will be touched on in the following chapters.

Corporations in Agri-Food

The role and actions of TNCs are among the most studied topics in contemporary sociology of agri-food (e.g., Bonanno, Busch, Friedland, Gouveia, and Mingione 1994; Bonanno and Constance 2008; Boyd and Watts 2007; Burch and Lawrence 2007; Heffernan and Constance 1994; Jansen and Vellema 2004; McMichael 2013, 2007). This literature shows the transformation of multinational corporations into TNCs, the significant level of concentration of productive capacity, and the creation of global networks of production and consumption associated with corporate expansion. These processes are salient factors in the creation of "the food from nowhere" phenomenon that largely defines contemporary agri-food. Additionally, this literature illustrates how TNCs were able to use neoliberal deregulation to increase their power over consumers, labor, and the state. The overt exploitation of labor remains one of the most fundamental aspects of the growth of TNCs. Environmental, food safety, and socioeconomic sustainability concerns are also listed as relevant consequences of the corporatization of agri-food.

In Japanese academia, the role and actions of transnational agri-food corporations began to be discussed in the late 1980s. This was one of the consequences of the growth of the international debate and the translation of numerous relevant books and articles into Japanese.[3] Following this injection of foreign empirical evidence and theoretical formulations, a wealth of local publications appeared in the 1990s and following decades (Agricultural Marketing Society of Japan 1996; Goto 2013; Hisano 2008, 2002; Isoda 2001; Iwasa 2005; Kishikawa and Park 2010; Komai, Dial, Yamauchi, and Kaku 1999; Nakano 1998; Otsuka 2005; Otsuka and Matsubara 2004; Rai 2012; Sekine 2008, 2006; Shimada, Shimowatari, Oda, and Shimizu 2006; Toyoda 2001).

A portion of this literature includes early works that, focusing on agri-food corporate management systems and related themes, introduced these international debates to the local audience and ignited a burst of empirical studies (e.g., Agricultural Marketing Society of Japan 1996; Komai et al. 1999). Stressing the

29

positive character of the adoption of corporate-style systems, Komai and his associates (1999) popularized discussions carried out at the Harvard Business School. They contend that the liberalization of commodity markets and the growing financialization of the economy are desirable developments that could lead to farmers' success and better preparedness to address business challenges. In this new climate, farmers, they maintain, should acquire greater awareness of their responsibilities in farm management and work toward expanding their farms' sizes and/or generate more value-added products. Simultaneously, these authors call for greater corporate social responsibility, particularly in terms of behaviors leading to better food security and food safety, the alleviation of hunger, the avoidance of risks, and the pursuit of environmentally sustainable development. Through separate studies, the Agricultural Marketing Society of Japan (1996) publicized the content of research on agri-food corporations produced in North America. Moreover, these studies introduced the methodology of commodity analysis as a tool to study corporate behavior and society and stressed the relevance of the adoption of a more systematic study of agri-food corporations in Japan. The Agricultural Marketing Society of Japan also provided a wealth of empirical studies on emerging contractual and partnership schemes in the production and commercialization of agri-food products, such as broilers and vegetables, carried out by Asian corporations operating in the Japanese market.

Continuing to focus on international issues, a second portion of this literature involves analyses on the expansion of TNCs in countries other than Japan, including the United States (e.g., Hisano 2002; Isoda 2001), Malaysia (e.g., Iwasa 2005), Indonesia (e.g., Rai 2012), South America, and other parts of Asia (e.g., Toyoda 2001). Isoda (2001), for instance, focuses on the U.S. grain market and its restructuring initiated in the 1980s. He illustrates the growth of powerful transnational agri-food corporations, which he terms "grain majors," and their power in the market and their ability to affect pertinent legislation. Recognizing their capability to counter corporate power, Isoda further investigates the restructuring of grain cooperatives. He contends that they remodeled themselves as a "grain complex" and in so doing are able to compete with TNCs. In addition, through the creation of new generation of cooperatives, these grain cooperatives promote the independence of local family producers. Hisano (2002) focuses on issues associated with genetically modified crops (or the use of GMOs in crops) and the appropriation of this technology and the pertinent regulatory sphere by agri-food corporations. He indicates that this process promotes the oligopolization of seed markets and wrenches their private control away from public oversight. He concludes by stressing the importance of countering privatization by establishing a democratic control of biotechnology based on citizen participation and consensus.

Investigating the development of export-oriented palm oil production schemes in Southeastern Asian countries, Iwasa (2005) (Malaysia) and Rai (2013) (Indonesia) probe the consequences of the introduction of these schemes as part of neoliberal structural adjustment projects. Heralded by many as successful strategies for development, they contend that these government-led and supported projects are actually destabilizing factors that worsen the socioeconomic conditions of small farmers. The international market-formulated palm oil prices create volatility while increasing farmers' debts and dependency. Additionally, the massive growth of oil palm plantations deteriorates the environment by inducing deforestation, loss of biodiversity, and floods. Accordingly, they conclude that these export-oriented agricultural development projects do very little for the alleviation of poverty, the creation of sustainable economic growth, and the social and political involvement of local farmers.

Paralleling the research of Iwasa and Rai but departing from their conclusions, Toyoda (2001) investigates the growing involvement of agri-food corporations in the production of various food commodities, including orange juice, fresh fruits, bananas, and shrimp in South American and Asian countries. He illustrates the problematic character of export-oriented modernization programs, as they often increase the economic gap between corporate agriculture and traditional farming dominated by small and subsistence operations. However, he also recognizes the positive impact that transnational agri-food corporations may have on the economic growth of family farms and communities by promoting farmers' involvement in international markets, their adoption of new technologies and inputs, and the creation of jobs for members of these communities. He concludes that the government's intermediary role between these two components of agri-food is crucial in the establishment of their productive coexistence.

A separate portion of this literature investigates Japanese food trading and food processing corporations and their global activities (e.g., Otsuka 2005; Shimada et al. 2006). Employing secondary data on the production and international trade of fresh agri-food products, such as seafood, chicken, and vegetables, Shigeru Otsuka (2005) probes the growing import of food items from Asian countries and the associated actions of Japanese corporations. He contends that the ensuing decline in Japan's food self-sufficiency ratio is not exclusively the result of pressure from foreign countries to open Japanese markets and the growth of foreign agri-food firms. Nevertheless, Japanese transnational agri-food corporations' actions and growth do play a role. Moreover, he maintains that the development of these corporations worsens the socioeconomic status of Asian farmers and is one of the reasons for the growth of inequality and the growing size of the lower classes in these countries. Ultimately, he concludes, these problems find their roots in the dominant process of globalism or market fundamentalism.

Also stressing the growth of large agri-food corporations, Katsumi Shimada and his associates (2006) indicate that a restricted group of Japanese trading corporations controls most of the imported agri-food products and agricultural inputs, such as feeds and chemicals. This is the continuation of the domination initiated with the pre–World War II *zaibatsu* system and, in some cases, it dates back to the Meiji era. Since the 1990s and with the acceleration of globalization, these corporations have drastically increased their foreign direct investment and formed joint ventures with local corporations in East and Southeast Asia. These activities are directed at the import of agri-food products or inputs for the production of processed foods. Additionally, these companies are involved in processes of vertical integration that include food retailers and restaurant chains as well as the creation of new corporate groups. As the concentration of the sector continues, these authors conclude, mergers and acquisitions characterize the restructuring of the production, distribution, and consumption of food in Japan.

A fourth and final segment of this literature refers to a growing number of works studying foreign and Japanese agri-food corporations that invest in Japan. As corporate involvement in Japanese agri-food became increasingly visible in the 2000s, analyses focusing on the consequences of these corporate actions on agricultural production and rural communities began to inform pertinent debates (e.g., Goto 2013; Kishikawa and Park 2010; Muroya 2007; Sekine 2008, 2006; Taniwaki 2011; Tsutaya 2000b). Often employing case-study methodologies and fieldwork, these authors document the growth of the corporate presence in Japanese agri-food and the concomitant deregulation promoted by the government. Additionally, they associate this corporatization of agri-food with the implementation of policies that prescribe corporate growth as a tool for the improvement of the socioeconomic conditions of rural areas.

The social geographer Takuya Goto (2013) studies corporate industrial strategies related to three commodities: tomatoes for the processing sector, broilers, and rush grass used for the Japanese traditional *tatami* mat industry. He contends that the initial emphasis on the purchase of domestic agricultural products was replaced by an industrial strategy that contemplates the acquisition of imported commodities along with the expansion of vertical integration. Vertical integration, he continues, evolves at different speeds across these commodities.

In the case of tomatoes and broilers, integration developed quickly and became an established factor. In the case of rush grass, it is less pronounced. These differences influence the independence of local farmers. Dwelling on this analysis, Goto concludes that while the globalization of agri-food is characterized by the hollowing out of production, corporate actions do include contractual and trading relations with domestic farmers that are employed in the production of quality agri-food items and to address risk management concerning food safety.

Studying corporate investment in fresh vegetable production in several Japanese locations in the 2000s, Kae Sekine (2006) investigates the case of a subsidiary of Dole Food Company, Dole Japan. She documents how this company—one of the first TNCs to invest in Japanese agri-food production—bypassed existing norms on farmland ownership by establishing joint ventures with local firms. Local political authorities, agricultural cooperatives, and farmers who became convinced of the beneficial effects that Dole Japan's presence would generate for the local economy, she continues, backed this move. Deregulation and the economic decline of local operations fostered this company's expansion. Yet Sekine indicates that disappointing earnings were quickly met with disinvestment plans and relocation of production sites. She concludes by underscoring the peril that the hypermobility of corporations represent to local farms and agricultural communities. Echoing Sekine's concern about corporate hypermobility, Osamu Taniwaki (2011) argues that the deregulation of farmland ownership promoted the growth of corporate investments in agriculture. But because returns did not meet expectations, some of these corporations quickly disinvested. He concludes that corporate hypermobility should be regulated, and rural communities and agricultural production need protection from the effects of deregulation and corporatization. Harada (2011) adds to the discussion by pointing out that the liberalization of farmland ownership promotes processes of securitization that are attractive for corporations and investors but accomplishes little for the sector and, above all, for rural communities.

Underscoring the positive contributions of corporate investment in agri-food, Kishikawa and his associates (2010) probe the behavior of several Japanese and foreign corporations, including Mitsui (trading), Ito En and Kirin (beverages), Uniqlo (apparel), and Nestlé (agri-food). They contend that corporate involvement in agri-food provides market opportunities for local farmers and, by generating employment and cash flow, revitalizes local communities. They recognize that corporate initiatives foster resistance led by residents, agricultural cooperatives, and local politicians. However, this opposition tends to fade once corporations have an opportunity to demonstrate the actual benefits

33

of their actions, including extension services and the branding of local products. Uniqlo, whose industrial strategy of low-cost mass production and mass sales generated poor outcomes, represents the exception to this trend. In effect, this company's initial investment in the sector was followed by a rapid exit that left local residents, farmers, and community leaders dissatisfied. These researchers conclude by arguing that, despite the overall importance of corporate investment, the possibility of development is enhanced by the constructive coexistence of corporations with local producers and community groups. Arihiro Muroya (2007) stresses the need for the coordination of the activities of corporations and farmers. He maintains that most corporations investing in agri-food are actually local small and medium-sized firms whose intention is to support the declining economy. Actions to address the faltering economy are carried out by local authorities that, to that end, welcome corporate investment, according to Muroya. As there is a convergence of interests in the creation of additional investment, he concludes that agricultural cooperatives should be called on to coordinate the activities of salient actors, including corporations and rural communities. Tsutaya (2000b) sees the enhanced presence of corporations in agri-food as a stimulus for local cooperatives that, because of this presence, are pressured to change their practices. Additionally, the fact that corporations tend to invest in high-value-added commodities rather than extensive crops makes them poor candidates for the status of major agricultural producers.

The wealth of contributions on the growing presence of corporations in agri-food is characterized by a duality. The view that underscores the positive contributions of corporate presence and investment in agri-food is contrasted by that of many researchers who stress the dangers associated with this corporatization of the sector. The events and instances presented in the following chapters corroborate these two groups' documentation of the corporatization of agri-food, the support that it receives from local and national political authorities and policies, and the multifaceted consequences that it engenders for the sector and its communities. Also in the following chapters, we will engage this debate by showing the problematic dimension of corporatization and its position in the context of the stability of the agri-food system.

Resistance to Dominant Patterns in Agri-Food

Resistance to the introduction of neoliberal measures and the growing presence of corporations in agri-food are also among the dominant focuses of recent agri-food international literature (e.g., Bonanno and Constance 2008; Constance, Renard, and Rivera-Ferre 2015; Wolf and Bonanno 2014; Wright and Middendorf

2007). This literature documents the declining power of labor unions, the increased exploitation of labor, but also the growth of alternative forms of agri-food. As these initiatives emerged in reaction to the expansion of corporate power, they have been criticized for accepting the logic of Neoliberalism and therefore offering limited opposition to corporate expansion. In recent years, this debate has been enriched by responses to these criticisms that stress the emancipatory dimension of alternative agriculture.

In Japan, resistance to dominant groups is contextualized within cultural parameters that distinguish it from trends that characterize other advanced societies. Accordingly, while resistance is not an exceptional behavior in Japan, labor relations, industrial relations, and opposition have been historically controlled through the phenomenon of "companism." This term refers to a situation whereby workers display solidarity and loyalty to the company that, in return, extends significant benefits to workers. This type of labor-management accord has worked effectively to pacify relations among social groups and stabilize society. Since the first postwar decades, companism has dominated labor relations to the point that welfare measures are largely created and administered at the company level rather than by the state. In this context, unionization takes place at this level, and unions and management work out agreements within the company rather than at the industry or national level, as happens in most advanced countries.

In agri-food, struggles of local peasants and farmers against dominant groups have a long history in the salient literature. For instance, Katsumata (1986) documents the numerous revolts that involved peasants during the Middle Ages. Similarly, Mori (2007) describes farmers' struggles against local rulers that occurred in Nambu Clan (in the current Prefecture of Iwate and one of the areas discussed in chapter 7) in the nineteenth century. These well-organized struggles generated significant change at the time. The documentation of farmers' resistance continued in the post–World War II era. Hosaka (1986) illustrates the broad opposition movement against the U.S.-Japan Security Treaty that saw the participation of workers, students, and intellectuals in street demonstrations and other forms of organized protest. Additionally, anti-Vietnam War political demonstrations were accompanied by pro-environment struggles, such as that against the construction of the Tokyo-Narita International Airport. In this struggle, farmers were joined by other groups, creating a broad-based coalition that called for the preservation of the large area of farmland allocated for the construction of the airport. Uzawa (1996) documents this struggle, which is symbolic of the limits of Japanese democracy and the undesirable consequences of the top-down model of industrialization that dominated the country in the first postwar decades. It is also emblematic of the subordination of farming to designs that stress the development of manufacturing. As is well known, Tokyo-Narita International Airport eventually opened in 1978.

Despite the limited political achievements of these late-twentieth-century struggles, they contributed to the establishment of movements that propose alternative forms of agri-food. As in other parts of the world, Japan experienced the emergence of such movements as civic agriculture and organic farming. In particular, the phenomenon of *Teikei*, or community-supported agriculture based on the partnership between farmers and consumers, achieved significant importance. In the literature, Furusawa (1994) and Orito (2013) define *Teikei* as a response to the modernization of Japanese agriculture and its negative consequences on the environment, food safety, and sustainability. In particular, Furusawa (1994) contends that *Teikei* draws support among farmers and consumers alike, as both groups backed the implementation of organic or environmentally friendly agriculture and participated in the coordination of planned (prepurchased) production schemes. In some instances, programs of consumer voluntary assistance to farmers were created. Some of these movements' initiatives, Furusawa (1989) also indicates, translated into direct political actions and the successful support of candidates in local and national elections. These electoral victories gave greater voice to opponents of the neoliberalization of agri-food.

Despite this mobilization, the literature stresses that *Teikei* remains a small phenomenon affected by some of the same problems associated with this type of initiative seen in other parts of the world. Orito (2013) points out that in Japan, the number of organic farmers remains relatively small and below levels recorded in Europe and North America. In 2010, it includes 0.5 percent of all farmers. Additionally, and studying a specific case of *Teikei*, Furusawa (1989) shows that this organization was affected by an identity crisis as large department stores and supermarkets began to sell organic products. This situation created at least two types of problems. First, *Teikei* operations began to face the competition of corporate chains. Second, they encountered distribution problems, as the minimum volumes of production required for broader distribution could not be met. In his case study, Furusawa further notes that consumers with enhanced sensitivities about food safety and the protection of the environment left this *Teikei* to join smaller and more politically committed consumer cooperatives (Furusawa 1989). Simultaneously, other studies (e.g., Jordan and Hisano 2011) stress that *Teikei*, as well as other forms of alternative agriculture, are at risk of being co-opted by corporations. Responding to these concerns, Yoshitaka Mashima (2011), the vice-president of the Japan Family Farmers Movement, or "Nominren," a member of Via Campesina, emphasizes the important role that alternative agri-food movements play in the opposition to neoliberal policies. He contends that *Teikei* but also the use of local agri-food products in public procurement (meals for schools, hospitals, and other public institutions) are elements that promote an "Economy of Solidarity"—a desirable alternative to the dominant free market philosophy.

Recent contributions (e.g., Demura 2008; Hamada 2013a; Tashiro 2005; Tsunashima and Ogawa 2013) stress the proliferation of new actions against the neoliberalization of agri-food. Tashiro (2005) identifies a factor that effectively opposes globalism in the resistance of agricultural cooperatives through the linking of producers and consumers. In particular, Tsunashima and Ogawa (2013) document how local and national fishing cooperatives successfully opposed the implementation of an SZR program in the Momonoura area in Ishinomaki City. As discussed in detail in chapter 7, this program was designed to attract corporate investment through the liberalization of fishing rights. Agricultural and fishing cooperatives have also organized demonstrations and other forms of opposition as the prices of agricultural inputs, such as fossil fuel and animal feed, sharply increased during the 2008 crisis (Demura 2008).

Overall, the literature on agri-food analyzes the history and actions of opposition to dominant groups and discourses in farming and fishing regions. It shows that this opposition has characterized various eras of the evolution of the sector and in recent decades, urban groups, consumers, and their cooperatives have supported it. The overall debate, however, has focused more on actions and movements that seek alternative forms of agri-food. Accordingly, and in contrast to Western debates, limited direct attention has been paid to resistance (the word itself is rarely used). As the neoliberalization and corporatization of agri-food increase, arguably more studies on resistance will soon be produced. Currently, though, and given the magnitude of the neoliberalization and corporatization of agri-food, resistance largely remains an understudied theme.

NOTES

1. Promoted by the school of critical theory, the concept of artificial negativity refers to the illusion of freedom that accompanies class domination in mature capitalism. Subordinate classes feel empowered by their material gains and ability to consume, only to find themselves trapped in consumerism and the commodification of social relations.

2. In so doing, this literature tends to gloss over the significant point that Neoliberal globalization is one—albeit dominant—of the possible forms of globalization (Bonanno and Cavalcanti 2014). Connecting globalization with Neoliberalism can be viewed as theoretically weak, as the two processes are not the same. The emergence of a common global culture, enhanced interaction and communication across the globe, and global sharing of ideas are

among the salient characteristics of globalization that cannot be considered as simply among the tenets of Neoliberalism. This position is also politically problematic, as anti-neoliberal critiques benefit very little from postures that dwell on localism, provincialism, and, in more radical cases, tribalism and fundamentalism.

3.   For instance, Bonanno et al. (1994) was translated in 1999; Burbach and Flynn (1980) in 1987; Friedmann (2005, 2003, 1994) in 2006; Kneen (1995) in 1997; Glover and Kusterer (1990) in 1992; Lawrence (2004) in 2005; and Magdoff, Foster, and Buttel (2000) in 2004.

CHAPTER 2

Agriculture and Fisheries in Japan from the Post–World War II High Fordism to the Neoliberal Era (1945–2010)

Introduction

This chapter illustrates salient aspects of the Japanese agri-food sector's evolution from the immediate post–World War II years to the end of the first decade of the twenty-first century. The objective is, through a synthesis of the literature on the socioeconomic growth of postwar Japan, to provide a brief socio-historical background to the topics discussed in the remainder of the book. It opens with a review of the conditions and development of agriculture and fishing during the post–World War II year of *High Fordism*[1] (Antonio and Bonanno 2000). This period includes the reconstruction process following the war's devastation, the years of rapid economic growth, and its end in the early 1970s. This section focuses on two periods: the beginning of High Fordism from 1945 to 1951 and the two decades from the early 1950s to the early 1970s that saw the rapid industrialization and formidable economic expansion of Japan. The second section covers salient developments of Japanese agri-food from the mid-1970s to 2010. It provides an illustration of the characteristics of the policy shift from Fordism to Neoliberalism and its consequences for the sectors in the context of the growth of globalization. It is divided into two subsections. The first covers the years from 1973 to 1985, while the second discusses the years of neoliberal globalization from 1985 to 2010. For the purpose of this analysis, we employed the periodization that the noted Japanese historian Shuzo Teruoka (2008) uses to study agri-food from 1945 to 2010 (see table 2.1). The concluding section documents the growth of the presence of transnational corporations and the establishment of a business-friendly pro-corporate environment in the pre-March 2011 period.

Table 2.1. Periodization of postwar periods in Japan (1945–2010)

Periods	Years	Features	Subperiods	Years	Features
Beginning of High Fordism	1945–1951	Military occupation by the Allied Forces Social and economic reforms	Demilitalization and democratization	1945–1948	Reforms for demilitarization and democratization
			bases of economic expansion	1948–1951	Reforms for economic expansion
High Fordism and rapid economic growth	1951–1973	Begins with Peace Treaty and Mutual Security Agreement with US Ends with the oil crisis and collapse of the Bretton Woods accord	Economic takeoff	1951–1955	Strong state interventionist policies (State monopoly capitalism)
			First rapid economic growth	1955–1965	Rapid economi growth led by growth in manufacturing Trade and currency liberalization in the 1960s Membership in the OECD (1964)
			Second rapid economic growth	1965–1973	Recession of 1965 and recovery through deficit spending and Vietnam War generated economic opportunities Japan grows to be the second largest world economy
Transition to neoliberal globalization	1973–Present	Further market liberalization and domestic neoliberal reforms in the economy	End of Fordism and low economic growth	1973–1985	Plaza Accord ends trade negotiations and resolves frictions with United States and other countries
			Beginning and establishment of Neoliberal globalization	1985–Present	Significant market liberalization and deregulation

From High Fordism to Its Crisis

The Beginning of the High Fordism Period (1945–1951)

Throughout the evolution of capitalism in Japan, agriculture and rural areas provided vital resources and assets, such as food, energy (many power plants are located in rural areas), labor, safe and abundant water, and a beautiful environment that were fundamental to the country's development as well as markets for industrial products, such as chemical agricultural inputs and machines. As the semifeudal, prewar social system dissolved, the steady supply of cheap immigrant labor to the growing urban areas and manufacturing sector, coupled with improvements in domestic food production, created significant impetus to the dramatic postwar socioeconomic recovery.

During the postwar military occupation by the Allied Forces (1945–1951), Japan was the theater of a number of reforms that altered its militaristic and semifeudal social and economic structure (Allinson 2004; Bailey 1996; Dower 1993, 1999; Teruoka 2008). While policies aimed at the demilitarization and democratization of the country characterized the first portion of this period, the years between 1948 and 1951 featured efforts to expand the economy. In the context of the emerging Cold War, Japan's economic growth was not only relevant for the country's domestic stability, but it was also central to the U.S. anticommunist campaign. It served as an example of the superiority of American-guided capitalism over Soviet style socioeconomic arrangements. In this context, American-led reforms focused on three areas. First, efforts were carried out to break Japanese monopolies—known as *zaibatsu*—that dominated the economy in the prewar decades.[2] Following the New Deal experience, American authorities deemed monopolistic economic concentration inefficient and antidemocratic, and these authorities acted to alter limited market access and participation. Second, pro-labor reforms were initiated. In an attempt to stabilize labor relations and provide social inclusion for local workers, the asymmetrical and often overtly exploitative power of management over labor was reduced, and labor's rights and conditions were strengthened and improved.[3] Finally, the Land Reform Program was carried out, resulting in the elimination of the semifeudal system of absentee landlords and tenant farmers (Allinson 2004; Baily 1996; Teruoka 2008).

As tenant farmers constituted 70 percent of all agricultural households, worked in harsh conditions, paid high rents to landlords, generated very low production and productivity, and remained poor with dismal hopes to own a farm, the Land Reform Program was pivotal for the improvement of their

41

conditions and those of agriculture as a whole (Endo 1966; Ino 1971; Teruoka 2008, 157–173). Ultimately, it resulted in the improvement of food production, the creation of a group of relatively more efficient family farms, and the release of the abundant surplus agricultural labor for urban employment in the expanding industrial sector. The Land Reform Program imposed by the American government remained strictly within the parameters of the market economy. It not only compensated landowners for the forced sale of land but also allowed them to retain a portion of the original property. On this land, new leasing contracts were signed featuring much reduced rates, cash payments to avoid servitude-style compensations to landowners, and measures that established and protected tenants' rights. Land was sold to farmers at very favorable prices. Political institutions for the supervision of local agriculture were reformed, and farmers were allowed to directly elect their representatives (Shimamoto 2011, 9–10).

After the reform, the portion of land occupied by tenants decreased to 13.1 percent (1949) of all cultivated land, down from the prewar 46.2 percent (1941). Simultaneously, more than 6 million landless agricultural workers gained land as property (Teruoka 2008, 165, 169–173). The economic conditions of farmers, tenants, and farmworkers improved significantly along with their social and educational levels. These improvements were the direct outcomes of emancipation from rent payment for land use, newly created programs that lowered the costs of higher education, and improved working conditions (Teruoka 2008, 172). These changes stabilized social relations and transformed rural areas into reservoirs of moderate conservative voters that, for years to come, supported the rule of the Liberal Democratic Party (LDP). While left-wing parties, such as the Japan Socialist Party (JSP), enjoyed some support among rural residents in the immediate postwar years (Waswo and Nishida 2002), the success of these LDP rural policies contributed to this party's victory over the JSP in the 1949 elections. Since then, the JSP has shifted its electoral focus from rural small-scale farmers to the urban industrial working class.

This land reform also allowed for the reintegration of 7 million World War II veterans and 6.5 million repatriates from the former colonies in the immediate postwar period (Tashiro 2003, 56). Through better educational levels and the expansion of industrial employment, many rural unemployed and underemployed obtained relatively good and stable jobs in urban areas. Simultaneously, the improved local situation and the flow of remittances sent back by these migrants further stabilized the conditions in rural regions. Ultimately, this rural to urban migration was fundamental to economic expansion during the *rapid economic growth* years of the 1950s and 1960s (Endo 1966).

Despite these positive results, the Land Reform Program was characterized by two major limitations. First, it was implemented on only a portion of the country's total land. In effect, 70 percent of domestic land was excluded. While this land was located in less productive yet accessible mountain regions, if reformed, it could have added to the total national production (Teruoka 2008, 173). Second, the way land was redistributed did not allow for land consolidation. As farms remained fragmented in various parcels of land, the use of machines and labor was inefficient. In addition to these limitations, the post–Land Reform years were characterized by the negative effects of rice price control and quota systems introduced by the American administration. Designed to maintain low and stable food prices for the growing urban/industrial population and coexisting with high agricultural taxes, these measures paid less than production costs and, ultimately, depressed returns for farmers (Ino 1971; Teruoka 2008).

The economically large, culturally and community relevant, and strategically important Japanese fishing industry was also reformed in the immediate postwar years (Hokimoto 2009; Kawai 2011; Ruddle 1984). The prewar system was regulated by legislation enacted in 1901 (the Meiji Fisheries Act), which addressed the existence of community-based exclusive fishing rights. Following the traditional organization of fisheries instituted during the *Edo* period,[4] this semifeudal system allowed villages to claim adjacent coastal waters as exclusive fishing grounds for the community. The prewar legislation instituted Fisheries Cooperative Associations (FCAs), which administered fishing rights and mandated membership for all local fishermen at the village or cove levels. This system, however, was ruled by local noblemen who controlled fishing and captured a substantial portion of the wealth generated from it (Kawai 2011, 21–22). As inequality characterized the sector, many fishermen remained poor and under the exploitative control of middlemen and wholesalers (Ruddle 1984, 168). These conditions further deteriorated during the Great Depression, and in 1933 the government intervened through a partial reform that allowed more economic freedom to FCAs. During the immediate prewar, and war, years FCAs were placed under the direct control of the central government (Hokimoto 2009; Ruddle 1984).

In 1945, the U.S. administration prohibited navigation for all Japanese vessels, including fishing vessels. Engineered to control the occupied country, this action quickly had to be revoked, given the importance of seafood in the traditional Japanese diet and the development of serious food shortages that challenged attempts to stabilize society and revitalize the economy (Kawai 1994, 53–55). The so-called *MacArthur Line* was employed to define the water space where fishing was once again allowed. Despite this change, the fishing zone remained small, at 60 percent of the country's current exclusive economic zone (EEZ),[5] and this limited the sector's recovery. In 1945, the output of the Japanese fishing industry stood at half of its prewar volume (1.8 million metric tons (mt) compared to 4.3 million mt in 1936).

The U.S. administration's plans to promote the economic growth of Japan provided impetus to the introduction of significant reforms in the late 1940s. In particular, the Fisheries Cooperative Association Act was passed in 1948, and the more comprehensive Fisheries Act was passed in 1949. These measures were directed to the general reorganization and development of Japan's water space, an increase in fisheries' production and productivity, and the democratization of management and operations. Known as "the land reform of fisheries," these changes paralleled in purposes and methods those implemented in agriculture (Kawai 2011, 35–36) and consisted of three steps. First, the government redistributed fishing rights authorized under the 1901 law. It paid indemnifications to fishermen whose rights were restructured and allowed the broader and more democratic participation of local fishermen in the sector. Second, and to limit concentration of power, fishing rights were implemented under the jurisdiction of FCAs. FCAs assigned the property of fishing rights to cooperative members, and this "collective" property was equivalent to the ownership of farmland instituted under the Land Reform. Only fishermen and fishing enterprises were permitted to claim fishing rights, and the prohibition to sell, rent, and/or transfer these rights to any third party was introduced (Kawai 2011, 27–30). Third, a more democratic regulatory system was set up. It involved the establishment of the Sea-Area Fisheries Adjustment Commissions that, along with the FCAs (now Japan Fisheries Cooperatives, or JFs), allowed direct participation of local fishermen in the management of fisheries. The postwar reforms established the foundations for the significant Japanese economic expansion of the coming decades and the integration of agriculture and fisheries into the world capitalist system.

High Fordism and the Rapid Economic Growth Period (1951–1973)

In North America and Europe, the 1950s and 1960s represented two decades of significant economic expansion and social stability. Defined by Talcott Parsons and likeminded functionalist theorists as a period in which the virtues of the American socioeconomic system and the U.S. world leadership were self-evident, these years represented the time when the Fordism regime reached its highest levels of stability and efficiency[6] (Antonio and Bonanno 2000). The combination of state intervention and economic planning, the success of the management-labor accord, and expanding markets and economic opportunities appeared to offer an endless path to development. Japan was part of this process, and the 1951 signing of the Peace Treaty and the Mutual Security Agreement with the United States signaled the beginning of its High Fordist era. Similar to the case of North America and Europe, the 1973 oil crisis and the collapse of the Bretton Woods accord brought Japan's Rapid Economic Growth period to an end. It is important to note that relevant differences exist between the types of Fordism applied in Europe and North America and that of Japan. In Fordist Japan, like in other parts of the advanced world, growth was directed by a strong "developmental state" (Johnson 1982). However, the uniqueness of the intervention of the Japanese state consisted of its policy to pick sectors and firms to be developed and support them through the actions of formidable economic and financial bureaucracies. It also featured the fostering of specific cultural traits that stressed solidarity and loyalty of workers to the firm and of the firm to its workers. Known as *companism*—or the alliance between wage earners and managers to promote the well-being of the firm—it significantly added to the exceptionality of the Japanese system. Ultimately, the productivist posture aimed at conquering export markets through state coordination departed from the European and American version of Fordism. The latter paid more attention to the control of the unwanted consequences of capitalism through the development of social welfare (Antonio and Bonanno 2000; Garside 2014; Lechevalier 2014). To be sure, the popular thesis of the Japanese state-directed development is challenged by the "flexible production" thesis. Originally articulated in English by David Friedman (1988), this theory contends that Japanese economic growth was actually the result of the ingenuity and innovations of a host of locally managed and operated small and medium-sized firms. Acting "from below," these group of companies generated a highly competitive network based on horizontal cooperation and the use of highly skilled labor. By adopting flexible production strategies, they were able to acquire a competitive superiority that differentiated the Japanese industrial sector from those of the other advanced industrial countries and, above all, the United States. It is also important to note that, to a significant extent, the formidable performance of the Japanese economy in the 1950s and 1960s owes its success to the growth of domestic demand. While it is undeniable that exports fueled Japan's economic expansion, domestic consumption contributed to about 60 percent of this period's national growth rate (Yoshikawa 2009). In the late 1980s and throughout the 1990s, this situation was reversed, and the contribution of exports to the growth rate exceeded that of the domestic demand. In the 2000s exports accounted for about 60 percent of the growth rate.

The years between 1951 and 1973 can be divided into three subperiods: the takeoff period (1951–1955), the first Rapid Economic Growth period (1955–1965), and finally the second Rapid Economic Growth period (1965–1973) (Teruoka 2008, 181). Each of these three subperiods featured different policies and patterns of development for the agricultural and fishing sectors. The first period (1951–1955) was characterized by a strong interventionist posture of the state. Following patterns already adopted in Fordist Europe, the Japanese state stimulated private economic activities but also intervened through direct investment and ownership of businesses. This State Monopoly Capitalism Policy was intended to propel Japan to a position of economic self-reliance and to maintain social stability (Mishima 2001a; Moriya 1971; Tabata 1990; Teshima 1966). By allowing foreign direct investment, technology, and equipment, the industrial structure of Japan was redirected away from traditional light industries, such as spinning and textiles, into the development of heavy mechanical and chemical production. In this process the Ministry of International Trade and Industry (MITI) played an active and important role by guiding the economy through the licensing of corporations, administrative assistance, and budget support (Johnson 1982; Vogel 1979). Japan's membership in the International Monetary Fund (IMF) in 1952 and GATT in 1955 provided further impetus to the country's rapid industrialization process. Internationally, Japan's economic expansion continued to benefit from America's intent to use it as a tool in the context of the Cold War. The Korean War (1950–1953) and the strategic importance of Japan proved to be a strong stimuli for the expansion of the economy. In this subperiod, the country's agricultural policy was directed to the twofold objective of increasing production and improving the low food self-sufficiency ratio[7] (Ino 1971). The 1952 Agricultural Land Act and the 1950 *Carl S. Shoup Tax Reform* provided the instruments to expand the production and productivity of family farms and reduce the burden of the tax system (Shimamoto 2011, 10; Teruoka 2008, 190–195). The augmentation of farms' efficiency and output involved primarily the production of rice, the country's staple food, but also wheat and livestock. These commodities—and rice in particular—were controlled through price-support programs. In the case of rice, prices for consumers were kept low through direct purchases by the government. Also targeted was the upgrading of infrastructure that included reclamation of farmland, irrigation and drainage projects, and the consolidation of paddy fields. Improved infrastructure allowed increased use of farm equipment and chemicals, whose availability was expanded through the growth of cooperatives. Production cooperatives were also instrumental in implementing price-support programs. As these programs were reduced, so was the relative importance of these institutions. Structurally, the size of farms increased slightly while the number of farmers decreased. Part-time farming became more prominent among operators of small farms (Teruoka 2008).

These part-time farmers sought employment in the expanding off-farm labor market. Accordingly, the growth of this off-farm employment contributed to the improvement of the socioeconomic conditions of rural communities by providing additional income to farmers' households. In many cases, development of road networks and popularization of cars supported the increase of part-time farming, as well as the establishment of corporations in rural areas. As in similar cases recorded in North America and Europe, economic expansion translated into a decline in community solidarity (Jussaume 1991, 156). Efforts to increase agricultural production and the food self-sufficiency ratio were, however, hampered by Japan's participation in the U.S. Food Aid Program in 1954. This program resulted in increased grain imports from the United States and reduced local production (Ino 1971; Kase 1993; Mikuni 2000). Additionally, U.S. imports affected the local diet that gradually Westernized, changing from being centered on rice, fish, and vegetables to being characterized by the augmented consumption of bread, vegetable oil, meats, and dairy products. This dietary shift was further promoted through public school meal programs.

During the second subperiod (1955–1965), the country's fast economic growth propelled Japan to become one of the world's major industrialized and developed economies (Allinson 2004; Endo 1966; Teruoka 2008). Growth in the automotive, home appliance, electronic, and petrochemical sectors accompanied early development in the steel, electric, and shipbuilding sectors. In 1960, the government formulated the *Trade and Currency Liberalization Plan*, which liberalized trade and capital mobility. Japan's membership in the Organisation for Economic Co-operation and Development (OECD) in 1964 cemented the integration of the country into the growing world economy. These changes created a pattern in which Japan's economic development centered on its newly acquired world prominence in the production of industrial goods. The export of industrial products was accompanied by significant imports of such agri-food commodities as wheat and grains, resulting in a positive balance of trade but also in a decrease in food self-sufficiency.[8] Throughout these years, the *zaibatsu* companies recovered from the postwar breakups and formed new groups of corporations known as *keiretsu*[9] as well as business organizations, such as *Keidanren*[10] (Federation of Economic Organizations), the Japanese Association of Corporate Executives, and Japan Chamber of Commerce and Industry.[11]

This renewed power was successfully employed to direct government policies to favor corporate economic interests and the creation of a "corporate state" featuring a strong state-corporation partnership (Moriya 1971).

Rapid industrialization further fueled rural to urban migration. During these years, farmers' and farm workers' outmigration provided needed labor to the industrial sector, promoted the development of part-time farming, and contributed to the improvement of the economic conditions of rural families (Misawa 1969). It also facilitated the mechanization and modernization of farms and the resulting increase in crop and labor productivity (Ino 1971; Teruoka 2008; Tsuchiya 1969). Simultaneously, outmigration generated rural population losses and a significant decrease in the number of full-time farmers and farms. Despite this decrease, farmland consolidation did not take place, and the size of Japanese agricultural operations remained small. Part-time farming and expectations of very lucrative farmland prices offered by urban developers motivated current and former farmers to keep their land. Improved economic conditions resulted in the end of rice shortages and changes in the local diet. High-quality rice, dairy, and meat products; fresh fruits and vegetables; and processed food became part of the everyday food consumed by the Japanese population. This Westernization of food consumption led to higher agri-food imports, while the income gap between farmers and industrial workers grew larger. Facing overall socioeconomic growth but also expanding inequality between urban and rural areas and between industrial and agricultural workers, the government was under pressure to intervene.

The elimination of the socioeconomic gap between agricultural and industrial workers and between rural areas and their urban, industrial counterparts was the objective of the *Agricultural Basic Law* (Ino 1971; Mulgan 2006). Enacted in 1961, this fundamental legislation guided the evolution of agriculture until 1999 when a *New Agricultural Basic Law* was introduced, accompanying Japan's membership in the WTO. The period's agricultural policy was productivist and interventionist. It contemplated the expansion of production and productivity through an overall attempt to increase the size and the output of farms and eliminate small and inefficient operations. At the time, two-thirds of all farms were less than 1 hectare in size, while only 4 percent exceeded 2 hectares (except in Hokkaido). While embracing GATT directives that suggested a more market-oriented approach, the Japanese authorities remained committed to the importance of domestic price control and import tariffs that exceptions to the GATT rules allowed. This regulated opening to market forces also included "selective" state intervention directed to the price support of some commodities, including dairy, meat products, fresh fruits, and vegetables. Rice was also a commodity targeted by state intervention. Following the Agricultural Basic Law's objective of balancing farmers' and wage workers' incomes, the LDP administration increased the price of rice by an average of 9.5 percent per year from 1960 to 1967 (Teruoka 2008, 225–227). While this state action strengthened LDP popularity among rural constituencies, it added to the state deficit, contributed to overproduction, and drew criticism from abroad for its protectionist posture (Jussaume 1991, 7–8).

The third subperiod (1965–1973) began in 1965 with Japan's most serious postwar recession (Teruoka 2008, 243–246). Deficit spending and the availability of credit promoted by the government along with the economic benefits resulting from U.S. involvement in the Vietnam War engendered a rapid recovery. The ensuing growth period, known as the second Rapid Economic Growth period, was sustained and propelled Japan to become the second largest world economy after the United States. The power of large corporations increased, and the burgeoning trade surplus created trade frictions with the United States and other countries. Japan's export-oriented economy and its multifaceted restrictive import policy in agri-food were the subject of negotiations and trade "retaliations"[12] (Hayami 1988, 1). Ultimately, U.S. requests to open the Japanese market to American agri-food exports and domestic corporate designs to provide cheap food for industrial workers motivated the Japanese government to reduce state intervention (Sekishita 1987). Japan's industrial growth continued, but its food self-sufficiency ratio declined. Following the policy initiated earlier with the Agricultural Basic Law, increased agricultural production was sought for selected crops only. The service sector increased its importance and emerged as a further outlet for the surplus rural population. Growth translated into increased wages but also rapidly increasing prices, including those of such items as housing and land. Emerging urban social problems, such as overcrowding; long commutes; and water, air, and sound pollution, were accompanied by the aging and shrinking of the rural population (Endo 1966). Responses to these problems included the emergence of antipollution movements and the election of reformist local governments throughout the country (Matsubara 1971; Shimizu 1995).

Facing urban overcrowding and pollution, corporations began to move their operations to rural areas. Cheaper labor, more affordable land, and clean and plentiful natural resources represented significant incentives for the corporate leadership to relocate plants. The ensuing shift in land and natural resource use further increased part-time farming and transformed many members of farm households into wage laborers. While some farmers were able to expand their operations, small farms and part-time farming remained the norm (Teruoka 2008, 250–252). Beginning in 1968, increases in rice productivity and declining consumption resulted in surpluses that encouraged the government to alter price-support programs and introduce production-adjustment measures. These policy changes prompted a decrease in farm income that was once again compensated by off-farm employment. The growth of part-time employment also contributed to the decrease of the gap between farm and industrial income that characterized the period.

During the first Rapid Economic Growth period, the fishing industry was also affected by the growth experienced by the rest of the economy. In 1952 and just preceding the signing of the San Francisco Peace Treaty, the MacArthur Line was abolished (Kawai 1994, 55). Over the following years, the lifting of this restriction, the increasing demand for food and resultant food shortages, the installation of industrial plants along the coast, and the construction of new trading ports prompted Japanese fishing boats to move to offshore waters. Deep-sea fishing grew significantly and included the development of a large tuna fishing industry (Bonanno and Constance 2008, 57–83; Kawai 1994, 65–66). At the coastal level, the loss of fishing space and fishing rights translated into economic problems and the outmigration of local fishermen. Reclamation and pollution generated by industrial expansion further impacted the socioeconomic situation in these areas (Kawai 1994, 70–72).[13]

Agriculture under Neoliberal Globalization and Its Crisis

The end of the Rapid Economic Growth period coincided with a prolonged economic crisis. Following international trends, attempts to address it centered on a shift from Fordist state interventionist policies to Neoliberal market-oriented policies. Continuing trade frictions with global partners and the appreciation of the yen further characterized the liberalization of the agri-food market and the so-called *Low Economic Growth period*. Ensuing concerns about food security, food safety, environmental protection, and land management quickly became the new challenges not only for Japanese agriculture and rural areas but also for all Japanese citizens. The ruling LDP lost credibility and strength; its neoliberal policies and pro-corporate posture stimulated popular resistance and efforts to promote social welfare and the environment (Allinson 2004; Bailey 1996; Teruoka 2008). For heuristic purposes, these years are divided into two periods. The first refers to the transition from the Rapid Economic Growth period to the globalization era. It begins with the collapse of the Bretton Woods system in 1973 and ends with the Plaza Accord in 1985. The second period opens after the signing of the Plaza Accord in 1985 that symbolizes the beginning of the Neoliberal globalization era in Japan.[14]

The End of Fordism and Low Economic Growth Period (1973–1985)

The conditions facilitating the Fordist regime came to an end in the early 1970s. The ideology of modernization and its promises of constant economic growth, emancipation of subordinate groups, and reduction of global inequality were delegitimized. The continuous existence of disparities, calls for equality, and actions to reduce the power asymmetry between North and South and between dominant and subordinate classes provided the instruments for the permanent crisis of the post–World War II system. The inability of developed nation-states to maintain high levels of domestic social spending and economic intervention engendered a fiscal crisis that negatively impacted corporate requests for state support and subordinate classes' calls for expanded and efficient welfare programs. The world oil crises (in 1973 and 1979), stagflation, rising unemployment, and social instability ushered the end of fixed exchange rates and Keynesian economic policies (Antonio and Bonanno 2000; Harvey 1989). By the beginning of the 1980s, Neoliberalism established itself as the new dominant political ideology. The rise to power of Margaret Thatcher in Great Britain, Ronald Reagan in the United States, and Yasuhito Nakasone in Japan marked this transition. As uncertainty and concerns about damaging economic downturns characterized the mood of the country during these years, Japan was able to extend its trade surplus. Technology innovations, labor restructuring measures, and cost reduction moves that offset the appreciation of the yen explain this outcome. Toyota's "just-in-time" system, the world-acclaimed business model of the time, symbolized Japan's success. Though less known, this restructuring resulted in a 6.5 percent contraction of wage workers in manufacturing between 1970 and 1980 (Teruoka 2008, 275–276). In effect, behind the glittering façade of corporate success and economic gains, workers' conditions deteriorated as the cost of living increased, wages stagnated, and stable jobs were eliminated and/or replaced with precarious, part-time, and low-paying employment[15] (Teruoka 2008, 275–276). Moreover, during this period, those who worked harder to keep their "good" jobs often feared *Karoshi* (Allinson 2004; Bailey 1996).

Despite the worsening conditions of urban employment, agricultural workers continued to leave farming. Mechanization and structural changes generated excess farm labor, and the total number of farms decreased. Indexed at 100 in 1965, farm labor stood at 65 in 1975 and 60 in 1980. A group of larger farms developed, and the Japanese agricultural structure became polarized following similar trends in major advanced industrial societies of the time (Bonanno 1987). Part-time farming grew further. Among part-time farmers, the proportion of the self-employed decreased while the proportion of those with urban wage

51

jobs increased (Teruoka 2008, 279; Usami 1990). Price-support levels for rice were increased in the early 1970s to respond to the worldwide food crisis. But they were rolled back by 1978, and land set aside and crop substitution programs were introduced. Farmers were encouraged to convert rice production to soybeans, wheat, and feed crops (Yokoyama 2000). The further diffusion of the Western diet, however, made these measures less effective, and rice overproduction became the norm. Because Japan's economic development policies required an emphasis on industrial exports, the adoption of price supports for agriculture became less feasible. Accordingly, agricultural policies focused on structural improvements and the deregulation of farmland. As urban and industrial uses of land increased, the price and pressure to make more land available also increased. As the 1980s unfolded, it was clear that the proclaimed objectives of the Agricultural Basic Law were far from being achieved (Teruoka 2008, 282–284). To be sure, compared to the immediate postwar years, the economic conditions of rural residents had significantly improved, and severe rural poverty was de facto eliminated. However, rural income growth was largely the result of increased off-farm work, and farmers' part-time jobs generated low wages and unstable employment.

Neoliberal Globalization Era (1985–2010)

The neoliberal reforms introduced since the late 1970s gave impetus to the globalization of social and economic relations, including agri-food (Bonanno and Constance 2008; Bonanno et al. 1994). Relaxation of barriers to the circulation of capital; commodities; and, to a much lesser degree, labor provided the conditions for decentralization of production processes, the creation of global networks of production and consumption, and the growth of transnational corporations (Antonio and Bonanno 2000; Bonanno and Cavalcanti 2011). The Plaza Agreement in 1985 and the related GATT Uruguay Round (1986–1993) and its eventual transformation into the WTO represented some of the salient policy steps taken under the new regime. As a result of these policy agreements, Japan was asked to allow a significant appreciation of its currency and further liberalization of the agri-food market. Promoted by U.S. plans to restrain international competition, restore American companies' market share, and dispose of U.S. agricultural surpluses, these requests resulted in the elimination of the 1961 Agricultural Basic Law and its replacement with the New Agricultural Basic Law in 1999. This new policy for agriculture fully embraced neoliberal ideology and practices that inspired globalization-oriented reforms worldwide. These conditions also led to the growth of Japan's "bubble economy" of the late 1980s and its eventual collapse in the early 1990s.

In the mid-1980s, Japanese industrial corporations had control of a significant portion of the U.S. market. The export of automobiles, machinery, communication equipment, and electronics had generated a large trade surplus for Japan and, simultaneously, significant problems for U.S. corporations and the U.S. economy (Sekishita 1987). Responding to corporate calls to act, the U.S. government imposed sanctions on Japan for "unfair trade practices" and demanded the appreciation of the yen that would reduce Japan's trade advantage. The United States' and other countries' corporate circles were looking for measures that would limit Japanese exports and allow better access of foreign products to Japan. The Plaza Agreement of 1985 sanctioned the appreciation of the yen and the concomitant devaluation of the U.S. dollar that virtually ended the Japanese spectacular post-war economic growth (Ikeda 2004, 380).

In response to the changed conditions, Japanese corporations introduced technical innovations and, more importantly, began, and subsequently increased, the relocation of production facilities to the United States and other countries. Accordingly, Japanese companies, such as Honda and Toyota, assumed a new "nationality" and became "American." Honda of America and Toyota Motor of North America located plants in the United States (and also Canada), hired American workers and managers, and promoted themselves as U.S. enterprises. These moves initiated a process of decentralization of production that remains a fundamental characteristic of neoliberal globalization and transnational corporations (Bonanno and Constance 2008). By assuming a new "nationality" and adopting transnational strategies and policies, the traditional identity between corporations and their native countries became increasingly blurred. The increased imports generated by corporate decentralization negatively affected domestic production. In agri-food, the appreciation of the yen also favored further growth of agri-food imports and made competition in the food market increasingly difficult for Japanese producers. It also further lowered domestic food prices, favoring industrial corporations' plans to reduce labor costs.

In this context, three important events oriented the Japanese agri-food policy in the neoliberal era (Mulgan 2006; Okada 1998; Teruoka 2008, 304–309). First, following the report of the U.S.-Japan Advisory Commission in 1984 and under international pressure, Japan further deregulated its agri-food market. In particular, it removed barriers to beef and citrus fruit imports in 1990 and 1991, respectively. These were commodities whose production was encouraged under the Agricultural Basic Law. Second, in 1986 the so-called Maekawa Report was adopted as a guiding principle for the development of agri-food. This report called for Japan to commit to the emerging neoliberal ideology by strengthening deregulations and adopting a low-interest monetary policy. Moreover, the report invited Japan to reverse its export-oriented economic strategy and protectionist agri-food policies in favor of postures that would emphasize expanded domestic demand and free-market competition. The report also called for the further modernization of farms to meet global market competition. Third, also in 1986, the Japanese Agricultural Policy Council issued its recommendations following the Maekawa Report. These recommendations stressed the importance of (1) adopting market mechanisms for all agri-food commodities; (2) improving the productive capacity of Japanese farms and enhancing their competitiveness; (3) considering consumer policies that would allow the consumption of quality foods; (4) improving rural life and society; and (5) addressing the issue of the aging rural population.

The economic reforms that followed contributed to the creation of the bubble economy of the second half of the 1980s and the long recession period of the 1990s (Asher 1998; Teruoka 2008, 310–313). Low interest rates, public investment, and speculation resulted in steep rises in stocks, land, and housing prices. The deregulation of the land market allowed a significant flow of investment that promoted the conversion of farmland into land for urban construction projects and the development of tourist resorts. These projects further attracted investment and ignited a speculative spiral in which land and other commodities as well as stock prices skyrocketed. Marking what would become one of the most distinctive characteristics of the phenomenon of financialization (Bonanno 2013), the transformation of land into a market asset inflated prices, detached them from the actual value of commodities, generated a significant amount of wealth for financial elites, and prevented many members of the middle and working classes from being able to afford a home.

In late 1980s, the end of the Cold War ushered in the rapid advancement of globalization, which involved neoliberal reforms, the strengthening of transnational corporations, and the establishment of the WTO system. Global neoliberalization signified increased wealth for corporate and financial elites in Japan and other countries of the developed North (but also in some countries of the South) and generated an optimistic view of socioeconomic growth, symbolized by the period's ideology of the Washington Consensus (Harvey 2005a; Robinson 2004; Stiglitz 2003). But these years also brought to the fore growing class disparities,[16] economic instability, food shortages, and mounting environmental problems. In Japan, as in other parts of the world, antiglobalization movements emerged, calling for social justice, the protection of the environment, sustainable economic growth, and enhanced social welfare.

While the United States recovered from the economic downturns of the 1980s and entered the "roaring 1990s" (Stiglitz 2003), Japan began a long period of recession. Known as the "lost decade," the 1990s revealed the dire consequences of the financialization-induced end of the bubble economy (Ikeda 2004). The prices of stocks, land, and housing entered a downward spiral; insolvency, bankruptcies, and financial instability became constant features of the Japanese economy. Even cooperatives in agriculture amassed significant debts that crippled them. Traditional measures of economic policy were ineffective. The introduction of very low interest rates did not translate into growth, and national and local governments increased their deficits. The value of the yen sharply rose. This exponential strengthening of the yen reduced the trade surplus, made exports difficult, curbed domestic production and employment, and prompted local corporate elites to introduce drastic restructuring measures. Labor was the primary target of this process. Eliminated were stable, relatively well remunerated blue and white collar jobs and the benefit systems that have traditionally accompanied these types of jobs.[17] Highly unstable part-time employment with limited benefits became a characteristic of the Japanese labor market. Members of the working and lower middle classes became accustomed to short work weeks and short-term employment contracts.[18] In this context, the unemployment rate more than doubled through the decade.[19] Discontent was countered by arguments stressing that restructuring measures were necessary to maintain Japan's global competitiveness. And as corporations kept on exporting jobs, capital, and production facilities and transnationalizing, the increasingly less popular ruling LDP continued to pursue its pro-globalization neoliberal agenda and governed the country with only a brief interruption from 2009 to 2012.

Throughout the 1990s and the 2000s, the Japanese government strongly deregulated the economy, and postwar Fordist agri-food policies were revised and/or eliminated (Mishima 2001b, 33; Teruoka 2008, 323). The measures that replaced them (such as the new Agricultural Basic Law of 1999 and Law for Stabilization of Supply-Demand and Price of Staple Food—the so-called Staple Food Law) positioned agri-food to follow policies inspired by free-market ideology. The results were a further decrease in production, the number of farms, full-time farmers, and cultivated land.[20] Additionally, the aging of the population and the worsening of the socioeconomic situation of farmers and rural communities completed the image of a sector in crisis.[21] To be sure, the introduction of mechanical and chemical innovations prompted a sharp increase in productivity. But this growth was insufficient to make Japanese agriculture adequately competitive in the world market while creating further concerns about environmental pollution and food quality. The declining value of production characterized important commodities, such as rice, livestock, fruits, and vegetables that once were protected by state intervention (Tabata 2008, 129). In 1990, the number of farms stood at 3.8 million, down from 6 million in 1955 (MIC 2008). This number further declined to 2.5 million in 2010,[22] indicating the serious economic—but also social—problems affecting the sector. Its ability to expand was seriously compromised (MAFF 2011a). Of the remaining farms, about two-thirds were part-time, as inadequate and declining farm income pushed farmers out of the sector. The resulting reduction in cultivated land brought it to a total of 3.4 million ha in 2010, down from 5.2 million ha in 1955. As the total number of farms declined, those considered larger farms (5 ha or greater, except in Hokkaido) increased in number between 2005 and 2010 (MAFF 2011a).

Dissatisfied with the declining farm income but also with the farm lifestyle, younger rural residents showed decreasing interest in agriculture. The resulting aging of the farm population emerged as one of the most significant problems of Japanese agriculture. Farmers' average age rose to 65.8 years in 2010 from 56.7 in 1990, while the number of farmers 65 and older stood at 61.6 percent of all farmers at the outset of the 2010s (MAFF 2010a, 2011a, 2011b). Agricultural income peaked in 1975 at 2 million yen per year per household. But, it decreased to 1 million yen by 1999 (Teruoka 2008, 336). Part-time farmers' off-farm income also declined, and pensions covered a greater portion of the total farm household income. In 2010, 35 percent of all farmers were identified as subsistence farmers. The reduced presence of farmers on the land contributed to the deterioration of environmental conditions, damages to the ecosystem, and the unchecked growth of wildlife (Makino 2010, 7–10; Yorimitsu 2011, 10–11). Administrative consolidation and decreased government spending further reduced the resources available to rural communities (Okada 2007, 223, 226; Tada 1999, 103–104).

The neoliberal economic reforms also challenged the existing public wholesale market system. Japan has an established history of public wholesale auction markets that were first formalized by the Central Wholesale Market Law of 1923 (Agricultural Marketing Society of Japan 1999; Takizawa et al. 2003). This act significantly modernized the then-dominant semi-feudal, middlemen-led wholesale market system by creating a publicly controlled auction market system featuring higher transparency and greater benefits to the public. Additionally, the new system allowed a significant number of small-scale producers and independent small and medium-sized retailers to participate in the market activities, establish business networks, improve transaction efficiency, and offer more regulated and fairer competition among stakeholders. Setting commodity prices through auctions emerged as one of the major and most beneficial functions of wholesale markets, as it limited the ability of large food and retailing corporations to influence price setting.

At its peak in 1985, the Central Wholesale Market included 91 markets (Agricultural Marketing Society of Japan 1999). Beginning in the late 1980s, however, the wholesale market system initiated a decline that brought its share of the trading of agri-food commodities down to historical lows. From 1989 to 2008, the trading of all fruits declined from 78 percent to 46 percent; vegetables from 85 percent to 74 percent; fish from 75 percent to 58 percent; and meat from 23 percent to 10 percent (Hosokawa 2012). The reasons for such a decline are associated with the neoliberalization of agri-food and the concomitant crisis of independent small and medium-sized producers and the concentration of retailing. More specifically, three events played important roles in the shaping of this situation. First, domestic and transnational supermarket chains increased their presence in the retail sector. Due to their size, they tend to bypass wholesale markets. Second, the liberalization of agri-food markets allowed a massive inflow of imported commodities that are not traded in these markets. Third, grouped under local production cooperatives and their prefectural and national level organizations, domestic producers began to sell their crops directly via contractual schemes (Sakazume 1999). Adding to these changes and since the early 2000s, some local governments have privatized their public wholesale markets, while the national government has liberalized the wholesale commission rates to enhance competition.

These policies and events triggered several relevant consequences. First, they engendered a market duality, featuring a pole of rapidly growing markets contrasted by a pole of fast declining yet still relatively numerous small markets with a limited group of middle-level markets (Hosokawa 2012). Second, as the importance of wholesale auction markets declined, their ability to set commodity prices diminished as well. The setting of agri-food prices has become increasingly influenced by corporate actions, with a loss of competition, transparency, and fairness. Finally, wholesale markets are still an important source of agri-food products for small retailers, who play an important role in the local economy and employment structure. Accordingly, their decline affects local communities in ways that cannot be compensated by the corporatization of agri-food.

Neoliberal globalization was resisted, and opposition movements emerged. In agri-food, paralleling similar projects that emerged in other advanced countries worldwide, various initiatives sought to create alternative systems of food production and consumption and to promote the balanced growth of rural areas. Such programs as green tourism and locally based developmental schemes (Abe, 1999; Japanese Association for Rural Studies 2008; Miyamoto, 1998; Yamada, Endo, and Hobo 1998), agro-ecology, organic farming, and safe foods (Tsutaya 2000a), farmer-to-consumer cooperation or *Teikei,* and Community Supported Agriculture emerged (Amemiya 2011; Ichihara 2006; Ikegami 2010; Jordan and Hisano 2011; Nakajima and Kanda 2001; Oyama 2004; Parker 2005; Yasuda 1986). Consumer cooperatives continued to pursue their objective of enhancing food safety through the creation of direct links with farmer groups and production cooperatives. However, they also faced difficulties under neoliberal globalization as they experienced strong competition from corporate supermarkets (Takizawa and Hosokawa 2000). Despite opposition, the Japanese administration kept its neoliberal policy and further liberalized agri-food markets by establishing bilateral and multilateral agreements, such as FTA, EPA, and TPP.

The Japanese fishing sector also experienced restructuring and an overall decline under neoliberal globalization. Although Japan could still count itself as among the seven largest EEZs in the world, its size was reduced to 200 nautical miles in 1977. Additionally, Japanese vessels lost access to a number of foreign fishing grounds, resulting in a reduction of the catch from international waters (Kawai 1994, 73–78). This loss of deep-sea catches—down to 1.3 million mt in 1992 from 4 million in 1973—was compensated by imports that grew from 1 million mt tons to 4.7 million over the same period. The strong yen, the liberalization of import quotas, and tariffs also contributed to this growth (Iwasa 2004, 202–203; Yamao and Torii 2000, 225–230). At its peak in 1984, the catch of Japanese fishing vessels stood at 12.8 million mt, but declined to 5.6 million mt in 2009 (Yamao 2011, 135). The economic crisis transformed consumer demand, and less expensive fish varieties replaced high-grade expensive fish (Masui and Jo 2003, 142). Technological progress in freezing, processing, and delivery systems, however, addressed the diminished quantity of fish and changes in demand. Additionally, the transnationalization of operations allowed general trading companies, such as Mitsubishi and Marubeni, and global companies in the sector, such as Maruha and Nippon Suisan, to reduce labor costs and source their subsidiaries for imports (Sekishita 1987, 315–316; Yamao 2011, 134). State support and investment declined. Loans and financing for fishermen became more difficult, and more than half the remaining state intervention was devoted to the construction of ports (Kawai 1994, 84–86). During this period, Japanese boats were criticized for their aggressive and overexploitative strategies in foreign waters. Charges of environmental and ecosystem damages stigmatized Japan's fishing fleet (Iwasa 2004, 208–209).

Economic growth along with policies that promoted labor migration to urban centers significantly contributed to the reduction of the number of fishermen. The loss of foreign fishing grounds following the resizing of the EEZ, the reclamation and pollution of coastal areas, and the increase of less expensive imports accelerated job losses. In this context, the number of families involved in fishing declined to 115,000 in 2008 from 250,000 in 1955 (MAFF 2010b; MIC 2008). While productivity increased, the income of fishermen remained low and stood at half that of urban wage workers in 1990 (Kawai 1994, 6). Economic hardship and difficult working conditions motivated younger members of families of fishermen to seek employment in other sectors. A reduced labor force and deregulation fostered the use of foreign workers, mostly from Indonesia and other areas of Southeast Asia (Iwasa 2004, 212–213). Responding to the worsening of economic and working conditions, fishermen organized and mounted protests (Isobe 1999, 213). Their protests centered on altering developmental policies that targeted coastal areas for the construction of industrial plants, tourist resorts, and nuclear power plants and the production of gravel. The safeguarding of the environment and the creation of alternative and sustainable patterns of development along with the desire to deliver better quality food to urban consumers inspired fishermen to carry out initiatives along these lines. Notable was the development of programs for the direct delivery of marine products to urban consumers and those that fostered fishermen's multiple activities, such as community-based tourism and hospitality services (Isobe 1999, 217).

Corporations in Agriculture

Contemporary agriculture is one of the most globalized sectors in the world. As it globalized, the power of transnational corporations increased significantly in all facets of production and consumption (Bonanno and Constance 2008). This is the case in Japan as well, even though Japanese agriculture remains characterized by the presence of a significant family/small business sector. This sector covers 98 percent of the total number of all Agriculture Management Entities[23] in the country (MAFF 2011a). However, as family farming becomes increasingly part-time and farmers leave the sector, the presence of corporate agriculture has acquired increasing importance.

Land tenure policies affected changes in the structure of agriculture. Easing and eventually reversing the policy that favored the control of farmland by farm families initiated with land reforms, the government took steps to facilitate the commercial availability of farmland during the neoliberal globalization era. To be sure, already in the 1960s legislation increased the maximum limits of farm size to favor large-scale production. Additionally, at the same time, the right to farm was extended to include legal persons with the exception of publicly traded companies (Shimamoto 2011, 13; Teruoka 2008, 222). These legal persons acquired the special legal status of Agricultural Production Corporations, which allowed them access to farmland. Further deregulation occurred in the 1970s. These measures promoted the leasing and sale of farmland with the objective of increasing the overall farm size (Shimamoto 2011, 16–18; Teruoka 2008, 260–261).

Despite these reforms, the corporate presence in agriculture and the number of large farms remained quite low, with some exceptions in the production of selected commodities, such as poultry, hogs, greenhouse horticulture, and some arable crops. The depressed price of rice and increases in land value generated by the construction boom of the 1970s limited the leasing of farmland (Shimamoto 2011, 19–20; Teruoka 2008, 293–294). To rectify this situation, the government introduced measures that allowed short-term leasing (up to three years). In this scheme, nonagricultural corporations were still excluded. Additional measures introduced in the 1980s further promoted structural changes. In 1992, the process of revising the 1961 Agricultural Basic Law was initiated. Under the 1999 New Agricultural Basic Law, the management model recommended for Japanese farms addressed the existence of corporate farming, and publicly traded corporations were recognized as having the legal right to farm in 2000 (Taniwaki 2011, 202). With this act, the land reform era's goal of an exclusively family farm agricultural sector was definitively abandoned (Teruoka 2008, 344). Measures designed to provide structural support and financial services to larger/corporate farms were also introduced in the 1990s, signaling a more overt national and regional government support of large commercial operations. The result was the concentration of land: the top 1 percent of all farms occupied 26.2 percent of total farmland in 2010 (MAFF 2011a). However, these farms remained relatively small compared to their counterparts in Europe and North America (the average size of Japanese farms stood at 2.2 hectares compared to 169.6 hectares in the United States and 14.1 hectares in the EU in 2010) (MAFF 2015), and although growing in size, they suffered from the consequences of intense global competition and indebtedness.

The liberalization of the farmland market and the corporate presence in farming were promoted by business circles—such as *Keidanren*, the most influential Japanese business circle—and the governing administration. In the 2000s, the administration of Prime Minister Koizumi of the LDP promoted neoliberal reforms that culminated in the establishment of Special Economic

Zones (SEZs). Their aim was to restructure and revitalize a number of economic sectors, including agriculture (Fujii 2007, 201; JAJA 2004, 10–11; Shimamoto 2011, 26–27; Taniwaki 2011, 202). In farming, the land-leasing system was implemented in 2002, allowing publicly traded nonagricultural corporations to have direct access to farmland. In this system, nonagricultural corporations were required to have at least one of their board members engaged in agricultural production and sign an agreement with the local government to lease agricultural land. The agricultural land available for leasing was limited to areas where land was abandoned by family farmers. However, ownership was not permitted to nonagricultural corporations. Local governments could unilaterally terminate leasing contracts in the event of violations of leasing rules by corporations.

Concerns over corporate leasing of land quickly emerged. Among those, fears that corporations would focus on short-term profit and disregard long-term developmental objectives, quickly abandon land cultivation in case of economic downturns, contaminate land through the illegal disposal of waste and toxic material, and affect water availability to rural communities surfaced (JAJA 2004, 27). Calls for a more careful evaluation of the consequences of implementing the SEZ system were made. However, the government quickly approved the expansion of SEZs nationwide and the further liberalization of agriculture in 2005 (Shimamoto 2011, 27). Despite these changes, which virtually bypassed the Agricultural Land Act, the Japanese business leadership remained dissatisfied and called for direct farmland ownership for corporations and a revision of the Agricultural Land Act. As the law was revised in 2009, the classical principle of farming by landed farmers disappeared from Japanese legislation (Harada 2011, 38; Taniwaki 2011, 203).

The changes to the legal system resulted in an increase in the number of nonagricultural corporations involved in production. In 2004, 71 corporations leased farmland in the SEZs occupying 132.4 ha. In 2009, this number reached 436 units on 1,356 ha (Muroya 2007, 16; Taniwaki 2011, 206) (figure 2.1). After the revised Agricultural Land Act was introduced in 2009, the number of nonagricultural corporations further grew to 144 and 1,071 in 2010 and 2012, respectively (MAFF 2013b). Among the corporations that invested in farming, food processing, distribution, and service companies constituted the most numerous group (figure 2.2).

Their objectives have primarily been related to vertical integration; reduction of transaction costs; and access to specialized agricultural products, such as organic fruits and vegetables. Construction corporations represent the second largest group. Following the real estate collapse of the 1990s, reduced economic opportunities in construction motivated these companies to search for

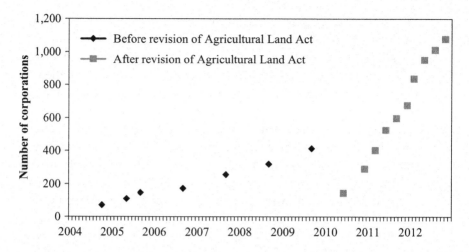

Figure 2.1. Number of corporations before and after the revision of the Agricultural Land Act. *Source*: Authors' compilation based on data presented by Muroya (2007) and MAFF (2013b).

alternative investments. The high demand for farm labor from spring to fall and the concomitant low demand for labor in construction during the same period, the presence of many part-time farmers among construction workers, and the availability of machine operators all facilitated the involvement of these companies in farming (JAJA 2004, 11–12). The remaining corporations consist of a variety of companies, including enterprises whose business activities center primarily on manufacturing, railroad, communication, and finance (table 2.2).

However, almost 60 percent of nonagricultural corporations involved in agriculture recorded losses by 2008 (Sadakiyo 2012). Despite the difficult business environment, the reasons for their presence in agriculture vary and include the construction of ecologically friendly and consumer-appealing images and recession-safe investment schemes. In a global market, these corporations' involvement in agriculture may be temporary, as the constant search for better financial opportunities characterizes their overall business posture. In effect, the financial sector is increasingly making attempts to create initiatives in the Real Estate Investment Trust sector for the right to future use of farmland (Iwamura 2008).

Corporations expanded their presence in the fishing sector as well. While some corporations operated in deep-sea fishing in the prewar era, the

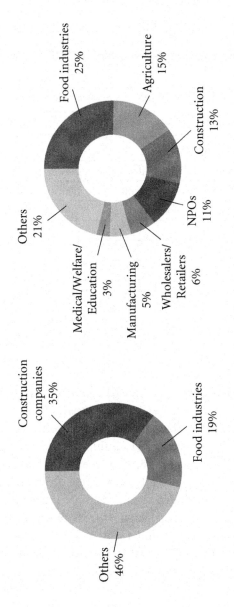

Figure 2.2. Types of corporations involved in agricultural production. *Source:* Authors' compilation based on data from MAFF (2013b).

Table 2.2. Large corporations with investment in agricultural production (2000–2011)

Type of Business	Name of Company
Agriculture	Japan Tobacco, Dole Japan
Food processing	Kagome, Mercian, Kewpie, House Foods, Kyusai
Food service	Mos Food, Monteroza, Watami, Saizeriya, Lawson, Yoshinoya, Skylark
Retailer	Seven & I Holdings, AEON, Coop Hiroshima, Hankyu Department Store
Trading	Itochu, Sumitomo, Mitsui, Mitsubishi, Marubeni, Nissho-Iwai, Toyota-Tsusho
Beverages	Sapporo Beer, Suntry Holdings, Kirin Brewery
Manufacturing	Toyota Motor, Nittobo, Showa Denko, Omron, Secom
Communication	NTT Communications
Railroads	Japan Railroad
Chemicals	Sumitomo Chemical
Finance	Promise

Source: Authors' compilation based on information available in Muroya (2007), Taniwaki (2011) and Tsutaya (2000b).

Note: These companies invest in agricultural production directly or through subsidies.

contemporary deep-sea Japanese fleet is nearly controlled and managed by corporate entities (Kawai 2011, 47). Coastal fishing, conversely, is still dominated by small family-owned operations. Despite their resilience and cultural importance, however, these small independent local units are decreasing in number and economic relevance (Hasegawa 2003, 153). The loss of water space due to reclamations, water contamination, and competition from corporate enterprises are factors that have contributed to their decline. The growth of publicly held companies was fueled by financial support from the government and by the granting of fishing rights—albeit under different conditions—in 2001. In recent decades, the decline of family-owned coastal fishing operations has been compensated by the growth of aquaculture. Introduced in the 1960s, production accelerated in 1970s and by the mid-1980s, it was three times greater than in the prior decade (Kawai 1994, 116). By 2003, total output reached 1.3 million mt at a value of 4.2 million U.S. dollars. It stood at about 22 percent of the total domestic fish production and 31 percent of the total value of the fish produced.

By 2011, the sector total revenue rose to 2.4 billion U.S. dollars. However, it declined by almost 4 percent from its peak in 2007. Given its size, aquaculture remains an important sector for small family-run fishing operations. Simultaneously, however, many of these family-owned businesses have been acquired by large corporations, such as Nippon Suisan (Hasegawa 2003, 153).

The evolution of fisheries paralleled that of farming. During the Rapid Economic Growth period, the fishing sector served as a reservoir of labor for the manufacturing sector and generated needed food for urban workers as much of its space was absorbed by industrial development. Similar to farming, the growth of large corporations, the power of food retailers, and the reduction of family units characterized the era of neoliberal globalization. A limited supply of labor and aging workers are the result of intensive restructuring that reduced the number of workers to about 200,000 in 2008, down from more than 1 million in 1949 (Yamao 2011, 146). Among the remaining fishermen, one-third of them are 65 years old or older. As small-sized family fishing operations still constitute the majority in this sector and play an important role in the economy of fishing villages, albeit with less influence in the food system, cooperatives have come to represent the most concrete alternative to corporate power. Since the 1970s, fishing cooperatives have supplied large food retailers and consumer cooperatives through increased contractual relations (Kawai 1994, 207–208). Today, cooperatives play an important role in local economies and in the resource management of coastal fisheries. They are also relevant in decisions regarding the type of fishing equipment, grounds, and sizes of catches; they also manage financial business (banking) and insurance, and sales of equipment, feeds, and fuel. Fishermen use cooperatives to ship their products to local wholesale markets near fishing ports that are eventually sold to larger urban wholesale markets and retailers. Transactions are based on consignment (Kawai 1994, 143; Masui and Jo 2003, 140). There were about 1,000 cooperatives, 471 regional wholesale markets, and 44 urban wholesale markets in 2011 (MAFF 2012a). The proportion of marine products shipped through wholesale markets stood at 58 percent in 2010 (MAFF 2012a, 2013a).

Conclusions

Overall, the increasing presence of corporations in Japanese farming and fisheries indicates the significant modernization of the sectors achieved since the end of World War II. These changes in the sectors are also a reflection of the importance of agriculture in the process of socioeconomic development in Japan. Manufacturing was the engine of the astonishing growth of the Japanese economy in the second half of the twentieth century. However, the roles of reservoir of labor for urban and industrial expansion, supplier of food and raw materials for industries and cities, market for chemical and mechanical products, and a diplomacy trump card for international negotiations made agriculture and fishing fundamental components of the Japanese economy and society.

After World War II, the Japanese economy depended on American support and was significantly affected by U.S. strategic interests. Agri-food was not an exception. It was reformed in the context of the economic recovery program planned by the United States and employed as a tool against communism during the Cold War. Through land reform, the semifeudal system of landlord and tenants was eliminated and Japanese agriculture began to feature capitalist economic relations and development. The Agricultural Land Act affirmed the principle of farming centered on family owned and managed operations. Their small size, fragmentation, and high production costs prompted the progressive rejection of this principle for a more commercial agriculture based on larger and more competitive farms. Changes in land tenure regulation and the introduction of leasing were featured in this process. Rural to urban migration was encouraged, and the farm and fishing sectors functioned as reservoirs of surplus labor for the expanding industrial sector and cities. Some owners of small farms stayed on their farms but relied on other employment to sustain their economic standing. This shift is credited with enhancing the development of more efficient agriculture production in the country. However, farm size and production remained undersized compared to other advanced countries. Paradoxically, this less than efficient status of agriculture worked well for the expansion of Japan's economy during the Rapid Economic Growth period.

As Japan's economy stalled in the 1980s and neoliberal measures were introduced, Japan's agri-food shrank rapidly. The state reduced its intervention in agriculture and progressively opened its market to international products. Less expensive foreign commodities and the concomitant need to maintain access to international industrial markets shaped the government's actions. Pressure to further liberalize the agricultural market mounted, and alignment with the world-dominant neoliberal requirements became a primary objective of the Japanese administration in the twenty-first century. Presently, farming faces a declining and aging labor force; competition for acquisition and control of farmland; and issues concerning environmental protection, sustainable development, and socioeconomic stability. To address these problems, the government proposes further market liberalization and expansion of the corporate sector. Financial and legislative support for corporations involved in agri-food are viewed as important tools to revitalize and rationalize the sector. As these proposals are discussed and some are implemented, concerns about the effectiveness and desirability of this posture increase. Of particular importance is the corporate sector's push to enhance its access to land and the concomitant design to revise existing farmland legislation (Harada 2011, 40). As worries about the use of land as a financial tool and the overall financialization of agri-food mount, further deregulation of the sector and Japan's participation in the TPP add to the contested terrain of agri-food development in the country.

NOTES

1. The term "Fordism" is commonly employed to define the state-regulated economy and society of most of the twentieth century. Its beginning is placed after the end of World War I, and its final crisis occurred the 1970s. High Fordism refers to 1945–1978. See note 6 below.

2. Some of these monopolies included familiar names, such as Mitsui, Mitsubishi, Sumitomo, Yasuda, and Nissan. Their contemporary economic clout reveals the lack of success of reforms promoted by the United States. In effect, the need to accelerate Japan's industrialization in the context of the Cold War motivated U.S. authorities to quickly abandon their antimonopoly campaign in the early 1950s (Allinson 2004; Baily 1996).

3. In the context of the Cold War, labor reforms and policy were directed toward economic growth. Trade unions, especially in the public sector, were strictly controlled and regulated. Additionally, the creation of company-based unions prevented the creation of a national union movement that, instead, characterized the development of other advanced economies in Europe and North America (Garside 2014).

4. This period (1603–1868) refers to the rule of the Tokugawa *shogunate*, and it is also known as the *Tokugawa Period*. It was characterized by the strict rule of shoguns (feudal lords) that fostered economic growth but also political isolationism. Throughout the period, enlightened rules promoted the arts and culture and introduced measures that protected the environment. The period officially ended in May 1868 with the fall of the city of Edo and the Meiji Restoration.

5. The EEZ covers a 200-nautical-mile distance from the coast and constitutes Japan's national waters. Fishing rights in the EEZ are regulated by Japanese law. Fishing grounds outside Japan and other countries' EEZs are considered international waters and are regulated through international agreements.

6. The period from 1945 to 1978 is known as High Fordism. This label is employed to differentiate it from early stages of the Fordist era that began in the early twentieth century (see Aglietta 1979; Antonio and Bonanno 2000). The combination of state intervention, Keynesian economic policy, and the labor-management accord came to fruition, generating high levels of socioeconomic growth and social stability in advanced countries.

7. The food self-sufficiency ratio—which is based on the ratio of required daily calories to produced calories—was adopted as one of the most important indicators of food self-sufficiency by the Japanese administration.

8. The decline in food self-sufficiency was also due to the abovementioned changes in the local diet.

9. *Keiretsu* refers to three types of corporations. The first type is based on the former *zaibatsu*, such as Mitsubishi, Mitsui, and Sumitomo. These corporations prefer horizontal integration. The second type includes companies headed by prominent corporations, such as Toyota. Vertical integration is preferred in this case. The third type involves groups based on financial entities, such as the former Sanwa Bank (acquired by Mitsubishi's financial group in 2006).

10.   The chairperson of *Keidanren* enjoys such as power that he or she is commonly referred to as the "prime minister of the business community." While *Keidanren* was established as an incorporated association under the jurisdiction of MITI in 1946 and has since functioned to connect MITI and major corporations, it has strongly influenced the actions of policymakers through donations, policy proposals, and evaluations of policies sponsored by political parties.

11.   These organizations' primary objective was lobbying.

12.   According to Kim (1987), at the time, the cost of the agricultural policy of Japan as a proportion of its GDP was well above that of Europe.

13.   As the unfolding of the Cold War promoted a flow of capital to Japan, the proliferation of nuclear arms associated with it engendered serious consequences, such as the notorious nuclear bomb tests at Bikini Atoll, which exposed more than 600 Japanese fishing boats and their fishermen to nuclear radiation (Kawai 1994, 57).

14.   In this chapter, our analysis covers the years up to 2010, as 2010 marks the last full year before the March 2011 earthquake, tsunami, and nuclear disaster at Fukushima. The post-2010 years are discussed in the subsequent chapters.

15.   Compared to the deterioration of conditions for wage and middle-class workers experienced in 1990s, the worsening of the status of workers in this period was relatively less severe. However, the term *Karoshi* (or death from overwork) was coined at the time and signaled its severity (Teruoka 2008).

16.   In Japan, inequality has grown since the 1980s. However, its Gini index remained consistently below that of the United States. In 2008, the Gini index for Japan was 0.329, while that for the United States was 0.38 (MHLW 2012a).

17.   In the 1990s, the government of the ruling LDP deregulated the labor market and allowed the percentage of contract workers to increase from 20 percent in 1990 to 25 percent and 37 percent in 1999 and 2014, respectively (Statistics Bureau 2015).

18.   These changes in the labor market directly affected the relative poverty rate, which increased from 12 percent in 1985 to 14.6 percent in 1997 and 16 percent in 2010 (MHLW 2010). By the mid-2000s, this rate exceeded the average of OECD countries, and Japan was ranked as the fourth worst country among all the 30 OECD countries after Mexico, Turkey, and the United States (MHLW 2012a).

19.   The unemployment rate increased from 2.1 percent in 1990 to 4.7 percent in 1999 (Statistics Bureau 2015). The definitions of unemployment used in Japan, however, differs from that used in the United States and the EU. Accordingly, Yamada (2013) points out that the unemployment rate in Japan would actually double if the definition adopted in the United States were used. Japan plans to revise its definition of unemployment to make it consistent with that of the other developed countries (*Nikkei Newspaper* 2014).

20.   The total size of the cultivated farmland decreased because of urban development that involved the construction of homes, plants, resorts, and roads and the end of farming activities in less favorable regions, such as mountainous areas.

21.   The value of total agricultural output decreased from 11.5 trillion yen in 1990 to 8.1 trillion yen in 2010, while agricultural income from production decreased from 4.8 trillion yen to 2.8 trillion yen over the same period (MAFF 2011a). From 1990 to 2010, the share of agricultural production as part of the value of total agricultural output decreased from 41.9 percent to 35 percent (MAFF 2011b).

22.   These data include commercial and subsistence farmers.

23.   "Agriculture Management Entities" is the technical term used by the Japanese Ministry of Agriculture, Forestry and Fisheries (MAFF) to define all enterprises involved in farming. This category includes family farms, large industrial farms, and corporate operations.

CHAPTER 3

Neoliberal Agri-Food Policies in the Aftermath of the 2011 Earthquake, Tsunami, and Nuclear Meltdown

Introduction

During the past two decades and despite changes in the country's governing body, the development of Japanese agri-food is characterized by the continuous adoption of neoliberal policies. Dismissing academic and political critiques of free market–oriented approaches (Brown 2015; Helleiner 2010; Krugman 2012a, 2012b; Lupel 2005; Mirowski 2013), Japan has continued on its road toward liberalization of input and resource markets and production processes.[1] Also, and contrary to situations that have recently characterized other advanced countries (Eargle and Esmail 2012; Rodriguez, Quarantelli, and Dynes 2007), Japan maintained its neoliberal posture as it began attempts to address the consequences of the Great East Japan Earthquake that hit eastern Japan on March 11, 2011, and caused a devastating tsunami and the explosion at the Fukushima Daiichi nuclear power plant. The impact of the Great East Japan Earthquake on the agri-food policy of Japan is the focus of this chapter.

Often, great disasters expose existing socioeconomic and structural problems. In North America and Europe, as well as in other parts of the world, recent natural and human-caused disasters prompted scholars and political leaders to call for enhanced state intervention. Assistance from the state was sought in the immediate aftermaths of these calamities but also in the reconstruction phases that followed (Button 2010; Hannigan 2012; Safina 2011). As part of a process of reconsidering the power of market-oriented measures, state intervention—the so-called neo-Fordist proposal (Bonanno 2014a)—has recently been viewed as a desirable solution for crises stemming from the financial, economic, and environmental spheres (Krugman 2012a, 2013a, 2013b; Raulet 2011; Underhill and Zhang 2008).

Despite recent (2013–2015) economic moves by Prime Minister Abe, the same cannot be said about Japan. The Japanese government's insistence on the continuous use of neoliberal measures in agri-food makes this a unique case. The decision to promote reconstruction programs for agricultural and fishing regions through the further strengthening of market deregulation, the key involvement of large private firms, and the reduction of state-sponsored measures for wealth redistribution make the Japanese situation prominent in the global panorama. Accordingly, the case of Japan can be described as characterized by the subordination of state intervention to corporate plans. As some public funds for the reconstruction of damaged areas were mobilized, their use followed neoliberal patterns, prioritizing corporate designs and visions over alternative ones.

The genesis, characteristics, and rationales for the development of these policies; the actors involved in these processes; and those affected by them are highlighted here. More specifically, the chapter reviews salient aspects of the damage generated by the triple disaster (earthquake, tsunami, and nuclear reactor meltdown), analyzes the reconstruction policies pertaining to the agri-food sector, and explores the postures and actions of such major actors as corporations, the state, farmers, fishermen, and consumers.

Genealogy of the Great Earthquake

A necessary first step in the analysis of the impact of the 2011 triple disaster should arguably be an attempt to propose a brief genealogy of the natural disaster reconstruction plans implemented in Japan in the recent past. Japan is an earthquake-prone archipelago located in the seam of the four tectonic plates: the Pacific, North American, Eurasian, and Filipino plates. Because it is an archipelago, Japan has experienced many earthquakes and tsunamis. Typhoons and volcanic eruptions have also caused damage in the past. Salient instances include the Great Kanto Earthquake in 1923, the Southern Hyogo Prefecture Earthquake of 1995, and the Mid-Niigata Prefecture Earthquake of 2004. These were all devastating disasters that resulted in a large number of fatalities and extensive damage (PRIMAFF 2012) (figure 3.1). Mistakenly viewed as the consequences of the inclemency of nature or the unpredictability of accidents, disasters overwhelmingly affect the weakest components of society and uncover its contradictory structure (Jones and Murphy 2009; Lundahl 2013; Okada 2012a). Additionally, reconstructions are accompanied by conflict among corporate groups seeking to foster their business interests, fractions of the nation-state that often—albeit not always—side with big business, and members of the working and middle classes (e.g., wage workers, farmers, and ordinary residents) who frequently offer voices of dissent and resistance. To further illustrate these points, we briefly review two of the most recent earthquakes and reconstruction programs in Hyogo and Niigata.

Southern Hyogo Prefecture Earthquake

The Southern Hyogo Prefecture Earthquake occurred on January 17, 1995, and hit the area around Hanshin and the two major and adjacent metropolitan areas of Kobe and Osaka. This powerful earthquake registered magnitude 7.3 on the magnitude scale (MS) (formerly Richter scale) and 7 on the Japanese Meteorological Agency seismic intensity scale (or JMA). At its epicenter, the earthquake caused damage inferior only to that caused by the Great East Japan Earthquake of March 11, 2011, and the Great Kanto Earthquake of 1923. At the time, it was the largest disaster to occur after World War II. The Fire and Disaster Management Agency reported more than 6,400 deaths, 44,000 people injured, 32,000 people displaced, and 250,000 houses either destroyed or damaged. It quantified the economic damage at about 10 trillion yen (100 billion U.S. dollars) (Hyogo Prefecture 2011).

The earthquake caused significant infrastructural damage, impacting roads; railways; the electric grid; and the water, gas, and telephone systems. Globally aired images of dangling highway overpasses captured the drama and shocked Japan and the world. More importantly, the instant TV coverage exposed the lack of protection that the highly advanced and concentrated urban settings offered against earthquakes. The urban industrial systems were designed to optimize economic and productive efficiency but lacked reasonable barriers against the perils of these types of disasters. Yet, not all components of these highly populated urban industrial areas fared equally. The vulnerability of the poor inner city neighborhoods stood out, as the damage in these areas was more severe, and spatial class segregation became a predictor of damage severity (Okada 2012b). As previously in the city of Kobe, significant investment promoted the development and concomitant gentrification of the downtown and waterfront areas; the lower classes and the poor moved to other areas, seeking more affordable yet less secure and much older homes. These structural conditions together with the social problems common to poor neighborhoods greatly added to the region's damage. More than 80 percent of all fatalities were caused by the collapse of old homes, many of them wooden structures lacking available antiseismic features (Reconstruction Design Council in Response to the Great East Japan Earthquake 2011).[2] Conversely, newly constructed and more expensive homes erected with codes established after 1981 suffered little damage. Furthermore, more than 40 percent of all deaths were elderly residents whose survival chances were hampered by inadequate escape routes and unavailable open spaces (Hyogo Prefecture 2011; National Geographic 2013).

While technical reports stressed that the safe use of space is a crucial component in disaster prevention, the adopted reconstruction program—appropriately named "Creative Reconstruction" (Nikkei BP 2011)—was oriented toward the furthering of large-scale developments, such as the construction of Kobe Airport and a great number of skyscrapers, to support interests associated with the economic growth of the area. These new construction projects were commissioned to nonlocal national developers and promoted through deregulation programs set up as parts of SEZs, schemes designed to attract corporate investment (Hyogo Prefecture 2011). Taking advantage of the LDP administration of Prime Minister Koizumi's introduction of the Special Zones for Structural Reform of 2002, the Hyogo Prefecture was first in line to establish special benefits to attract corporate investment. By 2011, there were seventeen SEZs in this prefecture. These neoliberal moves were also supported by public investment that affected local finances but did not produce the hoped-for improvements for local small businesses and residents (Okada 2012a). Discourses that viewed houses as exclusively private properties with no collective value informed reconstruction efforts (Okada 2012b). Accordingly, public intervention to support home rebuilding was minimal, and residents were left unassisted. As in the cases of other disasters, the social consequences were severe (Hannigan 2012; Lundahl 2013). Many of those who were evacuated to temporary housing could not rebuild and ultimately did not return to their original neighborhoods. Some lost their connection with their communities and friends. Socially disengaged, psychologically distressed, and facing economic problems, some never recovered from the quake. Simultaneously, these stories of tragedy engendered the growth of volunteer groups that created a bottom-up movement in support of the damaged communities.

Mid-Niigata Prefecture Earthquake

The reconstruction process in the aftermath of the Mid-Niigata Prefecture Earthquake in 2004 is equally telling of the importance of the socioeconomic dimensions of disaster recovery. This earthquake hit Niigata Prefecture on October 23, 2004, with a magnitude of 6.8 (MS) and seismic intensity of 7 (JMA), claiming 68 lives and injuring 4,795 people (Niigata Prefecture 2009). It destroyed or damaged about 17,000 homes, more than 100,000 people were evacuated, and the damage was estimated at 1.7 trillion yen (17 billion U.S. dollars)

(Kamemoto 2005; Uchida 2011). These problems were compounded by a series of additional disasters that affected the area during the same year. Floods, typhoons, landslides, and heavy snowfall all hit the area in rapid sequence. While the damage was less, and the people affected were fewer, than in the case of the Hyogo earthquake, the fact that the disaster involved a less economically developed rural mountainous region made its consequences more severe. In effect, a key aspect of the Mid-Niigata Earthquake was that it represented an example of the vulnerability of rural areas to disasters. These were the typical Japanese rural communities suffering from the decline and restructuring of the agricultural economy under neoliberalism (see chapter 2). Loss of farms, farmland, and farm income; the aging of the population; and outmigration were all local characteristics. Additionally, the consolidation of community administration entities, basic rural services, and agricultural cooperatives degraded the quality of life of local residents (Okada 2012b).

The delegitimizing government posture employed in the Southern Hyogo Prefecture Earthquake became a factor in the reconstruction of the Mid-Niigata areas. The then-LDP administration of Prime Minister Koizumi adopted the same "Creative Reconstruction" policy used in the Southern Hyogo Prefecture. It appropriated funds for large-scale development projects, supported corporate actions, and publicized the positive effects of "trickledown economics." Additionally, plans were made to upend the Agricultural Land Act, allowing direct access to farmland to publicly traded corporations and decreasing corporate limits to farmland ownership. However, opposition to expectations that large development projects would benefit corporations, negate economic opportunities for local small business and family farmers, and degrade the quality of life of local residents created political resistance that forced the government to partially change its original plans. Eventually, bottom-up processes of reconstruction that contemplated funds for small farms, community programs, and local facilities were adopted (Uchida 2011). Schemes that focused on preserving local social networks and the return of displaced victims were also supported, along with measures that allowed the use of public funds for the reconstruction of family dwellings. Succumbing to discourses stressing self-help and problems with state intervention, the allocation of these funds was characterized by too many restrictive conditions and ultimately was insufficient to address community needs (Okada 2012a).

As these reconstruction programs were heavily tinged with neoliberal colors, the reconstruction policy of the Great East Japan Earthquake and associated disasters can be viewed as the continuation of established patterns rather than an exception. However, as they relied on market mechanisms, pro-corporate postures, and discourses that privileged business over community and profit over social relations, their impact on the lives of residents is telling of the contradictory nature and consequences of neoliberalism.

The Great East Japan Disaster of March 11, 2011: Earthquake, Tsunami, Nuclear Meltdown

The Great East Japan Earthquake hit the Tohoku Region[3] in northeastern Japan (figure 3.1), creating a tsunami and a meltdown at the Fukushima Daiichi nuclear power plant. The earthquake damaged a broad area of 24 prefectures with a magnitude of 9 (MS) and a JMA level of 7 (Japan Meteorological Agency 2011; FDMA 2013). The tsunami was measured at 16.7 meters (55 feet). It was one of the most severe earthquakes in the world, and the fourth largest on record in the past 50 years. It was surpassed only by the Great Chilean Earthquake of 1960 (9.5 MS), the Great Alaskan Earthquake of 1964 (9.2 MS), and the Great Sumatra-Andaman Earthquake of 2004 (9.1 MS) (Reconstruction Design Council in Response to the Great East Japan Earthquake 2011). Eighteen thousand people were reported killed. An additional 2,700 people were reported as missing, while the number of those injured surpassed 6,000 (FDMA 2013). Approximately 400,000 homes were destroyed or damaged, and 340,000 people were evacuated. As difficulties for the evacuees mounted, an additional 2,300 deaths, including suicides and deaths from loss of social relations and social neglect—the so-called "deaths of loneliness"[4]—were recorded (Reconstruction Agency 2012). Severe fires in residential areas and in industrial complexes provided additional hardships to the surviving population and hampered rescue and recovery efforts.

The extensive damage to utility lines and industrial plants was accompanied by destruction of the agri-food complex. Farming, forestry, and fishing production processes came to a sudden halt. The Japanese Ministry of Agriculture, Forestry and Fisheries reported losses totaling more than 2.4 trillion yen (24 billion U.S. dollars), including 40,000 farms covering 24,000 ha (52,800 acres), 28,000 fishing boats, and 319 fishing ports (MAFF 2011c; 2012a). Seawater contamination of farmland and debris generated by the tsunami damaged 21,500 ha (47,300 acres) of the 24,000 ha of farmland affected in the three most damaged prefectures of Iwate, Miyagi, and Fukushima. Two years after the quake, only about 40 percent of the farmland was recovered, and only 26 percent of all previous farmers returned to the sector (MAFF 2012b, 2012c). Radioactivity continued to persist, and contaminated land was taken out of production indefinitely.

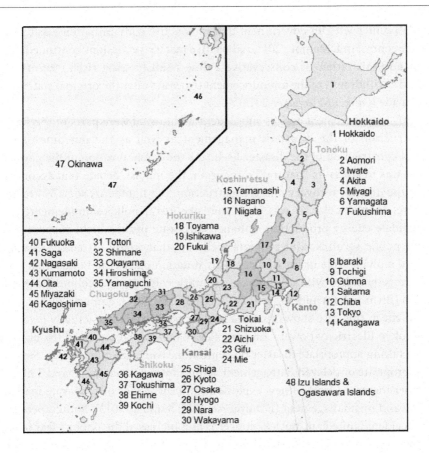

Figure 3.1. Map of Japan. *Source*: Authors' elaboration.

The complex nature of this triple disaster created significant recovery and reconstruction problems. Most experts considered the nuclear meltdown the most severe factor of this multiple disaster, as authorities considered it comparable with the Chernobyl nuclear accident (*Nikkei Newspaper* 2011d).[5] On March 11, 2011, the tsunami caused by the earthquake damaged the cooling system of the reactors at Fukushima Daiichi nuclear power plant, which caused the ensuing meltdown of the nuclear core and the explosion in the reactor buildings. This was the most serious accident in Japanese nuclear history with the release of 900,000 tera Bq (becquerels) of radioactive material in the air, land, and water (*Nikkei Newspaper* 2012e). As the half-life of the released radioactive material (cesium) is 30 years, the contamination is expected to affect generations to come. Additionally, and despite announcements from Prime Minister

Noda's center-left DPJ government that radioactive contamination was finally under control in December 2011, radioactive material emissions continued. The next administration of conservative Prime Minister Abe (LDP) eventually issued a withdrawal of the announcement two years after the original statement was made (*Sankei Newspaper* 2013).

This announcement and its subsequent withdrawal were parts of the social construction of the disaster's management as well as the outcome of the social construction of the disaster itself.[6] As the initial position of the government was to stress its "natural" dimension, the intense debate that accompanied the disaster recovery and reconstruction highlighted its socially created nature. In particular, it was clear that neoliberal policies implemented to deregulate energy production, enhance corporate profit, shield corporations from public scrutiny, and promote a climate that would attract investment played a pivotal role in the disaster. This situation places the Fukushima Dai-ichi tragedy in line with other recent calamities affected by neoliberal deregulation (Birmingham and McNeill 2012; Hindmarsh 2013; Samuels 2013).

In effect, this case shows that the nuclear policy of Japan actually deterred the Tokyo Electricity Power Company (TEPCO)—which managed the plant—from taking appropriate disaster prevention measures (Samuels 2013). Several inappropriate or delayed management actions by the government and TEPCO further increased fears of new explosions and suspicions of corporate malfeasance and mismanagement (Hindmarsh 2013; Samuels 2013). Simultaneously, the accident ignited antinuclear concerns and increased the public's fear of the many negative social and environmental consequences of nuclear waste and contamination. These concerns fostered questions regarding the neoliberal tenet that "economic growth first" represents a path that offers solutions to socioeconomic problems. In the case of rural residents and farmers, it was a reminder of the more serious socioeconomic conditions and their relative lack of political power in the rural regions. Increased distrust and fear mounted, providing impetus to organized protests against the use of nuclear power in the country (*Japan Press Weekly* 2012a).

Rooted in the 1945 atomic bombing of Hiroshima and Nagasaki by the United States, protest against nuclear power has a long history in Japan (Japan Council against Atomic and Hydrogen Bombs 2005). In the 1950s, protest ignited as Japan established its postwar domestic nuclear energy program. This pronuclear posture was shaped by U.S. policy and corporate interests highlighted by President Eisenhower's UN "Atoms for Peace" speech of 1953 and the economic gains of U.S. corporations, such as General Electric and Westinghouse[7] (Yoshioka 2011). The notorious 1954 nuclear tests of the Bikini Atoll further fueled opposition. This was a broadly based popular movement that originated from, and found support among, ordinary citizens. The antinuclear movement Peace from the Kitchen was organized by anonymous housewives and emerged as a symbol of the distance between the pronuclear position of the U.S. and Japanese governments and the local population's broader concerns about, and awareness of, the dangers of nuclear programs (Maruhama 2011). This movement was largely responsible for the organization of the first World Conference against the Atomic and Hydrogen Bombs in Hiroshima in 1955 and the establishment of the Japan Council against Atomic and Hydrogen Bombs in 1956 (Japan Council against Atomic and Hydrogen Bombs 2005). Those years were also characterized by other episodes of peaceful protest, such as the antinuclear document signing that originated locally in the Tokyo district of Suginami but quickly achieved national recognition (Maruhama 2011). These protest actions continued over the decades. Yet, and despite having support in Japan and aboard, they did not prevent the growth of the nuclear energy sector. In particular, support for nuclear power received a boost following the 1970s oil crises that allowed the government to enact legislation giving nuclear power primacy among all energy sources (Okada 2012b). Building on this policy and separating nuclear power from nuclear weapons, successive Japanese administrations and sector corporations were able to establish 54 nuclear reactors and legitimize their view among the citizenry. The meltdown of the Fukushima plant in March 2011 revived long-established antinuclear concerns and political mobilization.

Fearing a loss in the upcoming national elections and perceiving dissatisfaction from the left-leaning electorate, the DPJ center-left government decided to decommission a number of nuclear plants. As political pressure mounted, in May 2012, all commercial nuclear power plants went out of operation for the first time since 1970 (*Nikkei Newspaper* 2012f). While the Oi Nuclear Power Plant in the Fukui Prefecture was reactivated in July 2012, the DPJ government declared that it would close all nuclear power plants until the 2030s and that it would halt the construction of new plants indefinitely (*Nikkei Newspaper* 2012h).[8] The hypothesized political and time-buying nature of these moves did not satisfy opposition to nuclear energy sources and the management of those complex facilities (*Japan Press Weekly* 2012a). These opponents actively and regularly organized antinuclear demonstrations and petitions nationwide.

In the Fukushima region, farmers and fishermen continued to suffer the persistent negative consequences of the nuclear accident. Radioactivity was detected in all major food items, including rice, beef, seafood, vegetables, mushrooms, milk, green tea, and water. As "safe" radioactive levels were negotiated,[9] the commercialization of local agri-food products was prohibited, while fear of additional contamination added to the public's uncertainty. Consumers began to avoid all agri-food and even other products from the affected areas. Similarly, Japanese agri-food exports collapsed as countries importing Japanese agri-food commodities halted their commercial relations or significantly strengthened controls (MAFF 2012b). Debris removal became a seemingly insurmountable task in Fukushima, as locations to dispose of contaminated waste were unavailable. The Ministry of the Environment predicted that the contamination problems could not be solved prior to March 2014 (*Nikkei Newspaper* 2013a). As this date passed, problems continued to exist. In 2015, farmland decontamination was under way, but the process remained in its early stages. As of March 2012, TEPCO paid 120 billion yen (1.2 billion U.S. dollars) in compensation for damages to the agri-food sector against claims that exceeded 180 billion yen (MAFF 2012b). Moreover, as the payment process was contested, many claims were eventually adjudicated through litigation (*Nikkei Newspaper* 2013d).

More than four years after the quake, the overall conditions of the local economy remained in jeopardy. One year after the disasters, there were 626 firms in bankruptcy procedures and 340,000 people who could not return to their homes. This number included 70,000 cross-prefecture evacuees (*Nikkei Newspaper* 2012c, 2012g). As the effects of the disasters unfolded, outmigration escalated and the local economy continued to shrink. Okada (2012a) pointed out that this region's economy was already suffering from the negative consequences of globalization and the strengthening of the neoliberal posture of the Japanese government over the past two decades. The earthquake, tsunami, and the ensuing social problems hastened the devastating economic fallout from globalization and neoliberal policies.

Farming and fishing were the most affected components of the economy under the neoliberal regime. The loss of farms and farmers was accompanied by administrative consolidation processes that reduced the availability of social and commercial services and assistance. The slow pace of disaster relief programs as well the often-denounced limited involvement of local residents in the reconstruction decisionmaking process were outcomes of restructuring policies (Okada 2012b). As in the cases of the Niigata earthquake, the vulnerability of poor rural regions was exposed. The building of nuclear plants in these areas was part of a plan for economic revival of depressed areas whereby controversial projects were located in less developed and politically weak regions. Promises of job creation and the beneficial effects of economic multipliers concealed concerns about nuclear contamination, unsafe working and living conditions, and, ultimately, disasters. As these projects engendered deleterious consequences, the situation of these rural regions worsened. Simultaneously, dependency and regional exploitation continued. In the immediate aftermath of the disasters, components of the system supplying the automotive and electronic industries controlled by transnational corporations quickly recovered or were relocated. The recovery and reconstruction of farms and fisheries, instead, lagged (Okada 2012a). Moreover, the objective of supporting the interests of the Tokyo metropolitan area remained above the debates that plagued the affected rural areas. In essence, the reconstruction of the Tohoku Region was approached in the context of the traditional role of rural areas: the provider of energy, food, and labor to support Tokyo's urban population.

The end of 2012 was characterized by a change in the country's administration. The center-left DPJ of Prime Minister Noda lost the elections. As the LDP of Prime Minister Abe returned to power, it announced plans to reintroduce pronuclear energy policies and dismiss the moratorium on the construction of nuclear facilities and the use of nuclear power (Cabinet Secretariat 2011). It even announced programs to sell nuclear plant equipment abroad (*Nikkei Newspaper* 2013h, 2013j). Despite these differences, both administrations employed the "Creative Reconstruction" policy that prevailed in previous disasters (Okada 2012a). In effect, as discussions on the strategies to address reconstruction developed, the specially created Reconstruction Design Council in Response to the Great East Japan Earthquake[10] suggested the adoption of Creative Reconstruction as the reconstruction policy (Cabinet Secretariat 2011; Reconstruction Design Council in Response to the Great East Japan Earthquake 2011). The three points characterizing the Creative Reconstruction with regard to farming and fishing are highlighted in the next section.

Neoliberal Agri-Food Policy Proposals and Actions

Creative Reconstruction refers to three key points: (1) the creation of the SZR program; (2) the introduction of a new energy policy; and (3) changes in the tax code enacted to budget the reconstruction process.

SZR Program

The creation of the SZR program was part of the broader Basic Act on Reconstruction that the government passed in June 2011. Additionally, a new act for defining the characteristics of the SZRs was enacted in December of the same year (Reconstruction Agency 2012). These acts promoted a set of pro-corporate deregulations that established tax abatements and incentives, state subsidies, and convenient credit to promote corporate investment targeting reconstruction

(*Nikkei Newspaper* 2011a). The creation of the SZRs followed the same rationale employed in the creation of the SEZs of recent years. A move common to neoliberal restructuring, the creation of SEZs is based on the principle and practices that allow corporations—often transnational corporations—a wide range of rights and advantages through the formation of areas that offer special concessions. Often called a process of denationalization of the national territory (Sassen 1998), it permits corporations to freely move about and act in a given territory with limited control from, and obligations to, the local nation-state. In many instances, the nation-state further assists these corporations with direct economic intervention (Bonanno and Constance 2008).

In 2002, the economic restructuring promoted by the Koizumi LDP administration contemplated the introduction of the Special Zones for Structural Reform Act. This move was complemented by the introduction of Comprehensive Special Zones Act of 2011 by the Kan DPJ administration. While the former focused on stimulating local economies by easing regulations, the latter not only employed deregulation but also added tax abatements, public subsidies, and low-cost credit to its arsenal of available economic tools (*Nikkei Newspaper* 2013f). The SZR program followed the same pattern of these earlier measures, as its SEZ format promoted reconstruction through deregulation, tax abatements,[11] public subsidies, and easy credit. Its purpose was to support the 227 municipalities of 11 prefectures damaged by the disasters. As of April 2013, more than 60 areas requested and received SEZ status by the Reconstruction Agency (Reconstruction Agency 2013a).

While the adoption of SEZs was not new in Japan, the creation of the SZR program represented a milestone in the process of the neoliberalization of the agriculture and fishing industries. For a number of years, corporate business circles vigorously pushed for the opening of farmland markets and fishing rights to publicly traded corporations. Yet, views based on traditional understandings of the role of agriculture and fishing remained significant obstacles (see chapter 2). This situation was particularly prominent during the Niigata reconstruction process, where pro-corporate neoliberal moves were forcefully proposed as effective reconstruction strategies. It was argued that corporate plans could represent the needed solutions to the economic decline experienced by farming regions in the wake of market deregulation and reduced state monitoring. Proposals for the restructuring of the Agricultural Land Act were framed in this fashion (Okada 2012a). Following this posture, the SZR program contemplated the expansion of the size of farms as its primary objective for agriculture. In addition, as the program was approved, some corporations rushed to invest in agriculture (see chapter 6). Taking advantage of deregulation and public support, even nonagricultural major banks and some local banks became involved in the sector (*Nikkei Newspaper* 2012g). To be sure, the Abe Administration did not allow corporations to access the farmland market. Nevertheless, this was only a move to secure votes during national elections. The introduction of the SZR program allowed corporations not only to benefit from deregulation but also to enjoy the support of state intervention that they so vocally opposed. The mobilization of taxpayer-generated funds for the promotion of corporate designs is an example of the inherent contradiction of the reconstruction process in Japan. As corporate actions are framed in terms of the power of the private sector to solve the ineffectiveness of state intervention and provide the resources to address the state fiscal crisis, in reality corporate actions depend on public funds and institutional support of the state (see also chapter 7 for an example from the fisheries sector).

In the early stage of the debate at the Reconstruction Design Council, the governor of the Miyagi Prefecture and member of the Council, Yoshihiro Murai,[12] insisted on the necessity of reforming fishing rights through the SZR program and proposed further deregulation of the Agricultural Land Act (*Nikkei Newspaper* 2011c) (see chapter 7). These recommendations were in line with tenets of corporate business circles' proposals consistently formulated since the early 1990s and certainly before the 2011 disasters. After the 2011 disasters, major corporate business circles, such as *Keidanren*, the Japanese Association of Corporate Executives, and the Japanese Chamber of Commerce and Industry, along with such corporate think tanks as Mitsubishi and Nomura, organized special project teams and launched a number of policy proposals for the reconstruction of affected areas (Japan Association of Corporate Executives 2011; Japan Economic Research Institute 2011; Keidanren 2012; Mitsubishi Research Institute 2011; Nomura Research Institute 2011). The enactment of the Special Zones for Reconstruction Act represents the most advanced point of the current push for the neoliberalization of disaster reconstruction.

New Energy Policy

The future of the domestic energy policy has emerged as one of the most debated issues in Japan. As objections to the use of nuclear energy have developed and calls for the use of alternative renewable energy sources were made, the debate on the new directions that domestic energy policies should take is evolving in favor of corporate interests. In the wake of the 2011 disasters, the DPJ administration was forced to cancel established plans to increase the nuclear component of domestic energy sources from 30 percent to 50 percent. After the disasters and responding to mounting opposition from the public, the DJP administration began discussions on the most desirable mix of energy sources that should be adopted. Included in these discussions were questions about the proportion of nuclear energy in the mix and even proposals to terminate the nuclear program altogether. It was a clear reversal from traditional Japanese energy policy that historically relied on nuclear power.

Despite opposition from conservative shareholders, the DPJ government gained control of TEPCO by purchasing a majority stake for 1 trillion yen. As part of its reorganization, it was allowed access to government loans totaling several trillion yen (*Nikkei Newspaper* 2012d). Simultaneously, it also began plans to increase wholesale power prices to meet the increased cost of fossil fuels. Oil was needed to power thermal power plants that were activated to replace the closed nuclear plants. In this context, corporations were eager to negotiate new contracts with power companies to secure needed power. They also campaigned to obtain additional and more convenient sources of energy and called for the reopening of decommissioned nuclear plants. One of the strategies used to this end was the "threat" of relocating facilities to other areas or abroad. In the nuclear power plant areas, local political leaders immediately supported the reopening of plants, as they identified their closing as one of the most serious obstacles to local economic growth. In this economic climate, the DPJ government allowed the reopening of a number of nuclear power plants. After the national election in December 2012, the victorious LDP administration of Prime Minister Abe announced a reversal of energy policy of the previous administration. While Abe was virtually silent on energy policy issues during the electoral campaign, when his party returned to power, he announced plans to reintroduce nuclear energy and resume international sales[13] (*Nikkei Newspaper* 2013h, 2013j).

Serious concerns about the use of nuclear energy remained paramount among the general population. Accordingly, their presence required the mixing of pro-nuclear energy actions with moves in support of alternative energy sources. In this context, the LDP administration introduced policies in support of renewable power sources, such as solar, wind, hydraulic, geothermal, and biomass sources. It also established prices for their sale and promoted corporate investment that sought the opportunity to gain from the expansion of these markets. Special attention was paid to the solar sector, which analysts identified as particularly lucrative and the government supported with specific legislation. Stimulated by corporate pressure, the government set a price for solar power that was higher than that available in other advanced countries. As the law required power companies to purchase solar energy, producing companies benefited from the larger gap between production costs and sale prices. Accordingly, corporations rushed to create capacity for solar power, and solar panels appeared everywhere, including on farmland. While the MAFF has been reluctant to permit solar panels on farmland, it finally decided to align itself with corporations and deregulated the sector (*Nikkei Newspaper* 2013h).

The debate on the new energy policy included discussion on the use of information technology (IT). The IT industry was called into question as a provider of tools that could control and eventually lower the use of electric power. The construction of "smart communities" equipped with smart grids, smart meters, and energy using "advanced storing battery systems" was quickly adopted as the desired model for the reconstruction and the improvement of infrastructure in Japan. This view, along with hopes to export this technology abroad, received the support of the government and the private sector (*Nikkei Newspaper* 2013k). Corporate giants Hitachi, Toshiba, and Mitsubishi[14] became very active in this market, along with the Japanese subsidiary of IBM, IBM Japan. Their objective was to take advantage of the business-friendly environment and growing demand for alternative energy. Targeted were emerging markets in Asia (primarily China and India) and other parts of the world (e.g., Russia). Additional corporate objectives included earning credits for carbon dioxide emissions under the international carbon dioxide emission control regime and gain share in the energy financial markets (Energy and Capital 2013).

In this context, the construction of agricultural plant factories emerged as a new trajectory for reconstruction. The term "plant factories" refers to a production system recently popularized in Japan whereby fresh fruits and vegetables are produced in a closed growing environment that often operates without soil and through the systematic control of all components of the growth process (Lindhout 2010). It relies on technology that is possible through the IT monitoring of environmental components, such as temperature, humidity, light,[15] concentration of carbon dioxide, nutrients, and water supply, and the automatic collection of additional pertinent data. In 2008,[16] the construction of plant factories was first encouraged by the Ministry of the Economy and Trade and Industry (METI) as legislation promoting the interface among advanced IT technology, agriculture, commerce, and industry was approved. However, it became a centerpiece of agri-food restructuring efforts after the 2011 disasters. IT corporations, such as Fujitsu, NEC, Hitachi, Toshiba, and IBM Japan, have been actively investing in this sector, an effort that is also supported by basic research carried out at public universities.[17] After the 2011 disasters, corporations proposed to build plant factories in the damaged areas. The rationale behind this proposal rested on the impossibility of conventional agricultural production on contaminated farmland. The corporate proposal was supported by the government, and in the three most affected prefectures of Iwate, Miyagi, and Fukushima, some plant factories were erected with reconstruction subsidies (see chapter 6). For instance, in the heavily damaged Village of Kawauchi, a joint venture corporation, KiMiDoRi, was quickly established. This private company then built a plant factory with public and private funds (Endo 2014). While a local official spoke of this factory as a symbol of reconstruction and vitality of the area, it is difficult to foresee its future profitability without the support of significant public subsidies.

Changes in the Tax Code

As recovery and reconstruction efforts were under way, the mobilization of needed financial resources was debated. Pertinent discussions pointed to two primary alternatives. The "reconstruction for humans" approach stressed the importance of reestablishing social relations and environments in ways that bolstered residents' quality of life. This concept was opposed by the "reconstruction for business" view, which identified economic growth as the condition for the development of all other facets of social life (Okada 2012a). The latter received support from the government and corporate circles and was employed—albeit not exclusively—in reconstruction efforts.

The government estimated the costs of reconstruction as between 16 and 22 trillion yen (160 to 220 billion U.S. dollars). This estimate did not include the monetary damage from the Fukushima nuclear meltdown that continues to be difficult to assess (Reconstruction Design Council in Response to the Great East Japan Earthquake 2011). As budget negotiations evolved, 25 trillion yen were set aside for reconstruction for a period of five years (*Nikkei Newspaper* 2013k). To finance this budget, the government decided to sell assets—stocks of the Japanese Postal Service and the Japan Tobacco Company—and government bonds. It also inaugurated a new program of tax increases that raised the income tax by 2.1 percent for a period of 25 years for individuals and 2.4 percent for corporations. However, this additional corporate tax was imposed for only three years and eventually was reduced to only two years (*Nikkei Newspaper* 2011d). Strong objections that depicted this measure as unfair and as a way to allow corporations to be virtually exonerated from the financial effort to reconstruct did not affect the government's decision. In effect, it further reduced corporate rates by 5 percent before the new 2.4 percent levy was assessed. Following established tenets of neoliberalism, this move was justified by the argument that corporations should be supported in their efforts to maintain competitiveness and viability if economic growth is to be reignited. As a result, corporations benefited from substantial tax reductions following the disasters (*Nikkei Newspaper* 2011c).

In the fall of 2012, significant irregularities associated with the spending of the budget emerged. These irregularities involved the disbursement of about 1.2 trillion yen for projects that were located outside the damaged areas and did not have legitimate connections to reconstruction efforts (*Asahi Newspaper* 2013). Examples of these violations included the training of jail inmates, repairs at military bases, the construction of a freeway in Okinawa and rural roads in other locations, anti-earthquake upgrades for government buildings in Tokyo, and the renting of boats for actions against antiwhaling organizations. The government also allocated 300 billion yen from the reconstruction budget to METI. METI's task was to attract corporate investment to the effected locations. However, only 6 percent of these funds were allocated in the three most damaged prefectures, and 80 percent of the money was paid to transnational corporations, such as Toyota, Canon, and Toshiba (*Japan Press Weekly* 2012b). Additionally, the allocation of these funds was outsourced to the Nomura Research Institute, a private think tank with strong corporate connections. The government responded to the ensuing public outrage by admitting that expenditures were not allocated according to established requirements. However, the government also argued that the economically benign nature of the allocations would trigger a trickle down effect that would benefit the damaged areas. As indignation mounted, the government paid lip service to the protesters but recalled only a fraction of the allocated funds (*Nikkei Newspaper* 2012f).

Facing many difficulties, farmers, fishermen, and residents of the affected rural areas slowly attempted to reconstruct their everyday lives. In March 2013, estimates indicated that in 80 percent of the most affected areas, only 20 percent of the reconstruction process was complete (*Nikkei Newspaper* 2013i). Such major utilities and infrastructure as the Sendai Airport and highways were quickly repaired, but the amount of farmland (39 percent), agricultural production (40 percent), fishing ports (36 percent), total catch of fisheries (63 percent), and fish-processing facilities (69 percent) restored remained minimal (Reconstruction Agency 2013b). By the end of 2012, the public housing units available for disaster victims was only 5 percent of the total number of units that the reconstruction plan called for (*Nikkei Newspaper* 2012e). The reconstruction of single-family dwellings continued at an equally slow pace because of inadequate public funding[18] and often depended on self-help efforts. For farmers, fishermen, and rural residents, the reconstruction process was hard and slow.

Resistance to Neoliberal Agri-Food Policy Proposals

The aftermath of the disasters brought to the fore the different ideologies and discourses supporting the concepts and practices of recovery and reconstruction. Supporters of recovery envisioned the maintenance of the basic democratic principles that inspired land reform and the reorganization of fisheries after World War II. Land to those who actually farm, fishing rights to fishermen, and their control to local communities were viewed as primary principles to be promoted and enforced. Farming and fishing were seen as dimensions to promote the well-being of local communities and their members. In contrast, reconstruction was presented as an opportunity to get away from these principles and open farming and fishing to the presence of corporations that would have the rights and opportunities to use land and fisheries for their pursuit of capital accumulation.

The national government promoted the reconstruction approach and supported policies that enhanced deregulation, placed greater power at the disposal of corporations, and favored market relations. Some local governments, on the contrary, privileged alternative solutions based on the concept of recovery. Among the three most affected prefectures, the government of the Prefecture of Miyagi sided with the national government and enacted policies that promoted the reconstruction of corporations supply chains, created SZRs, assigned rebuilding contracts to large general contractors, and rebuilt only major fishing ports. In contrast, the government of the Prefecture of Iwate promoted projects that gave equal priority to all fishing ports, including those supporting small fishing communities, and assisted the reconstruction of small and medium-sized businesses in the area. In the prefectures of Iwate and Fukushima, local administrations decided to focus on the construction of low-cost temporary housing that employed local labor and used locally available materials (Okada 2012a). In the Prefecture of Miyagi, the construction of temporary housing was contracted to corporate prefab makers. In this context, reconstruction plans in agriculture and fishing became the subject of controversy. As the DPJ and LDP administrations associated reconstruction with neoliberal moves, others opted to resist these tendencies. Below are some instances of resistance to neoliberal reconstruction policies in agri-food.

Farmers

Three years after the disaster, farmers were still struggling to clear their farmland of physical debris, salt deposited by the tsunami, and radioactive materials. Despite the assistance of volunteers, land reclamation took place at a glacial pace. In Fukushima and adjacent areas, the issue of nuclear contamination of farmland and agricultural products remained overwhelming. In a number of areas, all farming activities were suspended indefinitely because of concern about radioactivity. In others where farming was allowed, controls were carried out employing standards set by the state. These standards were tightened in April 2012. However, major supermarket chains and consumer cooperatives established their own standards, which exceeded state standards (Kimura 2013). In a context in which fear of contamination dominated, even documented lack of radioactivity did not appease consumers and retailers—a situation that virtually denied market outlets to local products. Farmers responded by not only supporting the application of standards but also, and along with agricultural cooperatives, by holding informational and promotional campaigns about the safety of their products. The precarious economic conditions engendered by the disasters pushed farmers to support the creation of assistance programs. Although compensation programs were established by TEPCO and the government, they remained limited and operated with great delays. As in the case of other major disasters, many farmers migrated to distant regions in the hope of a future return to their hometowns. Simultaneously, migration from coastal areas to interior regions was supported by the government as a measure to control the consequences of the tsunami. However, these migration processes and programs encountered significant problems. Available land for relocation was in short supply. A portion of these immigrants decided not to return to farming. The limited availability of land created more difficulties for the construction of homes and associated necessary facilities. In some cases, migration was also resisted due to farmers' attachment to their land.

As farmers proceeded to reorganize their lives and activities, grassroots efforts that favored alternative reconstruction plans emerged. In the city of Soma and coastal areas of the Prefecture of Fukushima, the farmers' organization, Japan Family Farmers Movement (Nouminren), a member of Via Campesina, established the not-for-profit organization Nomado. Its objectives were to create direct sales of agricultural products and processed foods along with the establishment of a community cafe to serve as a location for community support (*Noumin Newspaper* 2013). Additionally, local farmers joined forces with farmers across the country to protest government plans to participate in the TPP. The TPP was viewed as a new step toward the further liberalization of agricultural markets and the reduction of farmers' protection against market fluctuations and downturns. This opposition consisted of gatherings, street demonstrations, and the support of candidates at the national political election who opposed the TPP (*Daily Tohoku* 2012). Overall, however, these oppositional efforts have not deterred the government and likeminded business circles from supporting the creation of SEZs, SRZ programs, and the construction of plant factories. Additionally, farmers remained split, as some groups of large farm owners joined forces with the government to support established reconstruction plans. In Sendai City, Miyagi, the authorities established SEZs and the creation of plant factories. This reconstruction program was supported by local large farm owners and about 20 large corporations, including such transnational corporations as Kagome and IBM Japan. Although local farmers encountered difficulties opposing the government's neoliberal reconstruction program, their resistance continued and took additional forms, such as the refusal to participate in reconstruction projects. The Sendai City case is analyzed in chapter 6.

Fishermen

Fishermen also faced serious problems. The first two years after the 2011 disaster were dedicated to removing debris from fishing grounds and repairing fishing ports, markets, processing facilities, and boats. In many instances, boats were completely destroyed, and new boats had to be purchased. As of the first half of 2013, the government announced that almost 80 percent of all aquaculture facilities and set net[19] operations were ready to resume activities. However, at the time, the total catch of local fisheries was 40 percent below pre-disaster levels. Simultaneously, only 36 percent of the repair of fishing ports had been completed (Reconstruction Agency 2013b). In Fukushima and surrounding areas, the radioactive contamination of the sea prevented fishermen from fishing. All the local seafood products were monitored for radiation, and strict standards were enforced. As in the case of farmers, fishermen cooperated with the implementation of food safety measures and brought to market only safe products. Yet as concerns over contamination continued, prices dropped, and the quantity of fish sold sharply decreased. Compensation programs set up by TEPCO and the government were also available to commercial fishermen, but these payments were slow to be distributed and their amount limited.

Compared to those by farmers, fishermen's protests against the creation of SEZs and the government reconstruction program were stronger. In Ishinomaki, in the Prefecture of Miyagi, the local governor created a SZR for the reconstruction of fisheries and introduced legislation that allowed corporations to compete with local cooperatives for the distribution of fishing rights. The local Federation of Fisheries Cooperative strongly protested these moves. They joined forces with national organizations, groups of activists, intellectuals, and residents to create opposition to the introduced legislation. This case is discussed in chapter 7.

Consumers

For some weeks following the disasters, dozens of food companies were not able to supply supermarkets and other retailers. Bottled water was in short supply, and food shortages occurred particularly in eastern Japan (*Nikkei Business* 2011). In the heavily populated Tokyo region, recurrent power outages affected residents and businesses for months, adding to the climate of fear and uncertainty. In this context, consumers' primary concern was radioactive contamination. To control fears and restore trust, the government instituted food safety control systems and issued official standards that established safe radioactivity levels (Kimura 2013). However, these measures' implementation was accompanied by problems as irregularities, scares, and food item recalls became frequent. Self-help increased as consumers brought food directly to laboratories for testing or personally tested it using portable radiation detection instruments.

Two types of actions characterized consumer behavior. First, some avoided all food items and agricultural products that appeared to have a connection with Fukushima or adjacent areas. Even members of *Teikei* (Japanese community-supported agriculture) decided to sever their relationship with all local farmers, including organic producers. Despite these commodities meeting government safety standards, consumers turned to imported food and agricultural products from western Japan and abroad (Consumer Cooperative Seikatsu Club 2013). Ultimately, contamination fears sensitized consumers to the vulnerability of modern food systems, the dangers associated with nuclear power generation, and the precarious conditions of rural areas and the country's farmers.

Second, the hardships experienced by farmers and rural residents engendered public support. Accordingly, another group of consumers strengthened their connections and solidarity with farmers. Members of the antinuclear movement, environmentalists, and also ordinary citizens—some who had never before bought agri-food products from Fukushima—supported local farmers. These groups also participated in voluntary activities in the affected areas. Despite these actions, the vast majority of consumers did not overtly oppose plans for reconstruction based on the creation of SEZs and further liberalization of agri-food markets associated with membership in the TPP. In effect, the general mood among consumers was to cooperate with reconstruction efforts and even obediently accept the tax increases.

Conclusions

This chapter stresses that the process of reconstruction following the recent disasters adheres to the neoliberal posture. Deregulation, the creation of SEZs and SZRs, corporate tax abatements and subsidies, and mismanagement of funds along with increased taxes on the general population characterize the government's reconstruction plan. The 2011 triple disaster also revealed preexisting problems set in motion by the implementation of pro-market measures over the past two decades. Accordingly, the social construction of the 2011 Great East Japan Earthquake appears clear. The emergence of these problems, however, did not deter DPJ and LDP administrations from pursuing their deregulation and pro-market and pro-corporate reconstruction plans. From this point of view, the solutions proposed for the 2011 Great East Japan Earthquake did not depart from the patterns employed in reconstruction efforts for the Hyogo and Niigata disasters.

Farmers and fishermen were left to face the brunt of the consequences of the disaster. Reconstruction plans did not prioritize these groups' needs, and the resources deployed and processes undertaken did not assist them to the required extent. More importantly, the 2011 Great East Japan Earthquake became a tool to accelerate the restructuring of the agriculture and fishing sectors. Through the reconstruction plan, agriculture and fishing were progressively transformed into new markets for goods and services provided by corporations. They also became new fields for financial investment. The government legitimized its posture through the use of a neoliberal discourse, which held that policies supporting corporate agriculture were necessary to enhance Japan's international competitiveness and membership in global food networks. This position was resisted by farmers, fishermen, and also consumers. Their resistance stressed that neoliberal restructuring efforts could not generate sustainable development, socioeconomic growth of the sectors, an appropriate national land conservation program, enhanced food sovereignty, and the overall well-being of the local economy and communities' social relations. These conditions and opposition are more closely examined in the following chapters.

NOTES

1.   In December 2012, Mr. Shinzo Abe assumed office as prime minister of Japan. Since then, Abe has promoted a set of interventionist economic measures intended to revitalize the Japanese economy. Known as "Abenomics," these measures consist of state intervention based on monetary and fiscal policies aimed at encouraging the growth of private investment and the improvement of market relations. The reduction of interest rates, quantitative easing, and the depreciation of the yen have been fundamental components of Abenomics. These measures

depart from the reduction of state intervention policies that he implemented during his first administration in 2006 and 2007. However, they are not so dissimilar from measures used in the United States since the 2008 financial crisis, which are advocated by neoliberal thinkers suggesting state intervention in support of the creation of markets and the growth of corporations (see the Introduction to this volume). In the United States, quantitative easing has stimulated the expansion of the stock market while keeping bond yields and interest rates at historical lows. Following this posture, Abenomics involves state intervention to support profit growth and the financial sector. In essence, Abe has remained a strong supporter of neoliberalism. Yet, his actions can be viewed as indicative of the difficulties associated with the application of neoliberal measures in the context of a stagnating or slowly growing economy (see chapter 9). Additionally, these measures differ from the type of state intervention that characterized the Keynesian economic policy of the Fordist era, as they do not contemplate relevant income redistribution actions and the expansion of the welfare state. In effect, the debate on the directions of the Japanese political economy in 2015 is characterized by uncertainties on how to define the course of action taken by Abe. A commentator summarized this situation by stating "'Abenomics' . . . is not just 'Keynesian' in approach but also 'neoliberal'" (Roberts 2014, 1). To be sure, other students of Japan classify Abenomics as Keynesian policy (see Xu 2013) or as neoliberal policy with Keynesian characteristics, as Neoliberalism and Keynesianism tend to converge (Hashimoto 2014). Following the classical tenets of Neoliberalism, our reading places Abenomics squarely in the neoliberal camp. In December 2014, new elections were held. Abe called these unscheduled elections to fortify his political position and control opposition. Abe and his LDP won those elections.

2.   Older homes featured heavy tiled roofs. Built to withstand the frequent typhoons that affect this region of Japan, these roofs were supported by relatively light wooden frames. As the wooden frames could not withstand the impact of the quake, the heavy roofs collapsed, destroying the unreinforced walls and floors. This is a process known as a "pancake" crash. Homes built with antiseismic codes fared well, as they featured reinforced walls and much lighter roofs (National Geographic 2013).

3.   Of all people reported dead or missing, 99.5 percent resided in the three prefectures of Iwate, Miyagi, and Fukushima. These are all located in the Pacific coastal region of Tohoku (FDMA 2013).

4.   *Kodokushi* is the Japanese term for lonely deaths. It generally refers to elderly individuals who live alone and have lost touch with family members. It is often associated with a person's lack of social relations. The earthquake and tsunami contributed to the increase of *kodokushi*.

5.   Specifically, the total amount of radioactive materials liberated in the Fukushima nuclear accident was six times smaller than in the Chernobyl nuclear accident (*Nikkei Newspaper* 2012a). However, the discharge of radioactive materials continued more than two years after the disaster.

6.   In his book, *World at Risk*, German sociologist Ulrich Beck (2009) stresses the importance of the "staging" of risk associated with possible disaster in terms of the overall management of the increasing risk component of contemporary society.

7.   The development of the nuclear power industry added to the reorganization of *zaibatsu*. For instance, Toshiba and Hitachi collaborated with General Electric and TEPCO in the Tokyo region, while Mitsubishi collaborated with Westinghouse and KEPCO (Kansai Electric Power Company) in the Osaka region (Okada 2012a).

8.   While the current (2015) government of the LDP has not activated nuclear plants as yet, it has initiated plans for activation of nuclear reactors in the near future. See discussion below.

9.   The government originally had established temporary limits for safe levels of radioactivity in food at 500 Bq/kg for grains, vegetable, meat, egg, and fish and 200 Bq/kg for water and milk; but it restricted them to 100 Bq/kg for general foods, 50 Bq/kg for milk, and 10 Bq/kg for water after April 2012 (MHLW 2012b).

10.   The Reconstruction Design Council is an advisory agency that was established with the premises that "From now on, it is important for Japan to aspire not to recovering merely but to making [a] creative effort in future-oriented manner;" and the aim "to draw a blueprint of reconstruction design for formulation of a guideline including a wide-ranging standpoint." Both statements are cited from the official website of the Reconstruction Design Council (see Reconstruction Design Council in Response to the Great East Japan Earthquake 2014).

11.   In the case of the SZR, the corporate tax was kept at virtually zero for five years for corporations operating under specific conditions that included the establishment of local subsidiaries employing more than five workers who were victims of the disaster (*Nikkei Newspaper* 2011b). This measure was promoted by the chairman of *Keidanren* just days after the earthquake (*Asahi Newspaper* 2011).

12.   Some researchers from the Nomura and Mitsubishi Research Institutes were invited by Governor Murai to serve on the Reconstruction Council of the Prefecture of Miyagi. Governor Murai, a fervent conservative and neoliberal, eventually adopted a number of recommendations for the reconstruction process proposed by these corporate advisors.

13.   In May 2013, Abe signed an agreement with Prime Minister Erdogan of Turkey to initiate the construction of new nuclear power plants in Turkey by a consortium of Japanese and foreign corporations (*Nikkei Newspaper* 2013q). As part of the agreement, the French corporation, GDF Suez, along with another Japanese company, Itochu, would be allowed to sell electric power in Turkey (*Nikkei Newspaper* 2013p).

14.   These three corporations are also the major makers of nuclear power plants.

15.   Many plant factories are equipped with light-emitting diodes (LEDs) as a source of light and do not use natural sunlight at all. LED is a technology invented in Japan and promoted for export.

16.   Koshio (2014) points out that this is the third wave of plant factories in Japan. The first boom occurred in the 1980s followed by a second one in the 1990s. Despite these repeated growth spurts, plant factories remain unpopular among farmers and also corporations, due to their lack of profitability.

17.   One of the objectives of the corporate-university collaborations is to generate large data sets on agricultural production that involve the use of IT services and products and that can be used in both plant factories and conventional agriculture. These data sets could not be collected and analyzed in the past because of technological limits. The availability of "cloud technology"—larger and more powerful operating systems—makes this data collection and analysis possible (*Nikkei Newspaper* 2013n). While plant factories are employed for the production of high-value-added commodities, such as tomatoes, strawberries, and lettuce, corporate efforts—see plans by Mitsubishi, Toyota, and Honda—have been also directed toward the production of generic crops, such as corn and soybeans (*Nikkei Newspaper* 2013g). Koshio (2014) underscores that some of these IT corporations, such as Hitachi and Toshiba as well as Mitsubishi, are also invested in the construction of nuclear power plants.

18.   New legislation allowed individuals to receive public support of up to 3 million yen for repair/reconstruction of their homes. However, this amount was largely inadequate to address local needs.

19.   Set nets are fixed nets that are held on shore by anchors.

CHAPTER 4

Evolution of Corporate Agri-Food Industrial Policies in Japan

The Cases of Dole Japan, Kagome, IBM, and Sendai Suisan

Introduction

The adoption of neoliberal policies promoted corporate entries into agri-food production. We illustrate this phenomenon through the review of four cases. The first illustrates the actions of Dole Japan. This is a subsidiary of the Dole Food Company, one of the largest global corporations in the fresh fruit and vegetable trading sector. The second case deals with Kagome. Kagome is a major tomato ketchup and juice maker with corporate roots in Japan; a worldwide market; and a global network of farms, contractors, and processing facilities. Third, we analyze the case of an IBM subsidiary, American IT, a transnational corporation that is registered as a non-agri-food corporation. But, like other IT corporations, it has entered the agri-food market. Fourth, we focus on Sendai Suisan, a seafood trading company. Sendai Suisan is a dominant corporation at the regional level in Tohoku. This case is relevant, as Sendai Suisan is the first private corporation other than fishing cooperatives to obtain fishing rights. These rights were granted in one of the SZRs established after the 2011 Great Earthquake.

Dole Japan's Industrial Policies and Actions from the Early Years to 2010

From the Early Years to the 1980s

Dole Food Company is a major transnational corporation in the fruit and vegetable business, including production, packing, processing, and worldwide shipping (Dole Food Company 2013a). It has subsidiaries in more than 90 countries, a work force of 59,000, and revenue totaling 6.9 billion U.S. dollars in 2010 (Dole Food Company 2013b). Originally founded in 1851 as a trading company with the name Castle and Cook in Hawaii, in 1961 it merged with the Hawaiian Pineapple Company established by James Dole in 1901 (Dole Food Company 2013c). It entered the banana business in 1964, when it purchased the majority share of the Standard Fruit & Steamship Company of New Orleans. From the 1960s, Dole Food Company[1] began a policy of foreign investment and established its global sourcing and worldwide marketing network in the fruits and vegetable sector. It operated primarily through acquisitions and production investment. Moreover, because of the introduction of technical innovations in storage and transportation and neoliberal policies, it took advantage of the elimination of trade barriers and production limits associated with the perishability of fruits and vegetables. These changes permitted the establishment of new global strategies and production areas.

In 1965, Dole established a branch office[2] in Japan and began to import pineapples and bananas grown on its plantations but also by independent growers in the Philippines.[3] In 1982, this branch was replaced by a subsidiary, Dole Japan[4] (Dole Japan 2013a). Taking advantage of Japanese economic growth and gradual market liberalization, Dole Japan easily expanded its import and wholesale business of fresh fruits and vegetables. These processes continued unabated until the 1980s (Sekine 2006; Sekine and Hisano 2009).

Changes in Market Structure and Business Strategies: 1990s–2010s

Change came in the early 1990s with the saturation and consequent collapse of the banana market due to the influx of Latin American bananas that followed a drought in the Philippines (Sekine 2006; Sekine and Hisano 2009). As a result, Dole Japan revised its business strategy and expanded its activities from exclusive involvement in the banana sector to wholesaling of a number of imported agri-food products. Its primary source of imports—particularly bananas—remained the Philippines.

Also in the 1990s, Dole Japan began to implement a strategy that envisioned the production of fresh fruits and vegetables through vertical integration without disregarding, however, the sourcing of some domestic production (Sekine 2006; Sekine and Hisano 2009). It further sought involvement in the processing and distribution sectors through the establishment of joint ventures with other corporations operating in Japan. This involvement in the sector upstream and downstream responded to opportunities generated by the implementation of neoliberal reforms (Sekine 2006).

Benefiting from the deregulation of the retailing sector, the business friendly climate, and the lifting of restrictions on the number of large-scale retailers allowed to operate in the country,[5] Dole Japan invested in the fresh fruit and vegetable processing and distribution sectors. From the 1990s to 2000s, it established three joint ventures with the Japanese corporations Itochu and Kyowa and through these joint ventures created a national network of facilities. The objective was to replace traditional wholesalers as suppliers of large-scale retail chains (Sekine 2006; Sekine and Hisano 2009). Simultaneously, Dole Japan sought to enter the domestic upscale market for fresh fruits and vegetables by establishing contracts with local farmers and organizing farm operations under its control (Sekine 2006; Sekine and Hisano 2009). Dole Japan never established full legal ownership of these farms. Yet it maintained control through actions at the financial, human resource, technical support, and marketing levels. This was the result of Dole's strategy to bypass then-existing legislation that prevented direct ownership of farms by corporations (see chapter 2).

This growth was not long lived. Dole Food Company was deeply affected by the global recession of 2008 and eventually opted to sell its world division of food processing (including canned food and beverages) and its Asian division of fresh fruits and vegetables to Itochu. This transaction was completed in April 2013 (*Nikkei Newspaper* 2013g). Itochu established a new holding company, Dole International Holdings, with headquarters in Tokyo. The 50-year collaboration between Itochu and Dole Food Company was instrumental in the 2013 acquisition of Dole's Japanese business by Itochu.

From Contract Farming to Franchise Farming

By 1998, Dole Japan began to sell domestically grown fresh fruits and vegetables supplied by about 1,500 local contract farmers. Farmers signed contracts with the company to produce and deliver about 30 different types of fruits and vegetables, with broccoli and tomatoes representing the most commonly traded commodities. By the following year, participation in this popular program soared, as more than 3,000 farmers signed contracts (Sekine 2008). Departing from the farmers' enthusiasm for contract farming, the informed public expressed concerns about the globalization of Japanese agriculture and the growing presence of foreign corporations (Nakano 1998). Despite the fact that the sustained growth of agri-food imports has been a constant for decades, the presence of foreign corporations and foreign workers in domestic agriculture became a troubling sign of a qualitatively relevant leap forward toward increased globalization and loss of national sovereignty.

Ultimately, contract farming turned out to be a losing proposition for Dole Japan (Sekine 2006; Sekine and Hisano 2009). A great number of farmers breached their contracts and sold their production in the open market. They sold to Dole Japan only when open market prices were lower than contract prices. When prices were higher, they sold to wholesalers through their cooperatives. In this system, Dole Japan lacked instruments to control farmers' behavior. Normally, in contract farming, farmers are controlled by corporations through the provision of inputs, extension assistance, and financial services. Dole Japan could not employ these tools, because assistance to farmers was provided by local agricultural cooperatives. As most Japanese farmers were cooperative members with strong ties to these organizations, it was easy for them to circumvent contractual obligations with Dole Japan. Additionally, this adverse situation was compounded by Dole Japan's inability to handle farmers' constant mixing of household expenses with business costs. This accounting problem—a traditional practice—and the losses generated by breached contracts caused Dole Japan to abandon contract farming and switch to a fully vertically integrated system based on franchise production. The term "franchise" was another instrument employed to bypass legislation that prevented the direct ownership of farms by corporations. By legally maintaining the independence of these farms but, de facto, controlling them, Dole Japan was able to establish a direct presence in the domestic agri-food production.

Between 2000 and 2008 and stimulated by the new business-friendly climate, Dole Japan opened 10 farms aided by the cooperation of such corporations as Itochu and Kyowa and a local wholesaler in Hokkaido (Sekine 2006, 2008; Sekine and Hisano 2009). The locations of these farms covered a wide sample of areas and climates to generate a year-round supply of fresh vegetables. The primary cultivation was broccoli,[6] but production also involved paprika, pumpkins, sweet corn, green soybeans, and sweet potatoes (Dole Japan 2013b). These vegetables were grown in open fields with the exception of paprika, which was produced in greenhouses. Despite Dole Japan's overt pronouncements about its contribution to the revitalization of the Japanese agriculture,[7] it showed a footloose attitude in its selection of farm locations and farm management. It did not hesitate to close down quickly or relocate three farms when they showed signs of unprofitability. The details of the domestic vegetable production by Dole Japan are analyzed in chapter 5.

Kagome's Industrial Policies and Actions from the Early Years to 2010

From the Early Years to the 1980s

Kagome is a major Japanese agri-food corporation with a dominant position in the domestic market for processed tomato products, such as juice, ketchup, and tomato sauce. Established in 1899 in Aichi as a producer of tomato sauce for the Japanese market, this company decided to invest internationally in the 1960s (Kagome 2013a). By the first part of 2010, it operated six subsidiaries in the United States, Australia, Italy, China, and Taiwan; sourcing, processing, and selling commodities in these countries as well as in another ten countries, including Spain, Turkey, Chile, and Brazil (Kagome 2013b). In Japan, the company has two headquarter offices located in Nagoya and Tokyo, eleven subsidiaries, eight production plants, and a research center. The latest available company data indicate that it has a work force of more than 2,000 employees and annual sales totaling 1.8 billion U.S. dollars (Kagome 2013c).

During the second half of the twentieth century and with the economic growth and westernization of the Japanese diet, the domestic market for tomatoes and tomato products evolved from that of an exotic vegetable to a mass consumption market. Kagome took advantage of this expansion and grew in tandem with this market. Originally, this company developed contract programs with local farmers to source tomatoes across the country. Under the 1961 Agricultural Basic Act (see chapter 2), contract farming for tomatoes and contractual arrangements for processing and mechanization were promoted as a strategy to provide a stable source of income for farmers (Nakamura 2002). Kagome and Nippon Del Monte,[8] two oligopoly corporations in tomato processing in Japan, established their sourcing networks across the country at that time.

Changes in the Market Structure and Business Shift: 1990s–2010s

Because of the gradual liberalization of tomato market in 1970s and 1980s, imported tomatoes and semiprocessed tomato products became more accessible as their volume doubled between 1988 and 2008 (ALIC 2011). Consequently, there was a reduction of the use of domestic products and the concomitant lowering of contract prices offered to farmers (Sekine 2014; Zhang, Bao, and Nomiyama 2011). Because of discounted contract prices and increased international competition, some tomato farmers abandoned the sector, contributing to its reduction and indirectly to the aging of the farm population. Low returns discouraged a significant portion of the new generation of farmers to stay in the business. Despite higher domestic prices,[9] Kagome continued to sign contracts with local farmers, particularly in the case of tomato juice. The quest for high quality, fresh, and safe local products motivated the company's strategic posture. Food scares involving imported products affected the perception of Japanese consumers, and Kagome responded by maintaining a "quality" local production marketing scheme. Tomatoes are a very popular vegetable in Japan and absorb about one-fifth of the average household budget devoted to the purchase of vegetables (ALIC 2011). However, while consumption remains stable, domestic production and acreage have decreased due to international competition and the dwindling number of farmers.[10]

In 1998, responding to a growing demand from retailers, Kagome began diverting surplus tomatoes from the processing sector to the fresh produce market (Kai 2012). This shift involved a variety of tomatoes that Kagome developed specifically for tomato juice and that was grown by contract farmers. In the 2000s, Kagome also began to establish its own farms for the production of an internally developed new variety of tomato for the fresh market. This move was in partial response to the weakness of independent farmers operating in the local market, the gradual deregulation of the Agricultural Land Act, and signals from the government encouraging the involvement of large corporations in agricultural production (see chapter 2).

Contract Farming and Direct Farming

In contrast to Dole Japan, Kagome retained its network of contract farming despite the establishment of company farms for the production of fresh tomatoes. Currently, Kagome operates about 30 production sites throughout Japan. This number includes three farms directly owned by the corporation and those under production contract (Kai 2012). Covering almost half (44 percent in 2009) of the total number of tomato producers, in the company's internal division of labor, contract farming remains an important—albeit diminishing—form of production of tomatoes for tomato juice (Zhang et al. 2011). Following the established patterns of contract farming, Kagome provides farmers with its own variety of tomato seeds, then purchases the entire production and provides the organized shipping networks (Kagome 2013d). Because farmers are often members of cooperatives, these cooperatives are entrusted with the negotiation of contract area, prices, and production plans with Kagome. While contracting generates a stable income for farmers, dissatisfaction is widespread, as escalating production costs and harsh working conditions make current compensations inadequate (Zhang et al. 2011). More importantly, famers are frustrated by a lack of autonomy after signing production contracts. Despite farmers' views, Kagome has promoted a system based on a discourse in which farmers are considered employees and their farms as parts of the company. Labeled as the company's "first line of factories," these farms' presence is considered central for the production of raw materials for their "second line of factories" in the food-processing sector. The justification for this position is provided in terms of the quality control that Kagome is able to maintain through this system (Kagome 2013e).

While Kagome continues sourcing, it radically reduced the volume of tomatoes purchased from contractors. The rationale for focusing its own production is twofold (Kai 2012). First, Kagome wanted to reduce the gap between the sustained demand for fresh tomatoes and the inadequate and varying supply too often affected by adverse weather and the declining number of farms and farm output. Second, it sought to enhance the control of the production process of fresh tomatoes to achieve better traceability and product safety. These are virtually the same reasons that motivated Dole Japan to promote production. In effect, these moves are part of a broader process in which market liberalization and the reduction of the size of the medium-sized and small farm sectors encourage agri-food corporations to invest in direct agricultural production.

Kagome directly operates three farms in the prefectures of Wakayama, Fukuoka, and Fukushima (Kagome 2013b), where it employs about 30 permanent and 420 seasonal workers (Kagome 2013f). At these three production sites, Kagome grows its original tomato varieties using large greenhouses with up-to-date technologies. In 2005 in Kitakyushu City, Fukuoka, Kagome established Hibikinada Farm with J-Power,[11] a wholesale electricity corporation (Kai 2012). J-Power also supported the investment by lending 15 ha of its own land. This farm produces two varieties of fresh tomatoes with two greenhouses on 8.5 ha and employs 150 workers. In the greenhouses, the production system and inputs, including water, fertilizer, and temperature, are entirely computerized with half of the water used generated by rain. It further operates sorting and packing systems that allow timely deliveries to large metropolitan areas, such as Tokyo and Osaka, as well as to regional markets in Kyushu. The high operating costs make this facility currently unprofitable, but Kagome continues to operate it at a loss. After 2011 earthquake, Kagome quickly reorganized its production sites. Kagome's post-earthquake reorganization project is analyzed in chapter 6.

IBM's Industrial Policies and Actions from the Early Years to 2010

From the Early Years to the 1980s

IBM is a global IT corporation based in New York City with a business network spanning more than 170 countries and employing 430,000 people (IBM Japan 2013a). Established in 1911 and named C-T-R Company, it was renamed IBM (International Business Machines Corporation) in 1924 (IBM Japan 2013b). In 1925, a subsidiary of the Morimura group, a *zaibatsu*, imported tabulating machines from IBM as part of the upgrading of its business. It also obtained the rights to represent IBM in Japan. In 1937, it became a subsidiary of IBM,[12] and in 1950, it was renamed IBM Japan. In 2012, it operated 86 offices and two research centers domestically, generated sales totaling 8.5 billion U.S. dollars annually, and employed more than 14,000 people (IBM Japan 2013c).

After World War II, IBM Japan played an important role for IBM's international business growth, not only because it served the second largest market after the United States but also because it generated the development of new products, such as the first notebook laptop in the early 1990s (IBM Japan 2013b). Because of its contribution, IBM Japan maintained a high profile in the corporation, and the vice president of IBM Japan was appointed as vice president of IBM in 1990 (*Nikkei Newspaper* 2012a).

Changes in the Market Structure and Business Shift: 1990s–2010s

While IBM was a virtual monopoly in the mainframe, large computer market until the late 1980s, in the 1990s it lost significant ground and had to restructure and downsize (*Nikkei Newspaper* 2012a). In 2004, it sold its PC business to Lenovo, a Chinese personal computer corporation, and focused on the software sector. Facing further competition, it decentralized operations to less expensive labor markets in Asia, primarily China and India, and outsourced business tasks. Under these conditions in the 2000s, IBM Japan lost its position of prominence and began to decline. Its largest level of annual sales was recorded in 2001, which it has never matched since. Management further restructured operations by radically downsizing through the selling or closing of divisions and subsidiaries. Significant layoffs of personnel accompanied this process. Despite these moves, the decline continued, and IBM Japan lost position not only in the IT market but also within IBM itself. By 2012, its annual volume of sales was less than a half of its peak year of 2001, while its net income totaled about one-fourth of that recorded in that year (*Nikkei Newspaper* 2012b). After a scandal involving unauthorized sales in 2005, IBM Japan lost autonomy and was placed under the strict control of IBM headquarters. In 2012 and for the first time in 56 years, a non-Japanese president was appointed. After the inauguration of the new president, IBM Japan aggressively continued the downsizing of its workforce.[13]

As part of the restructuring process, IBM sought to diversify investment. Traditionally, IBM operated in the hardware, software, and related service sectors. Its primary clients were large organizations in the public (government bureaucracies) and private sector (companies), which support their back-office service operations, such as automation and transaction processing. Recently, IBM initiated a program of investment in support business of front-office operations, such as marketing and customer services (*Nikkei Newspaper* 2013g). This shift reflects its corporate customers' moves to increase investment in the analysis of consumer behavior and to purchase IT tools to support it. IBM aims to integrate its back-office and new front-office operations to regain its prominence in the IT sector. IBM Japan also followed this new business strategy and strengthened the provision of tools and services for large data analysis.

New Business in the Agri-Food Sector

To revitalize business, beginning in 2009, IBM Japan marketed the concept "smarter planet." This program analyzes large data sets using cloud-computing systems delivered by mobile terminals, such as smart phones, tablets, and social network systems (IBM Japan 2013d). Targeted sectors are energy, transportation, urban infrastructure, medical care, and agri-food. In agri-food, IBM Japan began to invest in IT infrastructure and services for agri-food distribution. Mounting problems associated with food contamination scares and scandals, errors in the display of food information, and significant food losses[14] called for efficient traceability measures and matching IT support. Following the mad cow disease scare of 2001, traceability for beef has been mandatory since 2003, while it has been required for rice since 2010. Taking advantage of these events and legislative moves, IBM Japan reinforced its presence in agri-food distribution.

In the late 2000s, the growth of plant factories and their high technology requirements allowed IBM Japan to penetrate agricultural production through the provision of IT systems and services. Though the plant factory is not a new concept and some growth was recorded in the 1980s and 1990s, early developments were hampered by high operating costs and low profitability. However, in the 2000s, MAFF and METI initiated the promotion of plant factories and stimulated partnership between farming, manufacturing, and commerce. In

2008, METI introduced new measures to promote this partnership, and MAFF followed with similar actions in 2010. MAFF's objective is to increase farmers' stagnating incomes, while METI expects the grow plant factories to represent a new export industry. These ministries invested 150 million U.S. dollars for this project in 2009 alone.

In the aftermath of 2011 earthquake, the government released *The Comprehensive Strategy for the Rebirth of Japan* programmatic document and identified IT as a tool to increase agricultural production and productivity. Beginning in 2013, Prime Minister Abe implemented this strategy as part of the DPJ administration's reconstruction policy and efforts to foster the competitiveness of Japanese agriculture before joining the free trade system under the TPP. This action resulted in the actual involvement of a number of major IT corporations, such as IBM Japan, Hitachi, Fujitsu, NEC, and Toshiba, in agricultural production (see chapter 3). In this context, IBM Japan has plans to invest in a large complex of plant factories in one of the SZRs in the city of Sendai in the Miyagi Prefecture in cooperation with Kagome and twenty other major Japanese corporations, such as Sharp, Mitsui, Itochu, and the U.S.-based Seven Eleven. The details of the project are investigated in chapter 6.

Sendai Suisan's Industrial Policies and Actions from the Early Years to 2010

From the Early Years to the 1980s

Sendai Suisan is a prominent regional trading company of seafood products. The company was established in 1960 as a wholesale organization in the Sendai, Miyagi, central wholesale market and quickly extended its business to food processing, refrigeration, distribution centers, trading, and transportation and information systems for seafood products. As of 2012, it controlled 23 medium-sized and small corporations, employed 780 workers, and recorded annual sales totaling 450 million U.S. dollars (Sendai Suisan 2013). Benefiting from a strong yen and market liberalization, Sendai Suisan steadily increased its sales and its capital despite the overall crisis of the Japanese fishing sector (see chapter 2). In effect, Sendai Suisan's success did not involve any direct participation in fishing, as fishing rights were reserved only for fishing cooperatives and their members.[15]

Changes in the Market Structure and Business Shift: 1990s–2010s

Globalization and the implementation of neoliberal policies put pressure on traditional wholesale markets to reform. In the 1990s, the deregulation of large retail stores[16] resulted in the growth of the number of large supermarkets and, bypassing traditional wholesale markets, of the practice of direct procurement of fish from fishing ports. ITs technologies were heavily adopted by supermarket chains in their upgrading of distribution and transportation systems to accommodate the growth of cool chain production. In 2004, commission rates[17] for wholesalers were liberalized, providing additional power to supermarkets (Sumida 2013).

To address the new business climate, Sendai Suisan invested in the upgrading of its operations, adopting an overall strategy that stressed the modernization and diversification of its business. In 1998, it established a subsidiary for information services to support its distribution system. In 2000s, Sendai Suisan opened offices in various locations in eastern Japan and also established subsidiaries for distribution, trading, and food processing. After the 2011 quake, the governor of Miyagi Prefecture established a SZR in the city of Ishinomaki, Miyagi, and allowed corporations to have access to open fishing rights (see chapter 3). Sendai Suisan took advantage of this opportunity and obtained local fishing rights. This case is analyzed in chapter 7.

Conclusions

The four cases show that the development of neoliberal agri-food policies promoted the participation of corporations in agriculture and fishing. As the number of small and medium-sized farms as well as family-owned fishing operations decreased, the government sought the involvement of corporations in direct production as a viable solution for the revitalization of the sector. The concentration of production and distribution in the hands of a few large corporations, however, casts doubts on the ability of these corporate entities to contribute to sustainable development that is beneficial for local economies and the agriculture and fishing sectors. In chapters 5–7, we investigate this question through an in-depth review of these case studies.

Furthermore, the presentation of the cases suggests three fundamental points. First, the cases of Dole Japan and Kagome demonstrate that these corporations showed interest in investing in agricultural production. The establishment of contract farming and the acquisition of farms characterized this posture. The search for new business opportunities in a context in which deregulation and restructuring defined the agri-food and fishing sectors represents the primary justification for such a move. The development of contract farming was identified as a strategy to secure a stable supply of agricultural commodities. Yet the results were mixed. Dole Japan eventually had to almost completely abandon this initiative and concentrate its efforts on production through vertical integration (franchise production). Kagome fared better, but it also experienced problems with its contract farming operations. The difference between these two cases is explainable in terms of these companies' ability to control the resistance of farmers and their cooperatives. In contrast to Dole Japan, Kagome was able to mobilize instruments that improved its negotiations with agricultural cooperatives, permitted the control of farmers' contractual obligations, and placed local contractors in direct competition with farmers in other parts of the world. Ultimately, a complex set of factors linked to the local context determined the adoption and success of corporate production strategies.

Second, there has been a surge of interest in agri-food by companies that have not historically been involved in the sector. The case of IBM Japan is exemplary of this trend. Following a prolonged period of economic stagnation, Japanese-based corporations sought new investment opportunities to revitalize growth. Agri-food is recognized as one of these areas. Building on expectations of the emergence of a growing gap between world food supply and demand, IBM—as well as other non-agri-food corporations—identified agri-food as one of the world most promising growth sectors. IBM Japan plans to position itself as an important supplier of information and communication technology for production and distribution in this sector. In the case of IBM Japan, the need to search for alternative growth sectors was further motivated by the crisis that its parent company, IBM, experienced in its traditional field of IT corporate sales.

Third, given the interconnection between agri-food, other productive sectors, and the financial sector (see the Introduction and chapter 1), interest in agri-food and fisheries is not necessarily confined to production and distribution. In effect, the expansion of the financial sector motivated corporations to use agri-food products as assets to be traded in financial markets. The securitization of agri-food has opened new income and capital accumulation opportunities for large companies. Simultaneously, agri-food production is increasingly linked to nonfood sectors, such as industrial inputs, new sources of renewable energy, transportation, and commercial real estate development. In this context, involvement in agri-food may signify intent to enter one or more of these related markets. Sendai Suisan is a case in point (see chapter 7). It shows that the acquisition of fishing rights turned out to be an instrument granting access to new economic opportunities. For a long time, the unavailability of fishing rights was an obstacle to the industrial development of coastal areas, such as the establishment of industrial estates, airports, military bases, and nuclear power plants. Accordingly, corporate involvement in agri-food and fishing sectors may lead to broader business objectives with potentially significant consequences to local areas and populations.

NOTES

1.   Dole Food Company was taken private by David H. Murdock, who was the company's chairman of the board, in 2003 (Dole Food Company 2013c).

2.   As Dole established its presence in Japan, it entered into an agreement with the Itochu Corporation. The latter began to serve as Dole's sale agent (Tsurumi 1982).

3.   In Japan, commercial banana imports began in the early part of the twentieth century. Until the 1960s, Taiwan, a former colony, was the major producers of bananas for the Japanese market. The Philippines became the number one producers in the 1970s due to the development of banana plantations and contractual schemes by American and Japanese transnational corporations, such as Castle & Cook (later, Dole Food Company using the brand name "Dole"), United Brands (Chiquita), Del Monte (Del Monte) and Sumitomo Corporation (Banambo). The 1963 liberalization of the banana market signaled the expansion of banana consumption in Japan (Tsurumi 1982).

4.   The name of Dole Food Company's subsidiary in Japan is Dole. For heuristic purposes, in this book we refer to it as Dole Japan.

5.   These reforms accelerated the process of concentration of the sector as a great number of small and medium-sized retail stores were eliminated, while the traditional wholesale system entered a final period of crisis.

6.   Broccoli was a primary commodity for Dole Japan in terms of both import market share and know-how for shipping and distribution. Dole Japan's strategy was to increase its broccoli domestic market share.

7.   Dole Japan created the brand I LOVE, which was an acronym for "I live on vegetables." This brand was introduced in 2004 for domestically grown vegetables to stress Dole's commitment to rural development (Dole Japan 2004).

8.   The word "Nippon" means "Japan" in Japanese. The Nippon Del Monte Corporation was established in 1961 as a 100 percent subsidiary of Kikkoman, a Japanese transnational agrifood corporation that operated globally in the soy sauce, spice, and beverage markets. It introduced Del Monte's technology under a partnership contract (Nippon Del Monte 2013). In 1990, Kikkoman obtained the rights to use and sell Del Monte's trademark in Asia and Oceania and named its subsidiary Nippon Del Monte in 1991 (Kikkoman 2013).

9.   In 2010, there was a 4.8 percent price spread between imported and domestic tomatoes for processing (MAFF 2012d).

10.   The area devoted to tomato production declined 11 percent between 1990 and 2006, while production decreased 3 percent in the same period. These figures suggest an increase in productivity, mostly due to better harvesting techniques, the introduction of advanced varieties, and contracting with more productive farms (ALIC 2011).

11.   J-Power was a former governmental corporation that was privatized in 2004 (J-Power 2013).

12.   In 1980, IBM established the IBM Asia Pacific Holdings in Tokyo. IBM Japan became a 100 percent subsidiary of IBM Asia Pacific Holdings, which, in turn, is a 100 percent subsidiary of IBM Corporation.

13.   Following the economic crisis of 2008, IBM Japan dismissed about 1,300 employees (Nikkei BP 2008). According to trade unions, IBM Japan is expected to reduce its workforce by several thousand units over the 2012–2015 period (*Akahata Newspaper* 2012). In 2012, its

notorious employment policy was discussed in the Parliament and sharply criticized by then–Prime Minister Noda.

14.   In 2009, 20 percent, or 1,800 mt, of all available food was discarded in Japan, and an estimated 500–800 mt of this food (6–10 percent) was still edible (MAFF 2012e).

15.   The revised Fishery Act now allows corporations to be involved in fishing. However, corporations still need to become members of fishing cooperatives to obtain fishing rights.

16.   The 1974 Act, "Measures by Large-Scale Retail Stores for the Preservation of the Living Environment," regulated the establishment and hours of operation of retail stores larger than 500 m² of floor space. This legislation was reformed in 1994, liberalizing the operation of all retail stores with less than 1,000 m² of floor space. The entire regulation was finally abolished with the "Law Concerning the Adjustment of Retail Business Operations in Large-Scale Retail Stores" Act of 2000. Under the new legislation, retail stores larger than 1,000 m² are allowed to set their own hours of operation with prior notification to the Governor's Office (METI 2000). One of the consequences of this deregulation was the further concentration of the sector, as many small and medium-sized retail stores closed down.

17.   Before 2009, the commission rate was established at 5.5 percent for marine products across the country.

CHAPTER 5

Dole Japan's Agricultural Production

Introduction

This chapter analyzes three case studies pertaining to Dole Japan's direct involvement in agricultural production by investigating the corporation's strategies and actions and the opposition that it encountered from local farmers, farmers' cooperatives, authorities, and other local actors. In the first section, we analyze the system of operation of Dole Japan's farms, its branding strategies, sales, and impact on local farming. The second section reviews the case of one of Dole Japan's farms, the I LOVE Nittan Farm located in the prefecture of Hokkaido in northern Japan. We illustrate how Nittan Farm successfully expanded its size, displayed significant power in negotiations with local government agencies, and established itself in the local farming sector. In the third section, the case of Izumi Farm in the prefecture of Kagoshima in the Kyushu region is investigated. Following a pattern virtually opposite that of the Nittan Farm, Izumi Farm failed to increase its size and could not consolidate available land. This outcome, we contend, is the result of the opposition from landowners that motivated Dole Japan to quickly shutter operations at this farm. Dole eventually relocated it to the Prefecture of Nagasaki in the Kyushu region, responding to local leaders' invitations to move their operation to the area. The fourth section presents the case of the I LOVE Tome Farm located in Miyagi Prefecture in the Tohoku region. Tome Farm is the only farm that produces paprika in greenhouses, as all other Dole Japan farms grow vegetables in open fields. Primarily, the case of Tome Farm illustrates the discrepancy between expectations about corporate-induced socioeconomic growth harbored by local government officials and the actual, and much less beneficent, consequences of the establishment of this farm.

Organization and Strategies of Dole Japan's Franchise Farms

Franchise Farms Organized across the Country

Dole Japan's failed attempts to establish contract farming (see chapter 4) led to the implementation of production through vertical integration by adopting the franchise system. In 2000, Dole Japan opened the first franchise farm in Fukushima, the I LOVE Farm Odaka. Between 2000 and 2008, Dole organized ten franchise farms across the country (figure 5.1) with the objective of creating a year-round supply of domestically produced vegetables (figure 5.2).

Broccoli was identified as the most strategically relevant crop for the company. To promote the cultivation of broccoli, one of the farms, Tomisato Farm, was designed as an experimental farm, while another one, Echizen Farm, served as a training farm (table 5.1). In the late 1990s and before it initiated direct production, Dole Japan imported broccoli from the United States, China, and Australia year round for a market share of 40 percent of all imported broccoli (Sekine 2006, 2008; Sekine and Hisano 2009). During that decade, imported broccoli represented about half of the entire domestic demand, with Dole Japan controlling 20 percent of it. While Dole Japan successfully established these ten franchise farms, half of them ceased producing[1] for Dole by 2011 (table 5.1).

The rapidity with which these corporate farms were established, and later closed, stands in sharp contrast with the persistence of family farms. It is an indication of the different approach to farming of the two types of operation and illustrates the implications of the mobility of transnational corporations. More importantly, it indicates the difference in the understanding of the relationship between economic activities and commitment to the socioeconomic expansion of rural communities. While transnational corporations often accompany their investment with pronouncements about their contribution to local socioeconomic growth, the swiftness with which disinvestment occurs in an economic slowdown is telling of the actual meaning of such corporate statements.

Organization and Control System of Franchise Farms

Dole Japan maintains a complex system of organization and control of its franchised farms. This system is summarized in figure 5.3. In 1998, when Dole Japan began acquiring domestic vegetables from contractors, it established an administrative corporation, Hokkaido Sanchoku Center, for the purpose of managing its activities in this sector (Sekine 2006, 2008; Sekine, Boutonnet, and

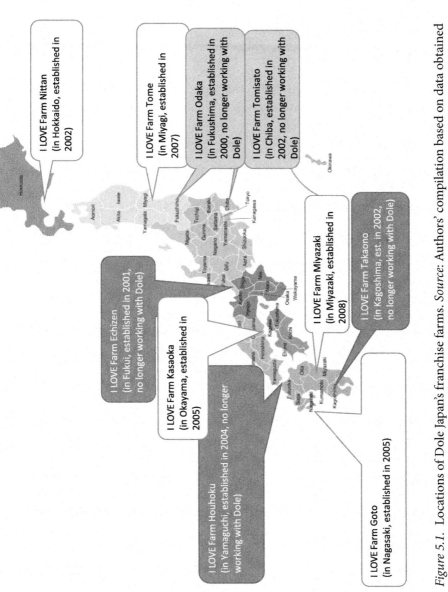

Figure 5.1. Locations of Dole Japan's franchise farms. *Source:* Authors' compilation based on data obtained through original interviews with Dole Japan representatives and Dole's webpage (http://www.dole.co.jp; accessed July 18, 2013).

I LOVE Farm Nittan (in Hokkaido, established in 2002)

I LOVE Farm Tome (in Miyagi, established in 2007)

I LOVE Farm Odaka (in Fukushima, established in 2000, no longer working with Dole)

I LOVE Farm Tomisato (in Chiba, established in 2002, no longer working with Dole)

I LOVE Farm Echizen (in Fukui, established in 2001, no longer working with Dole)

I LOVE Farm Kasaoka (in Okayama, established in 2005)

I LOVE Farm Houhoku (in Yamaguchi, established in 2004, no longer working with Dole)

I LOVE Farm Goto (in Nagasaki, established in 2005)

I LOVE Farm Miyazaki (in Miyazaki, established in 2008)

I LOVE Farm Takaono (in Kagoshima, est. in 2002, no longer working with Dole)

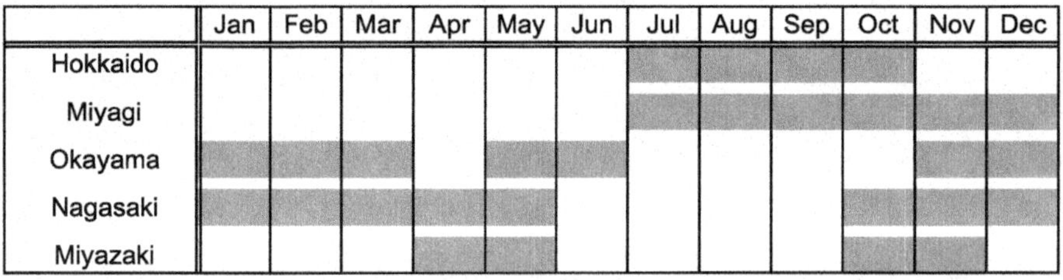

	Jan	Feb	Mar	Apr	May	Jun	Jul	Aug	Sep	Oct	Nov	Dec
Hokkaido							▓	▓	▓	▓		
Miyagi							▓	▓				
Okayama	▓	▓	▓	▓	▓	▓						
Nagasaki	▓	▓								▓	▓	▓
Miyazaki				▓	▓	▓						

Figure 5.2. Production calendar of Dole Japan's franchise farms (2012). Shaded areas indicate production windows. *Source*: Homepage of Dole Japan's website (http://www.dole.co.jp; accessed July 18, 2013).

Hisano 2008; Sekine and Hisano 2009). This corporation assumed a Japanese name to strategically allow Dole Japan to establish rapport with local political and community leaders as well as with farmers. The concern was that farmers would resist doing business with a foreign transnational corporation. As the Hokkaido Sanchoku Center became operational, it was assisted by the corporations Itochu and Kyowa and a wholesaler of fresh fruits and vegetables in Hokkaido.[2] Its primary role was that of intermediary between Dole Japan and local actors and between Dole Japan and its franchise farms. Specifically, it provided human resource management, allowing personnel from Dole Japan to be transferred to, and work in, the center and franchise farms. This cooperation focused on the provision of financial and technical assistance and relied on the collaboration of a major nursery company, Takii Shubyo. The center employed personnel from Takii to advise franchise farms. Because of this technical support, these franchise farms employed primarily unskilled workers and in so doing reduced labor costs. In return, the center received payments equal to 5 percent of total farm sales (Sekine 2006; Sekine et al. 2008).

In 2003, Dole Japan established a financial corporation, Agri Produce, to invest in its franchise farms (Sekine 2006; Sekine and Hisano 2009). Agri Produce was located in Tokyo at the headquarters of Dole Japan and staffed with personnel that held dual appointments at Dole Japan and Agri Produce. Thanks to this complex organization and to multiple intersecting directories, Dole Japan could concentrate on sales and franchise farm production (figure 5.3). In this scheme, however, Dole Japan did not invest directly in its franchise farms. Instead, it allowed its Japanese partners to invest through the center. This strategy responded to the same logic of avoiding conflict with local actors previously mentioned. It also represented a successful attempt to bypass and overcome legal hurdles regarding direct corporate ownership of farms as imposed by the

Table 5.1. Dole Japan's franchise farms

Farm Name	Location	From	Until	Mission	Area (ha)	Product
I LOVE Farm Odaka	Fukushima	2000	2011	Production	22	Broccoli and sweet corn
I LOVE Farm Echizen	Fukui	2001	2008	Training	5	Broccoli and sweet corn
I LOVE Farm Nittan	Hokkaido	2001	Present	Production	375	Broccoli, sweet corn, and pumpkins
Izumi Farm	Kagoshima	2002	2005	Production	9	Broccoli
I LOVE Farm Tomisato	Chiba	2002	2011	Experimental	5.5	Broccoli, onions, and cauliflower
I LOVE Farm Houhoku	Yamaguchi	2004	2008	Production	12	Broccoli
I LOVE Farm Kasaoka	Okayama	2005	Present	Production	94	Broccoli
I LOVE Farm Goto	Nagasaki	2005	Present	Production	123	Broccoli and sweet potatos
I LOVE Farm Miyazaki	Miyazaki	2008	Present	Production	53	Broccoli and green soybeans
I LOVE Farm Tome	Miyagi	2007	Present	Production	0.7	Paprika
Contract farming	Japan	1998	Present	Production	238	Broccoli and other vegetables
Total	Japan	1998	Present	—	884	Broccoli and other vegetables

Source: Authors' compilation based on data from interviews with Hokkaido Sanchoku Center (July 2004), Tome Farm (September 2012), and Dole Japan's Homepage http://www.dole.co.jp retrieved at http://www.dole.co.jp/ilove-yasai/index.html on July 9, 2013.

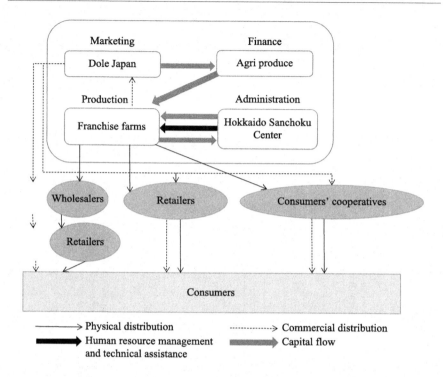

Figure 5.3. Organization of Dole Japan's vegetable production and distribution. *Source*: Authors' compilation based on data from interviews with Hokkaido Sanchoku Center representatives, July 20, 2004 and July 18, 2005.

Agricultural Land Act. According to this act, a single corporate investor could not own more than 10 percent of an individual farm.[3] For instance, in the case of Nittan Farm in Hokkaido, there were four local investors that established the farms. These individuals eventually became the four directors of the farm. Yet this original multiple investment was possible through financing made available by the center. Using this strategy, Dole Japan was able to establish direct control over its franchise farms and make decisions on crop varieties, volume, seasonal schedules of production, agricultural inputs, and purchase prices, despite the intended meaning of the Agricultural Land Act.

Branding Strategy and Sales

In 2003, Dole Japan created the I LOVE (I live on vegetables) brand to market vegetables grown by its franchise farms and contractors domestically (Sekine 2006; Sekine and Hisano 2009; Sekine et al. 2008). All Dole Japan's franchise farms assumed this brand name. Dole promoted the I LOVE brand products through production and market strategies based on consumer-friendly claims that proposed an image of social responsibility and support of Japanese agriculture (Dole Japan 2013b).

In promotional statements, the personnel assigned to the I LOVE brand were described as engaged in the selection of production locations and in the organization and direction of production and distribution processes. That is, Dole Japan directly organized and controlled farm production and distribution according to corporate plans. The image associated with this production was one of accountability, traceability, safety, and quality. Dole Japan stressed its efforts to disclose production histories, maintain procedures that met safety and quality standards, and allow consumers to have instruments to verify these claims. In effect, Dole Japan tagged its I LOVE produce in ways that allowed consumers to trace these products' production history and characteristics on the website of Dole Japan (Dole Japan 2013b). Additionally, production was presented as environmental friendly through the description of methods used that minimized their environmental footprint. Yet, detailed information on the standards employed was not available to the public. Therefore, consumers had to rely exclusively on the company's self-evaluation without the assistance of any third-party assessment. Third-party certification has emerged as the most commonly used system to verify the quality and characteristics of production[4] (Bain 2010; Busch and Bain 2004), but in this case, it was not employed. Simultaneously, adopted standards for the use of chemicals simply adhered to, but never exceeded, requirements established by existing legislation. Following a well-documented pattern in the use of certification schemes, the claimed quality of products reflected only the application of minimum legal standards. Essentially, no extra quality was added to the products.

Moreover, Dole Japan claimed to contribute to the growth of Japanese agriculture through "increasing production" and the "training of young agricultural producers." In effect, Dole Japan expanded the production areas of its franchise farms from an insignificant low of 2 ha in 2000 to 884 ha in 2011 (Dole Japan 2013b). Yet this claim concealed the fact that Dole Japan also shut down some of its farms that were considered unprofitable. Its pronouncements were silent on the consequences that the closing of these farms had on local rural communities, workers, and the overall well-being of Japanese agriculture. Additionally, the fact that Dole Japan did not hesitate to close down farms shows that the commitment to rural communities and agricultural development was secondary and, in fact, a by-product of the company's primary objective of profit making. While this posture may not be condemned per se—after all, for-profit companies should seek profit—these pronouncements about the contribution to rural community development were instrumental at a minimum.

Despite the actual production standards, the brand I LOVE was successful and convinced Japanese consumers of its superior quality. Accordingly, by the mid-2000s, Dole Japan could add a premium to the price of its I LOVE broccoli. While ordinary broccoli sold at 150 yen (1.3 U.S. dollars) per head, the branded broccoli was priced between 298 and 398 yen (2.56–3.56 U.S. dollars) (Sekine 2006). Furthermore, Dole Japan began to sell the I LOVE products to members of consumer cooperatives. These have traditionally been among the most conscious consumers in the country with strong concerns about food safety and quality and a pro-environment preference. Similarly, the brand appeared on the shelves of major supermarket chains, local retailers, and wholesalers (Sekine 2006; 2008; Sekine and Hisano 2009; Sekine et al. 2008). Through its domestic production, Dole Japan could finally win the confidence of skeptical and demanding consumers. Previously, these consumers' preference for local products had been the primary reason for the poor results of Dole Japan's imported broccoli.

Impact on Other Production Sources and Markets

Dole Japan's agricultural production grew successfully because of the company's ability to enlist the cooperation of major retailers and win the confidence of consumers. In 2011, Dole Japan planned to devote 884 ha to the production of I LOVE vegetables. It included franchise and contract farms and covered 6.6 percent of the entire domestic production of broccoli (Dole Japan 2013b; MAFF 2013c). While it may appear to be modest, this share was very large for a single producer. Additionally, because Dole Japan established a year-round distribution system, it could ship off-season crops from traditional supply regions, such as the Prefectures of Aichi and Saitama. According to Dole Japan's own sources, Dole Japan's seasonal share of the domestic production of broccoli reached almost 50 percent (Interview 2004a, 2006a), and it controlled 45 percent of the total Japanese market for broccoli (domestic and imported products). Relying on this dominant position, Dole Japan could command favorable terms in its negotiations with retailers and cooperatives (Sekine 2006; Sekine and Hisano 2009).

Individual broccoli growers, farmer organizations, and cooperatives in traditional broccoli-producing areas, such as the Aichi Prefecture, began spot selling to Dole Japan because of its dominant position in the market. Also broccoli producers located near Dole Japan's franchise farms sold their products to, or entered in contractual relations with, the company. In 2004, Dole Japan sourced 74 percent of domestic vegetables from franchise farms, 22 percent from contractors, and 4 percent from spot transactions with agricultural cooperatives (Sekine 2008).

The Case of Nittan Farm in Hokkaido

In Hokkaido in 2002, Dole Japan established its largest farm, Nittan Farm, near the town of Mukawa.[5] Hokkaido is renowned for its vegetable production as well as the production of other agricultural commodities, such as rice, dairy products, meat, and seafood.

Agriculture in Mukawa, Hokkaido

Mukawa is located in a predominantly agricultural region on the Pacific Ocean side of Hokkaido Island (see figure 5.1). Its economy is based primarily on the production of rice and vegetables but also on the breeding of racehorses (Mukawa Town 2004). Because of its cool summer temperatures, Dole Japan deemed this area quite suitable for broccoli production (Sekine 2006). Its investment in the area came at a time when a prolonged crisis had severely impacted the region's agriculture. The consequent loss of farm populations was so severe that the government officially designated the area as underpopulated (Mukawa Town 2002a). According to a survey conducted by the local agricultural authority, only 15 percent of all farm families planned to continue farming (Mukawa Town Agricultural Committee 2002). Moreover, because of the declining price of rice, farmland value had continuously depreciated during the past few decades (Mukawa Town Agricultural Committee 2004a). The local agricultural cooperative, JA Mukawa, attempted to respond to the crisis by promoting a reconversion to greenhouse horticulture centered on such crops as vegetables and flowers. However, a significant portion of farmers remained involved in open-field vegetable and grain production and therefore, did not benefit from this initiative. Traditionally in this region, a four-year crop rotation system[6] had been employed to enhance soil fertility. However, because of the combined effect of the aging farm population and the hard work associated with this type of farming, farmers gradually shifted to a three-year crop rotation that resulted in declining land productivity (Interview 2004b). In this context, for the local communities, Dole Japan's Nittan Farm appeared as the much-needed answer to the crisis of local agriculture (Sekine and Hisano 2009).

Establishment of the I LOVE Nittan Farm

Before the establishment of Nittan Farm in 2002, Dole Japan was sourcing broccoli from contractors in the adjacent town of Atsuma (Mukawa Town 2002b). Because of this presence in Atsuma, Dole Japan planned to locate Nittan Farm there. Accordingly, Nittan Farm proceeded to apply for the required permit to become a certified agricultural producer. Certification would have allowed Nittan Farm access to favorable production conditions, such as low-cost financing, tax abatements, and the support of the local authority in negotiations for farmland transactions. However, the municipal government of Atsuma delayed action on this application for one year, prompting Dole Japan to respond by relocating the farm to Mukawa (Sekine 2006).

The Administration of Mukawa received this application favorably, granted Nittan Farm the status of certified agricultural producer with the associated favorable business conditions for the first year of operation. In return, Nittan Farm committed to contributing to the local agriculture and economy through the implementation of a crop rotation system centered on broccoli production, environmentally sound soil improvement, the creation of jobs, and the use of local contractors (Sekine 2006; Sekine and Hisano 2009). The town of Mukawa and JA Mukawa cooperative also expected that local residents and cooperative members could sell agricultural products to supermarket chains and consumer cooperatives through Dole Japan.

In 2006, Nittan Farm cultivated a total of 400 ha, the vast majority of which was leased to contain costs. Leases from local farmers were signed for three-year terms with contracts negotiated and supported by the local government and agricultural committees[7] (Sekine 2006). Yet Nittan Farm paid higher rates (70,000 yen/ha, or 603 U.S. dollars/ha) than the then-current rates of 56,000 yen for prime land and 39,000 yen for average land. Additionally, it leased land that was originally zoned for alternative uses (housing and industrial development) but lacked demand for these purposes. Nittan Farm was managed by a president and three directors, all with a background in agricultural production and holding joint appointments with the Hokkaido Sanchoku Center (Sekine 2006). In addition, there were six full-time technicians who had degrees from agricultural schools and a number of part-time workers. The Hokkaido Sanchoku Center also provided technical advisors who worked for Takii or were skilled farmers. During production, there were visits to the farm by Dole Japan personnel and the president of Hokkaido Sanchoku Center.

Table 5.2. Production at I LOVE Nittan Farm

Year	Area (ha)	Harvest		Sale million yen	Permanent employees	Part-time workers
		million heads	metric tons			
2002	63	1.5	525	150	8	60
2003	100	3.0	1,050	280	9	120
2004	240	8.0	2,800*	—	10	250
2005	323	—	—	—	—	—
2006	400*	12.0	4,200*	—	—	

Source: Authors' compilation based on data from interviews of key informants at the Hokkaido Sanchoku Center, July 2004.
* Estimated by personnel at the Hokkaido Sanchoku Center.
Note: No data available for entries marked with —.

Agricultural Production on the I LOVE Nittan Farm

Nittan Farm consistently expanded its size and number of workers (table 5.2). In 2004, it employed 260 workers, the majority of them part-time workers. These part-timers had virtually no previous farm experience and worked under the supervision of technicians from the farm and the center. They worked on such tasks as seeding, transplanting, fertilizing, and harvesting. Additionally, they performed post-harvest production tasks, such as classifying, packing, cooling, and transporting products. Given the labor-intensive nature of broccoli production and shipping, Dole Japan and Nittan Farm strictly separated farm operations reserved for skilled workers from those that could be performed by unskilled labor. The goal was to reduce labor cost by increasing the use of inexpensive, unskilled part-time workers. Claiming a limited supply of local farmworkers, Nittan Farm began to hire workers from adjacent cities, such as Sapporo, Chitose, and Tomakomai (Sekine 2006). As wages were not raised and Nittan Farm could not hire enough workers, the farm began recruiting marginal urban workers with no farm background, including housewives and high-school students. The ample reserve of labor in the area allowed Nittam Farm to be successful but frustrated the aspirations of the area's out-of-work qualified farmers. Ultimately, through this system, Dole Japan was able to replace more expensive experienced farmworkers with cheap part-time workers.

In 2005, Nittan Farm employed 11 ha of land it owned to establish a nursery; 240 ha of leased land for broccoli production; and an additional 83 ha of leased land to grow sweet corn, lettuce, and Chinese yams for fresh consumption

Table 5.3. I LOVE Farm Nittan's share of local farm output (2003)

		Rice and Other Crops		All Crops Except Rice	
		(10 million yen)	(%)	(10 million yen)	(%)
Towns	Atsuma	559	27.9	233	39.8
	Mukawa	456	22.8	253	43.2
	Monbetsu	986	49.3	100	17.1
Three-Town Total		2001	100.0	586	100.0
I LOVE Farm Nittan		28	1.4	28	4.8
Mukawa		456	100.0	253	100.0
Nittan Farm		28	6.1	28	11.1

Source: Authors' calculations based on MAFF data (2004) and interveiws with personnel at I LOVE Nittan Farm, 2004.

(Sekine 2006). In 2003, the farm produced broccoli with a below-average productivity of 8.3 mt/ha. The average in Japan was 10.5 mt/ha. Only a year later, however, it dramatically improved to 11.7 mt/ha. Moreover, increases in productivity were accompanied by improved quality. In 2004, only 8 percent of the entire broccoli production was sold under the I LOVE brand. In 2005, this percentage quadrupled to 30 percent (Sekine 2006). These improvements were mostly the result of an economic incentive-based organizational system centered on target goals and stimuli to better them. These incentives, however, were confined to the director and technicians and did not apply to part-time workers. Once harvested, the broccoli was sent to the adjacent packinghouse for cooling and packing. It was shipped by refrigerated trucks directly to major wholesale centers. In 2004, 30 percent of all products were sold in the Tokyo metropolitan area, 25 percent in Osaka, and 10 percent in Nagoya (Sekine 2006). The farm also sold directly to a consumer cooperative and local retailers in Hokkaido.

Local Agriculture and the I LOVE Nittan Farm

The impact of Nittan Farm on total local farming output was significant. In 2003, the farm's sales totaled 280 million yen (2.4 million U.S. dollars) and constituted 1.4 percent of total agricultural sales of the three municipalities where its farmland is located (table 5.3). If rice and animal production are excluded, Nittan Farm's sales reached 5 percent of the total sales in the area and 11 percent of the entire production in Mukawa.

Nittan Farm's presence also affected the local farmland market. While the leasing price authorized by the local agricultural committee for rice paddies

Table 5.4. Farm lease prices in Mukawa Town

		1992	1995	1998	2004
Rice paddy	Yen	226,670	216,670	191,670	180,000
	Percentage change	100.0	95.6	84.6	79.4
Other crops	Yen	39,000	39,000	39,000	60,330
	Percentage change	100.0	100.0	100.0	154.7

Source: Mukawa Town Agricultural Committee (1992, 1995, 1998, 2004b).

Note: The farm leases are for 1 hectare and averaged over three different leases according to the fertility of the land.

declined 20 percent between 1992 and 2004, the leasing price of land devoted to other cultures increased by 55 percent during the same period (table 5.4). As indicated above, Nittan Farm leased land at 70,000 yen/ha, a price that was significantly higher than the average price of 39,000 yen/ha and the 56,000 yen/ha paid for prime land. While economically beneficial to farmers and landowners that did business with Nittan Farm, the inflated land prices negatively affected farmers who wanted to lease land in the open market. In effect, Nittan Farm's posture represented a strategy to entice local farmers and landowners to do business with the farm and reduce their concerns about doing business with foreign firms.

As a result, local institutions, farmers, and community members responded positively to the farm's presence. For instance, representatives of the local agricultural cooperative, JA Mukawa, were pleased with the increased volume of business. In 2006, the cooperative's sales to the farm exceeded 86 million yen (740,000 U.S. dollars), representing 12 percent of its total sales (Sekine 2006; Sekine and Hisano 2009). Nittan Farm became the cooperative's largest client. Local government officials were happy with the estimated growth in tax revenue and employment. Farmers expressed satisfaction for the technical assistance, while local residents were grateful for the community support. Nittan Farm provided technical assistance to farmers (for example, its compost-based crop rotation system and a system for the use of animal waste from local racehorse farms) that increased land productivity (Sekine 2006). It also allowed local farmers to use its greenhouses at no cost during the off-season. These greenhouses functioned as community nurseries. When some local residents lost their homes due to a fire, Nittan Farm allowed them to live in some of its facilities. And when a primary school[8] was closed, Nittan Farm rented the vacated space. Given these positive feelings about Nittan Farm's contribution to the local economy and community, it is not difficult to explain the limited opposition that it encountered.

To be sure, problems existed. Contrary to commitments made to local government officials, Nittan Farm neither employed local agricultural contractors nor met expectations concerning the growth of local employment. The strategy of paying low wages and offering only part-time jobs discouraged qualified local workers from seeking employment. In effect, Nittan Farm sought the use of temporary, inexpensive labor. Ultimately, and contrary to its original pronouncements, Nittan Farm invested in the area but created conditions that were not amenable to social and economic growth and, more importantly, did not represent a committed long-term presence. This is a characteristic of Dole Japan and a situation that is further explored through the case presented in the next section.

The Case of Izumi Farm: From Kagoshima to Nagasaki

This case shows the flexible approach to agricultural production adopted by Dole Japan. It probes the instance of Izumi Farm that was originally established in the Prefecture of Kagoshima in the Kyushu Region and later relocated to the Prefecture of Nagasaki and renamed I LOVE Goto Farm (see figure 5.1).

Agriculture in Takaono in the Prefecture of Kagoshima

Kyushu is an important agricultural region in Japan. In 2002, Dole Japan established Izumi Farm in the town of Takaono,[9] in the Prefecture of Kagoshima. Takaono is located on the Izumi Plain on the northwestern coastal section of the prefecture. The plain is often affected by typhoons and droughts. Yet its flat terrain, concentrated farm structure, and irrigation projects established after World War II make it a desirable farming area. It is known for its production of rice and is one of the most important grain-producing areas in the region (West Izumi Land Improvement District 1972). While the total number of local farmers has decreased, this decline has not been as pronounced as in the rest of Japan, and some younger farmers have been willing to replace their retiring parents on family farms. The plain is also known as a nesting ground for wild birds, such as the hooded crane (Izumi City 2004).

From Contract to Franchise Farming

Dole Japan's first presence in the Izumi Plain area dates back to the early 1990s. Prior to commercializing fresh fruits and vegetables under its brand name in the late nineties, in 1994, Dole Japan began signing production contracts with local farmers aided by the Hokkaido Sanchoku Center[10] (Interview 2004c, 2006b). These contracts called for the cultivation of broccoli by rice producers during the winter months in rotation with rice to be planted in the summer. The program grew over the next 10 years from the original 4 ha to 49 ha, making the area the most important broccoli-producing area in the prefecture (Sekine 2008).

In 2002, Dole Japan established Izumi Farm as a franchise operation for the production of broccoli in the polder of the Izumi Plain. This particular area was chosen because it was deemed suitable for an efficient use of agricultural machines. Dole Japan selected the same type of land in the Prefecture of Okayama, where it established Kasaoka Farm (see table 5.1). Izumi Farm leased its land and had only two full-time workers on its payroll: the president and a technician. The rest of the personnel consisted of part-time workers. This flexible management contemplated the signing of contracts for the leasing of machines, nursery services, and packing.

According to the mission statement of Izumi Farm, its business was to sell fresh fruits, vegetables, grains, and processed food produced on the farm or purchased elsewhere and to gain contracts for agricultural works (Izumi Farm 2002). The farm president was also the president of the Hokkaido Sanchoku Center, and the other full-time employee was also affiliated with the center. To maintain control of the farm while bypassing the Agricultural Land Act, the president was listed as controlling 40 percent of the farm capital. The technician and the center were listed as owners of 50 percent and 10 percent of the farm, respectively. As this technician was employed by the center, and the center was controlled by Dole Japan, the manner in which Dole Japan circumvented the law was evident.

Izumi Farm leased land from farmers with the assistance of the local agricultural cooperative, JA Kagoshima Izumi. In 2002, however, it leased land without the consent of the local agricultural committee, creating tension with this institution (Sekine 2008; Takaono Town Agricultural Committee 2002). The Izumi Agricultural Committee opposed the leasing of land for only the winter months, arguing that land should be leased and used for the entire year. Additionally, it expressed concerns about the fact that the farm president did not reside in the community but lived far away in Hokkaido. The all-local farmer committee feared that this corporate involvement would be detrimental to local agriculture.

Contrary to the situation in Izumi, the administration of Takaono supported the farm. Largely the result of the long-term association between JA Kagoshima Izumi and Dole Japan, this support quickly translated into the awarding of the certification of agricultural producer to the farm and good business relations with JA Kagoshima Izumi. Izumi Farm employed the JA Kagoshima Izumi packing center and delivered broccoli to Dole Japan through this cooperative's prefectural level organization.[11] As part of the negotiation with the city of Takaono, Dole Japan committed to "protect local agriculture and farmers," and "pay taxes" (Interview 2006c; Sekine 2008). However, two years later, in 2004, Izumi Farm suspended its business arrangements with the cooperative, citing poor performance that did not warrant the payment of the required commission (Interview 2004c, 2005a; Sekine 2008).

As indicated above, labor on Izumi Farm was almost exclusively provided by part-time workers hired through the local public "Silver Human Resource Center,"[12] an employment agency that provides various types of relatively low-skilled jobs to senior citizens. These jobs include housekeeper, private teacher, and agricultural laborer. Many of these workers were senior citizens and women. Their pay was about 645 yen/hour (5.56 U.S. dollars/hour at the time) (Interview 2006d; Sekine 2008). While low, this wage rate was in line with the legally established local minimum wage.[13] However, Izumi Farm benefited from the large local reserve of labor, as this surplus supply prevented wages from increasing. Also, given the availability of this large labor supply, it was easy to popularize the view that these part-time jobs constituted an important advantage to workers. In effect, despite the precarious and unstable nature of this employment and the limited contribution that it provided to the local economy, workers and residents saw the jobs as convenient. They felt that these low-quality jobs were better than no jobs.

Relocation of the Farm and Its Consequences

In 2005, Dole Japan shut down Izumi Farm and relocated it in the city of Goto in the Prefecture of Nagasaki. It provided three reasons for this move. First, Izumi Farm had faced a number of natural disasters that hampered production. These included salt damage generated by recurrent typhoons and crop damage stemming from the large number of birds in the area. In effect, because of these occurrences, farm productivity remained quite low. While the average domestic productivity of broccoli in Japan was 10 mt/ha, the productivity of this farm was 0.4 mt/ha in 2003, 3.2 in 2004, and 2.6 in 2005. The fact that Izumi Farm was located close to the coast made these recurrent problems more severe than had been foreseen and difficult to overcome. To address the issue, Izumi Farm management began to purchase produce for resale, acting as a de facto wholesaler. In 2004, the share of its own production consisted of 150 million yen (1.3 million U.S. dollars), representing only 5 percent of farm total sales (Takaono Town 2004).

Table 5.5. Izumi Farm's production targets and actual results

		2002	2003	2004	2005	2006
Area (ha)	Target	10	30	50	60	80
	Result	7	9	9	9	—
Yield (mt)	Target	—	200	334	400	534
	Result	—	4	29	23	—
Permanent workers (number)	Target	0	1	2	3	3
	Result	0	0	0	0	—
Part-time workers (number)	Target	10	15	20	25	30
	Result	16	37	41	43	—

Source: Authors' compilation based on data from Izumi Farm (2006).

Note: No data available for entries marked with —.

Second, the relationship between Izumi Farm and local landowners reached a low point in 2005, when Izumi Farm's plan to expand its operation ran into the opposition of local landowners. Table 5.5 shows the gap between Izumi Farm's farming targets and results. Between 2004 and 2005, Izumi Farm repeatedly negotiated with 20 farmers but could not reach an agreement. This was the case even though it offered 400,000 yen/ha, which was a much higher price than the standard lease price of 220,000 yen. Ultimately, while Izumi Farm planned to cultivate 60 ha of land, the actual land used was only 9 ha in 2005 (table 5.5). According to the chair of the local land improvement association (Interview 2006c, 2006e; Sekine 2008), Izumi Farm's inability to obtain land was the result of the assumed incompatibility between the cultivation of rice and of broccoli. Izumi Farm's high use of compost for the production of broccoli was viewed as incompatible with good paddy rice production. Farmers felt that the level of nitrogen released to the ground was too high. Also, local farmers resented the fact that Izumi Farm leased land without the authorization of the local agricultural committee. Even considering the support of JA Kagoshima Izumi, local farmers felt that the necessary consensus had not been achieved.[14]

Finally, the administration of the Prefecture of Nagasaki fervently invited Izumi Farm to relocate there. Beginning in 2004, the prefecture's administrators initiated a promotional campaign to convince Dole Japan's representatives to visit and eventually select area sites for the location of the farm (Interview 2006f; Sekine 2008). Together with the problems experienced in Takaono, this offer appeared quite appealing to Dole. To be sure, farming was not particularly developed in this area, which was considered unfavorable for agricultural production. However, and because of the crisis of farming, there was abundant farmland in Goto. Local farmers produced mulberry for the silk industry, sweet potatoes for alcohol production, and tobacco, all of which were in a structural decline (Goto City 2006). In this context, many of the farm families were expected to give up farming once their older members retired. As the prices of crops remained unattractive, Goto's unused land increased, reaching 830 ha in 2008 or about 14 percent of the total farmland (Inoue 2010). Dwelling on this land oversupply, Dole Japan contemplated leasing a large quantity of farmland at very a reasonable price and making Goto a production hub for broccoli.

As Dole Japan closed Izumi Farm, the administration of Takaono rescinded the farm's certification of agricultural producer and asked that a 9 million yen (90,000 U.S. dollars) low-interest loan that the farm received be paid back immediately. While small, this loan was politically important and financially significant, given the economic status of Izumi Farm. Dole Japan intervened and paid the loan. While most of the land previously used by Izumi Farm remained unused, the real negative impact of the relocation was felt by farmers who could not lease their land and lost their production contracts, part-time workers who lost their jobs, machine contractors, and the JA Kagoshima Izumi that lost business. While these negative consequences were predictable and similar to those recorded in other locations, this case is an illustration of the vicious circle that corporate mobility generates for rural communities. It can be summarized accordingly: When local communities oppose corporate moves, the corporation disinvests. As it disinvests, the local economy is destabilized, jobs are lost, and local administrations find their efforts to revitalize the economy nullified. When the corporation moves its operations and invests elsewhere, it recreates the same unstable conditions in the new location, whereby local opposition triggers a new round of disinvestment and a new move.

Establishment of the I LOVE Goto Farm in the City of Goto, in the Prefecture of Nagasaki

Dole Japan reopened Izumi Farm in the city of Goto in the Prefecture of Nagasaki in 2005. It was renamed the I LOVE Goto Farm. Goto is located on an archipelago 100 km from the port of Nagasaki (see figure 5.1). In the same year, Goto Farm began broccoli production on a 2 ha plot with good results. It received its license of certified agricultural producer in 2006 and expanded its production area to 108 ha in 2009 (Inoue 2010). It employed seven permanent staff members and 120 part-time workers at peak times. Four of the seven permanent staff members were located in the city. In 2009, its broccoli harvest

124

topped 750 mt with a productivity of 6.9 mt/ha. While this productivity level remained well below average, Goto Farm production was sizable, generating 250 million yen (2.5 million U.S. dollars) in annual sales. The farm also leased land on five-year contracts, paying 50,000 yen/ha. Dole Japan also signed production contracts with about three dozen local farmers on 5 ha of land and expanded this program to 79 farmers on 25 ha in 2006 (JA Goto 2006).

Originally, Goto Farm employed the local agricultural cooperative's packing house for its broccoli. As the relationship with the JA Goto cooperative deteriorated, it established its own packing house with half the costs covered by public subsidies (Inoue 2010). Concerned over the growth of unused farmland, the government made subsidies available to those who would cultivate additional land. Goto Farm took advantage of this program. As a result, in 2009, the farm operated 38.5 ha obtained through subsidy programs. This land represented 28.4 percent of the total amount of land included in these initiatives (Inoue 2010). Despite this institutional support, Goto Farm's business relationship with the JA Goto cooperative was eventually broken off in late 2000. Disagreements on the price of contracted broccoli paid to local producers angered local farmers and motivated the cooperative to oppose any new deal with the farm (Inoue 2010). Local farmers also opposed Goto Farm's expansion on local land and the support it received from the agricultural committee. In effect, the problem denounced by local farmers was the lack of public incentives for farming. They considered the availability of government support more desirable than private investment. Once the government intervened, they welcomed the support and took advantage of it.

The Case of the I LOVE Tome Farm in the Prefecture of Miyagi

Located near the city of Tome, in the Prefecture of Miyagi, the I LOVE Tome Farm is the only Dole Japan franchise farm involved in greenhouse production. Its primary crop is paprika. Originally scheduled to produce by employing a large greenhouse, Tome Farm's plans were revisited following economic problems experienced by Dole Food. Eventually, it operated with a medium-sized greenhouse that was, however, supported by local government and national subsidies.

Agriculture in Tome, Prefecture of Miyagi

The city of Tome is located in the northeastern portion of the prefecture of Miyagi, about 70 km from Sendai City, the prefectural capital (see figure 5.1).

Its relatively limited winter snowfall and abundant water resources, such as lakes and wetlands,[15] make it particularly suitable for greenhouse production. The area's most important agricultural crop is rice, followed by vegetables (specifically, cabbages and cucumbers) and beef (Tome City 2008). The municipality of Tome ranks first in number of farmers and second in agricultural annual sales in the prefecture. However, the overall number of farmers is declining due to the aging[16] of the farm population, as fewer young people are entering agriculture.

In Tome, before Tome Farm was established, paprika was a relatively unknown crop. Since the mid-2000s and under the administration of Governor Murai, Miyagi has been actively attracting corporate investment in agriculture. In this context, two large paprika farms were established. Richfield of Tomita Technology[17] and Vegi Dream of the Toyota Group were established in 2005 and 2008, respectively. These farms were located in Kurihara, a town adjacent to Tome (Northern Tohoku Regional Development Office 2009). When Dole Japan opened its greenhouse farm in Tome City, there was momentum to establish corporate paprika farms.

Establishment of I LOVE Tome Farm

In 2000, Dole Japan began to import paprika from South Korea. Korea is the largest exporter of paprika to Japan, producing 63 percent of the total volume imported. A distant second is the Netherlands, with 22 percent (MFJ 2011). As the quantity of paprika imported from Korea normally decreases during the summer, Dole Japan planned to produce it domestically to supply this unmet demand (Interview 2012a; Sekine 2012). In the mid-2000s, it established a franchise farm in the city of Misawa, in the Prefecture of Aomori on the northern tip of Honshu Island. This location was selected because of its cool summer climate, which is suitable for paprika production. However, excessive snowfall made the use of greenhouses virtually impossible, as they crashed under the weight of the snow.

Seeking an alternative to the Misawa farm, in 2006, Dole Japan and representatives of the administration of Tome met to discuss the possible establishment of a franchise farm in the area. At the meeting, Dole Japan was encouraged to pursue the initiative and to locate its facilities in a local industrial park—Naganuma Industrial Park—whose creation was meant to attract corporate investment to the area (Interview 2012a, 2012b; Sekine 2012). Additionally, it began mediating among key actors to create optimal conditions for the achievement of this goal. Specifically, representatives of the city of Tome were able to promote agreement among Dole Japan, local farmers, the city council, and the prefectural government. In this vein, several steps were taken. First, the Tome administration encouraged the Prefecture of Miyagi to change the zoning category for the land selected by Dole Japan. This land was originally zoned as forest and nonprime farmland and then changed to prime farmland. This change was achieved rather quickly, and the new category allowed Dole Japan to obtain national government subsidies. Second, the city purchased land from forty-nine local landowners and improved it through the enhancement of infrastructure, including the building of a water reservoir. These improvements were paid for with city funds after overcoming the original opposition from the city council. City officials were eventually able to find an agreement with the council and free these funds in March 2009. Also in 2009, Tome Farm signed a contract with the city to lease some of this land for a 10-year period. Third, in 2008, the city administration granted Tome Farm the status of certified agricultural producer and the financial privileges associated with it, including a grant for 110 million yen (1.1 million U.S. dollars) for the construction of the greenhouse. The total cost of the project was 230 million yen (2.3 million U.S. dollars).

Local residents did not share the same enthusiasm for Tome Farm with city officials. The residents were concerned that the establishment of the greenhouse and its intensive operation could cause environmental damages. In particular, they were worried about the chemical contamination of local water by the outflow of pesticide and waste created by the operation's hydroponic system. Tome Farm and city officials held town meetings to illustrate the safety measures associated with the greenhouse operation. They pointed out that the greenhouse would not discharge contaminated water, as it adopts a water-recycling system that virtually eliminates pesticide and fertilizer residues. Additionally, the use of pesticide is minimized through the use of biological pest control.[18] This information campaign was eventually successful, as it addressed local residents' concerns.

Agricultural Production on the I LOVE Tome Farm

In 2010, Tome Farm began greenhouse production of paprika. The greenhouse uses rock wool and a groundwater circulation system that mixes water with fertilizer for hydroponic cultivation. It also adopts an automated system for the control of the environment that regulates temperature, humidity, and level of carbon dioxide (Interview 2012a). When the temperature reaches 25 degrees Celsius, the automated system opens the windows and roofs or deploys curtains to reduce exposure to the sunlight, resulting in improved thermal efficiency. The original annual production goal for the three varieties[19] of paprika produced was set at 600,000 fruits to be harvested from 20,000 plants[20] (Interview 2012a).

However, problems with the available technology have not yet allowed the achievement of this production target. The same problems prevented the farm from effectively producing paprika during the winter months, when high fuel costs hampered profitability. Simultaneously, neighboring Vegi Dream and Richfield farms were able to successfully produce year round. Tome Farm sells all its class A paprika to Dole Japan at a fixed price established through contracts. Dole Japan sells this paprika to national and local supermarket chains. Eighty percent of paprika is shipped to the Tokyo metropolitan area, while the remaining 20 percent is shipped to Hokkaido.

Local Agriculture and the I LOVE Tome Farm

Tome Farm is led by a president who is also employed by Dole Japan. There are also five permanent workers, three of them recruited through the local unemployment office. During peak season from June to December, the farm employs four female part-time workers who are hired through the local Silver Human Resource Center. These women are from local farm families and are experienced in farming. Permanent and part-time workers are responsible for virtually the same tasks, such as harvesting and packing. The limited size of the greenhouse and the small number of local workers hired created dissatisfaction among city officials, who expected a more robust contribution to the economy of the community. In particular, a greater number of permanent workers, diffusion of advanced technology, and spin-offs were expected. In this context, Tome Farm responded by presenting the image of a firm that is committed to local socioeconomic development. It became a member of the local Association for the Promotion of Industry and participated in the association's festivals. Additionally, it opened the farm to the public through the organization of tours. Approximately 20 tours per year were organized and included visits from agricultural cooperatives; municipalities; and various schools, such as primary schools, a school for the disabled, and agricultural vocational schools.

Dole Japan established Tome Farm, relying on the local administration's financial and political support. The discourse proposed by local officials centered on the theory that economic incentives would attract corporate investment that, in turn, would promote community development. This theory—albeit with some reluctance—was accepted by skeptical administrators (for example, the city council) and concerned residents. However, these expectations were only partially met by the performance of the farm. The Great Recession of 2008 significantly affected Dole Food, which had to scale back its plans. Accordingly, it established a much smaller operation than originally planned, leaving most of the land that it leased unused (Interview 2012a). Plans to hire additional workers were also slashed. This is a situation that indicates the uncertainty associated with the global market and the consequences of financial fluctuations. It is also an illustration of the limits of socioeconomic development policies based on public support of transnational corporations. The effects of these limits and the damages inflicted on the local community and agriculture became painfully clear to the Tome area public officials (Interview 2012b).

Conclusions

The three case studies on Dole Japan's franchise farms illustrate at least four interrelated points. First, current agri-food in Japan is characterized by corporate hypermobility. While this is a trend common to most regions of the world, it assumes particular relevance in a context that has been historically characterized by a significant control on the part of public institutions. In the cases presented, Dole Japan was able to rapidly organize ten franchise farms across the country and move its operations once conditions were not favorable. The relocation of Izumi Farm is telling of the vulnerability of agriculture and rural communities to corporate hypermobility. Dole Japan closed Izumi Farm after only three years of operation. Arguably, Dole Japan is not at fault for closing this farm, as eliminating unprofitable units is a rational business decision. However, the incompatibility of corporate profitability and the balanced socio-economic development of communities—including the well-being of workers—emerges as an evident characteristic of the current situation and the ideology and policy that support it.

Second, corporate investment programs were carried out with substantial political and economic support of local and national governmental agencies. Additionally, Dole Japan was able to use this support to bypass the intent of existing legislation—the Agricultural Land Act—that forbade substantial control of agricultural production by corporations. This process occurred despite pronouncements from both corporate and governmental representatives about the fundamental desirability of market-based policies and mechanisms. As calls for the application of free market neoliberal policies continued, requests for state support escalated, showing a pattern of theoretical inconsistency and, above all, political instrumentality on the part of Dole Japan. Simultaneously, they show the commitment that some local political leaders have to neoliberal strategies of socioeconomic development and their inability to redirect these strategies in a situation characterized by lack of success.

Third, these cases illustrate that a key component of Dole Japan's industrial strategy is to operate its farms by using less expensive factors of production.

Additionally, the search for convenient economic, social, and political conditions is one of the primary variables affecting investment. Known as "global sourcing," this posture is maintained despite the abovementioned claims of support for local socioeconomic development. The consistently adopted policy of leasing land and machines indicates that the exploitation of local resources takes primacy over alternative approaches stressing cooperation, interdependence among stakeholders, and long-term stability. It is clear that local actors are aware of this posture and demonstrate their dissatisfaction. Yet, rather than addressing this issue substantively, Dole Japan proposes discourses that attempt to legitimize its position. As dissatisfaction remains among local farmers, workers, and community members as well as some political leaders, it is possible to argue that the industrial policy of Dole Japan and the overall ideology that supports it show a crisis of legitimation developing. Additionally, the refusal of local farmers to do business with Dole adds to the evidence that a crisis exists.

Finally, Dole Japan's involvement in farming has been characterized by the overwhelming employment of part-time wage workers. Often women and other marginalized members of the labor force, these workers represent the most common choice of labor in global agri-food. The use of marginal labor by Dole in its production efforts in Japan follows patterns applied in other corporate projects around the world. The mobilization of a large "reserve army of labor" has characterized the expansion of global socioeconomic relations in agri-food and other sectors. The mobilization of this global labor force has created labor surpluses that have impacted virtually all regions of the world, including, certainly, Japan. Accordingly, workers have seen their employment conditions and remuneration deteriorating while the growth of corporate profits remains robust. Additionally, as opposition to low wages materializes, the corporate response of employing surplus marginal labor has been effective. This situation points to a discrepancy between existing theories of development and current conditions. As more labor is mobilized globally, low wages are paid, and better remunerated and stable employment is eliminated, the conventional statement that investment would promote employment and community growth does not reflect reality. Similarly, local authorities' efforts to attract corporate investments are met with few and poorly paid new jobs. This combination triggers a vicious spiral that impoverishes communities and residents, increases the financial crisis of local administrations, and, ultimately, leads to results that are opposite those originally envisioned.

NOTES

1. According to Dole Japan's website, some of these farms may be in operation but are no longer part of the Dole Japan's supply system.

2. The name of this company is not revealed as per the request of its management.

3. In 2009, this act was revised and the limit increased to up to 50 percent (MAFF 2012f).

4. For a summary of the copious literature on certification, see the 2011 special issue of the *Journal of Rural Social Sciences* (volume 25, issue 3) and a 2013 issue of the *International Journal of Sociology of Agriculture and Food* (volume 20, issue 2).

5. The town of Mukawa was consolidated with the neighboring town of Hobetsu in 2006. The pronunciation of the new town's name remained Mukawa, but its Japanese language spelling was altered.

6. In this system, farmers produced soybeans, red beans, potatoes, pumpkins, wheat, and sugar beets.

7. In Japan, local agricultural committees consist of elected members who are farmers. They provide support to farmers through a number of activities. Before 2009, one of their duties consisted of setting rates for the leasing of farmland. There were two types of leases: one for rice paddies and another for other crops. For each of these types of contracts, the local agricultural committee established three different prices according to land productivity. In 2009, this system was ultimately abolished and leases were liberalized by the revised Agricultural Land Act.

8. In Japan, the sustained low birth rate has created an excess of primary and junior high schools that are now routinely consolidated. This is particularly the case in rural school districts. Alternative uses for these school buildings are often sought as components of local revitalization efforts. In this case, Nittan Farm rented the building to use it as a warehouse and to lodge some of its personnel.

9. In 2006, the town of Takaono and the neighboring municipalities of Izumi and Noda were consolidated. The new town was named Izumi City.

10. This Hokkaido Sanchoku Center is a legally different entity than the Hokkaido Sanchoku Center discussed in the case of Nittan Farm. It is an older corporate entity with a prior business connection with Dole Japan.

11. In Japan, agricultural cooperatives are hierarchically organized at the local, prefectural, and, ultimately, national levels.

12. This agency works exclusively with senior citizens 65 and older and is present in almost every rural community in Japan.

13. The minimum wage in Japan varies by prefecture. In 2013 in Kagoshima, the minimum wage was 665 yen/hour (Kagoshima Prefecture 2013).

14. This failed negotiation is indicative of the importance of obtaining the respect and trust of local farmers if a corporation wants to conduct business locally and of the ability of local residents to respond to unwanted corporate initiatives.

15. The area is known for its wetlands, which are registered under the Ramsar Convention. The local residents refer to region as the "village of water."

16. In 2007 in Tome, 72.4 percent of all farmers were 60 years old or older (Tome City 2008).

17. Tomita Technology is a medium-sized corporation specializing in farm equipment and aluminum lifeboats. Located in Yokohama, in the Prefecture of Kanagawa, in the early 2000s, it initiated a program of investment in agriculture, including the production of paprika and

tomatoes in greenhouses. Currently, Tomita Technology also imports greenhouses from the Netherlands, invests in environmental control systems for greenhouses, and provides consulting services. Together with Vegi Dream of Toyota, it is the leading producer of paprika in Japan. (*Sankei Newspaper* 2009).

18.   For the I LOVE brand, Dole Japan established its own standards for pesticide use. In Japan, the use of pesticide is strictly regulated by law with the intent of reducing the quantity employed. Tome Farm uses an average quantity of pesticides and uses 48 pesticide applications per year, which is common practice in conventional agriculture in the region. While Tome Farm has not been cited or singled out for any pesticide contamination of the local water supply system, the actual I LOVE standards for pesticide use are not as strict as the brand image would have the public believe.

19.   These varieties are imported from the Netherlands.

20.   Harvested paprika fruits are precooled overnight and sorted and packed the next day. Tome Farm uses a quality classification from A (higher) to C (lower) while using five ranks for size, color, and shape. Nearly all (97.5 percent) of the production is classified as class A paprika, and 70 percent of this production is commercialized through the I LOVE brand. Through this system, consumers can access information on production such as pesticide use. The remaining 30 percent is sold as generic. The B and C classes of paprika are sold to local school meal centers and agricultural cooperatives' shops.

CHAPTER 6

Corporate Agri-Food Industrial Strategies in the Aftermath of the Disasters

Introduction

In the aftermath of the Great East Japan Earthquake of March 11, 2011, neoliberal-inspired reconstruction policies were quickly adopted, and new business opportunities for corporations were created through the establishment of SZRs (see chapter 3). These policies centered on the "Creative Reconstruction" proposal that saw in the deregulation and reduced public oversight of private initiatives the necessary formula to reignite economic growth and social development. While state financial intervention was necessary to subsidize and trigger an inflow of private investment, the proposal was viewed as a move that would actually reduce state expenditures and provide a more robust economic expansion.

Considering this context, in this chapter, we analyze the case of corporate-sponsored agri-food production for the fresh market in Sendai City, in the Prefecture of Miyagi. This initiative was originally conceived to promote a business-friendly environment in which local farmers and corporations, such as Kagome and IBM (see chapter 4), would cooperate and, as a result, promote the growth of agriculture and the sustainability of local rural communities. Despite these plans, local farmers and residents became dissatisfied with this project and eventually opposed it. The chapter begins with an illustration of the general conditions of agriculture in Sendai City, the local consequences of the Great East Japan Earthquake, and the associated recovery process. In the second and third sections, we analyze the Sendai City SZR program and the founding of Michisaki Farm, respectively. The latter is a production project involving local farmers and corporations. In the fourth section, we illustrate farmers' and local residents' resistance to this pattern of reconstruction, and we provide a review of salient contradictions associated with this process. We stress that local resistance hampered corporate plans, which had to be scaled back. Reduced employment and land utilization resulted from this move. Simultaneously, the lack of tangible benefits for local farmers and residents and their limited involvement in the decisionmaking process were decisive factors in the emergence of dissatisfaction with, and opposition to, reconstruction plans. We demonstrate that resistance remained uncoordinated, as both grass-roots mobilization and institutional support did not materialize. In the conclud-ing section, we offer some analytical comments on these events. We contend that this neoliberal theory–inspired process of reconstruction required strong state involvement despite pronouncements about the saliency of private initia-tives, and the process engendered consequences that did not satisfy local farmers and created problems for corporations.

Agriculture and Disasters in Sendai City, in the Prefecture of Miyagi

Sendai City and Its Agriculture

Sendai City[1] is recognized as an economic, political, and cultural center of the Tohoku region (Sendai City 2013a). In 1989, it was appointed as the first and sole "city designated by government ordinance" (*seirei shitei toshi*)[2] in Tohoku. Its population has been constantly growing and surpassed 1 million inhabitants in 1999 (Sendai City 2013a, 2013b). As major corporations developed their busi-ness in the Tohoku region by establishing branch offices in Sendai, the econ-omy in Sendai became known as a "branch office economy."

While the region of Tohoku is an important supplier of agricultural products to local and national markets, such as the Tokyo metropolitan area, Sendai City has developed a suburban type of agriculture. According to the *Basic Plan for Sendai Agriculture* (Sendai City 2007), Sendai City's agriculture is multifunc-tional. Agriculture, therefore, is not simply about production—it is also a space of communication between urban residents and farmers, a disaster prevention system, and a green area to be used by the local population. In 2010, the city area listed more than 3,000 commercial farmers and a total of 5,000 ha of cultivated farmland, of which more than half was devoted to rice (MAFF 2010c).

The Disasters and Their Consequences for Sendai City Agriculture

The prefecture of Miyagi was among one of the areas most damaged by the 2011 Great Earthquake and Tsunami. There were more than 10,000 people killed and an additional 1,400 missing. The fact that 18,000 people died in all of Japan and 2,800 were missing is telling of the impact of the disasters in this prefecture (FDMA 2013). The tsunami that followed the quake inflicted the most severe damage to the local agriculture. It inundated 15,000 ha of farmland, which constituted two-thirds of the total farmland affected and 11 percent of total farmland in Miyagi. The estimated damage totaled more than 550 billion yen (5.5 billion U.S. dollars) (Ichinose 2011; MAFF 2011d; Miyagi Prefecture 2012).

The prefectural capital, Sendai City, was also severely damaged: 900 people were killed, 30 missing, 2,300 injured, and almost 140,000 buildings were estimated to have been destroyed or damaged (Sendai City 2013c). As the city sits on the Pacific Ocean, a significant portion was damaged by the tsunami. At its height, it reached 7.2 m (23.6 feet) and inundated 1,800 ha of farmland, causing severe seawater and debris damage that totaled 40 billion yen (about 400 million U.S. dollars). The total amount of damage for the city area agriculture, forestry, and fishery reached 73 billion yen (730 million U.S. dollars) (Sendai City 2013c). Farming facilities and infrastructure, such as waterways, drainage pumping stations, greenhouses, elevators, and machines, were destroyed, damaged, or washed away. This, however, was not as significant as the loss of lives that so severely affected the farming community and the survivors' willingness to continue farming.

The consequences of the explosion in the Fukushima nuclear reactor building and the ensuing radioactive contamination were not as harsh in Sendai City as in other southern municipalities in Miyagi. However, after the explosion, the MAFF detected 181 Bq/kg of radioactive cesium in farmland located in Sendai (MAFF 2012g). In April 2011, the Miyagi Prefecture officially announced that it detected unsafe levels of radioactivity in shiitake mushrooms (Japanese mushrooms) cultivated in Sendai and halted their sale (Sendai City 2012a). As the Prefecture of Miyagi is adjacent to Fukushima, the prices and sales of many agri-food commodities from Miyagi, including those from Sendai City, declined, even though the products brought to market were not contaminated. All beef produced in Miyagi and Sendai City still remains under mandatory testing for radioactivity, and samples from all other products are tested (Miyagi Prefecture 2013).

Recovery and Reconstruction

The government of Sendai City in cooperation with the Sendai Agricultural Cooperative (JA Sendai), the Land Improvement District of Eastern Sendai, the Miyagi Prefecture, and researchers assessed the damage and worked to develop an effective plan for the recovery and reconstruction of local agriculture. This plan contemplated the strongest level of intervention on the eastern side of the city, given that this was the most severely damaged area (Sendai City 2013c). By the end of 2011, the debris removal was complete, mostly through the efforts of more than sixty local farmers temporarily employed by the city (Sendai City 2013c). Subsequently, 1,600 local farmers began work to reclaim the sludge- and salt-contaminated farmland, supported by a nationally funded program that paid for this work and for lost farm income (Sendai City 2013c). Salt-tolerant colza was planted on this land. Such facilities as waterways and drainage pumping stations were also reconstructed through national and prefectural grants. Moreover, the city provided funds for the reconstruction of greenhouses. However, to promote farm efficiency and productivity, only large farms that met specific production standards were included in this program (Sendai City 2013d). Funds for the replacement of damaged equipment were also awarded selectively and only to organized farmers. Farmland reclamation was 78 percent complete by the end of 2013, and the city planned to finish it and restart farming on all inundated farmland by the end of 2014. However, fine debris still remained and represented a significant obstacle to the resumption of farming activities (Interview 2012a).

Following the Creative Reconstruction approach, Sendai City planned to rationalize the existing farming structure (for example, the size and number of farms). It initiated a program aimed at increasing the size of local farms through the consolidation of land parcels. The ultimate objective was to enhance these farms' "efficiency" and "competitiveness" (Sendai City 2013c). Through a process of redistribution and exchange of land,[3] the city planned to increase land parcels from 0.3 ha to 1 ha. The national government and the Prefecture of Miyagi paid 98 percent of the cost of this consolidation project, while the rest was funded by Sendai City (Tohoku Regional Agricultural Administration Office, Sendai City, Sendai Agricultural Cooperative and Land Improvement District of Eastern Sendai 2011a). While this program appeared beneficial to farmers, more that 20 percent of them did not favor it. In 2012, 77 percent of farmers supported the program, 15 percent opposed it, and 8 percent were undecided (Interview 2012a). Many of those who opposed the program were small farm holders practicing subsistence agriculture. These farmers were not interested in increasing the size of their operations. Others were not interested in altering the size or trading their parcels of land as required by the program. Ultimately, Sendai City failed to obtain the consensual support of farmers, and interest in the project remained tepid.[4] Yet this administration intended to complete the project, hoping to count on the vote of the two-thirds of farmers and landowners as required by law (Tohoku Regional Agricultural Administration Office, Sendai City, Sendai Agricultural Cooperative and Land Improvement District of Eastern Sendai 2011b).

Special Zone for Reconstruction in the Prefecture of Miyagi

The creation of the SZR was approved by law in December 2011 and became the centerpiece of the national governments' reconstruction program (see chapter 3). In Sendai City, attempts to further promote the involvement of corporations in the agri-food sector materialized with the proposal for the establishment of a SZR for the Eastern District of the city. As indicated above, this was the most affected part of the municipality. This SZR proposal contemplated a model for the development of the agri-food sector that included joint activities between corporations and local large farm operators (*Nikkei Newspaper* 2011b). As formulated, it immediately gained the support of the national government and was approved in March 2012 (Sendai City 2012b).

The Sendai City's SZR, named "Special Zone for the Development of the Agri-Food Frontier," was among the first zones authorized in the disaster-affected areas. Its plan contemplated the primary objectives of promoting the growth of agricultural production, productivity, and profitability and enhancing employment opportunities, particularly for younger members of the work force (Sendai City 2013c). More specifically, the plan encouraged farmers to incorporate their farms, work together with private corporations, produce value-added commodities for domestic and foreign markets, adopt state of the art technology, and integrate agricultural production with food processing and marketing (Sendai City 2012b). Overall, the SZR covered 3,000 ha of farmland and included coastal areas severely affected by the tsunami.

As of the end of September 2013, 16 projects were certified for support in Sendai City (Sendai City 2013e). Through this program, farms could receive funds if they invested in new agricultural equipment and facilities and employed victims of the disasters. Farming, agri-food processing, agri-food distribution and marketing, recyclable energy projects related to agriculture, and agricultural research centers were included among the qualifying sectors for employment subsidies (Sendai City 2012b). Additionally, farmers could receive abatements and exemptions for a variety of taxes, including city property tax, prefecture corporate enterprise tax, prefecture real estate tax on new purchases, and national income and corporate tax (Sendai City 2012b). The new law for the SZR also contemplated the deregulation of existing farmland legislation. However, in the case of Sendai City's SZR, this option was not exercised, as the local administration recognized that the deregulation of this legislation was sufficiently implemented through the measures introduced in 2009 (Interview 2012b).

The Case of Michisaki Farm: The Kagome- and IBM-Sponsored Project

Among the initiatives that were proposed after the disasters, those involving the development of a new farm—Michisaki Farm—gained particular attention. Jointly operated by such corporations as Kagome,[5] IBM Japan, Sharp, Mitsui, Itochu, Tohoku Electric Power, and Seven Eleven and local large farm owners, this collaboration was described as a symbol of the reconstruction of Sendai City. Nationally, it was heralded as the prototype of the more competitive, technologically advanced, and environmentally friendly agriculture to be established in the region.

The prestigious newspaper *Nikkei* devoted an in-depth presentation of this initiative in its September 1, 2011, edition (*Nikkei Newspaper* 2011b). Previous announcements of the project were publicized by the same source in April. According to the September article, the project called for the leasing of 23 ha of farmland to build a very large (10 ha) system of greenhouses,[6] counting on the technical assistance of Kagome and IBM Japan. Kagome's involvement consisted of the implementation of the greenhouses' hydroponic production platforms, which were designed to avoid contact with seawater-contaminated soil and to maintain high levels of productivity. IBM Japan's role consisted of the delivery of the greenhouses' IT-based production control systems. Additionally, the project included the construction of a food processing plant adjacent to the greenhouses and the use of solar power on smart grids and smart meters to increase energy efficiency (*Nikkei Newspaper* 2011b). Public finance corporations, such as Japan Finance Corporation and the Development Bank of Japan, supported the financing of the project.

Local Large Farms' Participation in the Project: The Case of Butai and Rokugo Azzurri Farms

Along with corporations, this project included the participation of some large farms, such as Butai Farm and Rokugo Azzurri Farm (Interview 2012c, 2013a; Sekine 2013). These large farms were incorporated in Sendai City and sold their products to large retail and restaurant chains, bypassing the mediation of the local cooperative. Their presidents promoted policy aimed at the creation of a "profitable agriculture" and, to that end, they joined forces with some other local farmers. The president of Butai Farm, Kiyoshi,[7] was a wealthy fifteenth-generation farmer in Sendai City. His farm had a stage that was employed for a religious festival held on the farm.[8] This celebration signaled that Kiyoshi came from a family with a long tradition of farm ownership, controlled a large amount of farmland, and commanded the recognition of local farmers (Interview 2012c). He inherited his farm in 1984 at the age of 22 and incorporated it in 2003. Most of the farm growth occurred in the early portion of the 2000s, when it doubled its annual sale from 70 million yen (700,000 U.S. dollars) to 120 million yen (1.2 million U.S. dollars).

Prior to the disasters, Butai Farm produced rice and vegetables on 15 ha[9] and also purchased agricultural products, including imported fruits and vegetables, at wholesale markets (Interview 2012c). Domestic rice and vegetables were purchased from contract farms in eastern Japan.[10] These products were processed or sold to large retail chains, such as Aeon[11] and Seven Eleven Japan, restaurant chains, takeout food, and food-delivery services as well as firms that prepare hospital meals. Butai Farm also opened two restaurants under its direct management in Sendai and Tokyo, and it acquired two retail stores of a food-delivery service chain. It employed fifteen full-time and 120 part-time workers prior to the 2011 quake.

Butai Farm was profoundly affected by the earthquake and tsunami (Interview 2012c). Sixty percent of its farmland and warehouses were inundated, and most of the harvested rice was lost. The total amount of damage was estimated at 450 million yen (4.5 million U.S. dollars). To rebuild, Kiyoshi decided to restructure. First, he divided Butai Farm's activities and created five new companies to benefit from the tax abatements and incentives associated with the SZR. He included these companies in the Butai Farm Group.[12] Second, to establish one of these corporations, he created a joint venture, Butai Agri Innovation, with the multinational corporation, Iris Oyama.[13] This company's mission was to purchase rice from contract farmers, operate a rice milling and packing plant, and sell rice through Iris Oyama's retailing channels. It covered domestic and foreign markets, including China (*Nikkei Newspaper* 2013e). Third, Kiyoshi organized a consortium of multistakeholders for large-scale production, processing, and marketing of agricultural products. The consortium included Butai Farm and its subsidiaries as well as a local university, the radioactive inspection center, distributers, some food retailers (such as Seven Eleven Japan and Aeon), and consumer cooperatives (Interview 2012c). In essence, Butai Farm evolved from a large family farm into regionally dominant, differentiated firms with particular power in the rice and vegetable markets. It was able to exit the traditional agricultural cooperatives' network to gain independence in the broader agri-food sector.

Owned by Saburo,[14] Rokugo Azzurri Farm[15] was incorporated in 2004 and established a partnership with Butai Farm (Interview 2012c, 2013a). Prior to the 2011 disasters, it produced vegetables, mainly lettuce. It also purchased vegetable produce from fifty local farmers to supply the large retail chain Aeon (Interview 2013b). Moreover, it specialized in pest control and employed radio-controlled helicopters for pesticide applications on Sendai City's fields and in the neighboring prefecture of Fukushima.

The tsunami also severely damaged this farm and caused the death of Saburo's younger brother, who worked on the farm (Interview 2013b). At the time, Saburo had become familiar with the farming activities of Saizeriya, a company with primary interests in the restaurant business.[16] After TEPCO's Fukushima Daiichi nuclear power plant meltdown, Saizeriya closed its farm in Fukushima and opened a new farm in Sendai City (Saizeriya 2013b). In April 2011, it offered a technical training program at this new 1.2 ha greenhouse tomato farm that was attended by Saburo and ten other local farm owners (*Kahoku Shinpo Newspaper* 2012). Saizeriya's new farm was able to create a new and profitable brand: the "Tomato of Reconstruction." This brand attracted a steady demand by projecting an image of social responsibility and care. Ultimately, the initiative was a success, and the farm was able to recover the losses caused by the closing of its Fukushima operation. The interaction among key actors that took place through this program was fundamental to the establishment of Michisaki Farm. Saburo introduced Saizeriya's tomato production technique to Michisaki Farm,[17] and this farm sold its tomatoes to Saizeriya (see the next section).

Establishment of Michisaki Farm

In September 2011 and prior to the establishment of Michisaki Farm, a meeting took place among Butai Farm, Rokugo Azzurri Farm, Kagome, IBM Japan, and the local energy corporation Kamei (Interview 2013b; Sekine 2013). Representatives of Sendai City, the Sendai Agricultural Cooperatives, and the Tohoku Regional Agricultural Administration Office of the MAFF also attended as observers. Kiyoshi chaired the meeting, with Saburo providing key organizational support. The representative from IBM Japan served as the meeting's secretary. This gathering led to the creation of Michisaki Farm. In July 2012, the farm was officially established with a 17 million yen (170,000 U.S. dollars) original investment (Interview 2013b). Kiyoshi and Saburo were among the five local large farm operators who participated in this project.[18] Saburo ended up contributing the majority of capital (15.5 million yen or 155,000 U.S. dollars) and became president of the farm. The farm obtained its Certified Agricultural Producer status in September 2012 and with it access to discounted loans and administrative support from the local government. Its products reached the market for the first time in July 2013.

Despite pronouncements about major contributions to the project and reconstruction of the area, Kagome soon withdrew its participation. Disagreements with the other farm owners and participating farmers were cited as reasons for this action (Interview 2012c, 2013b). In effect, during the early stages of the farm establishment process, Kagome began pressuring farmers into signing exclusive production contracts that would allow the delivery of virtually the entire harvest to this company. Additionally, Kagome asked farmers to purchase some of its agricultural infrastructure and products, such as greenhouses and environment control systems. In return for signing these proposed deals, it would provide technical and financial assistance. The response of farmers was negative. Many of them viewed this move as a deliberate plan to transform the farm into a de facto subsidiary of Kagome. They believed that they would lose their autonomy. Additionally, farmers viewed Kagome's action as one sided and ultimately disrespectful of their opinion and interests. The insistent request that farmers purchase expensive products with virtually no negotiations or discounts was often cited as an example of this company's unfriendliness and arrogance. Ultimately, Kagome's deals were rejected, and the company dissociated itself from the farm.

After Kagome's withdrawal, the Mitsubishi Group joined the project (Interview 2013b). Through its foundation, Mitsubishi offered financial support but also material and technical assistance through one of its subsidiaries, Mitsubishi Plastics Agri Dream. The Mitsubishi proposal was received positively and ultimately accepted. Contrary to the case of Kagome, the farm's leadership and its members deemed Mitsubishi's posture as one that would allow the farm to maintain its independence in its business strategies and farming operations.

Farmers' Dissatisfaction

Despite these developments—and arguably because of them—the Michisaki Farm project engendered dissatisfaction among local farmers (Interview 2012a, 2012c, 2012d, 2012e, 2013b). The coalition of large farm owners and corporations created uneasiness among farmers that found fertile ground in the significant level of uncertainty that dominated the mood of the farm community after the Great Earthquake. The severity of the damage incurred and the problematic future made the already difficult existence of farmers appear even more precarious. Specifically, the news of the establishment of the technically advanced, financially strong, and large Michisaki Farm was viewed as the addition of a formidable competitor to an already tight market. Local farmers felt that they could not compete for farmland, water resources, and most importantly, production and market outlets. In addition, many of these farmers were simply fearful of the strong corporate presence in the sector. They felt that this program, rather than supporting local agriculture, would penalize family farm owners to the benefit of a large corporate farm. It was felt that the plan to promote production and productivity had bypassed them and translated into a threat to their persistence in farming.

Moreover, this corporate- and government-sponsored program was carried out without the support of the broader farming community and the Sendai City's agricultural cooperative, JA Sendai (Interview 2012a). The fact that the traditionally powerful agricultural cooperative and members of the farming community were not consulted on the Michisaki Farm project was interpreted as an act of unilateralism. Unilateralism is frequently perceived as a violation of established cultural norms that demand the achievement of consensus on important community decisions. Dating back to traditional rice cultivation and the shared management of natural resources associated with it,[19] the absence of consultations and mutual agreement negatively affected farmers' perceptions.

Opposition

Farmers' dissatisfaction with the creation of Michisaki Farm translated into opposition to this project. For example, the farm's attempt to lease land from members of the community of Yotsuya in the Shichigo District of Sendai City did not go well (Interview 2012a, 2012c, 2012d, 2012e, 2013b). One of the reasons for the selection of Yotsuya as a possible location for some of Michisaki Farm's activities relates to the fact that Yoshio,[20] one of the original founders of the farm, owned land in the area. Yoshio enthusiastically made his land available to the farm and promoted the farm's presence among the local residents. To this end, he initiated a campaign to convince other local farmers to do the same and allow Michisaki Farm to lease their land. His request was met with strong opposition. Yoshio was singled out as the community's opponent and was de facto ostracized. Feeling this ostracism and the associated sense of community exclusion, Yoshio not only desisted from requesting farmers' support but also chose not to rent his land. Following communal tradition, he eventually severed all ties with Michisaki Farm (Interview 2012a, 2012c, 2012d, 2012e, 2013b).

Two additional reasons fueled dissatisfaction and opposition to Michisaki Farm. First, farmers were concerned about losing their independence. That small and family farm holders want to keep their independence as sector concentration intensifies is a fact that has been well documented through time and across space.[21] And in this case, local farmers saw in the establishment of Michisaki Farm a decisive step toward their being reduced to the status of hired labor. Additionally, independence and their desire to earn a living through hard work played a primary role in their uneasiness about renting their land to the farm. Becoming rentiers and receiving a monthly payment without any tangible work was not compatible with their preference for laboring for a living. Second, farmers were afraid that an agreement with the farm would negatively affect the value of their land and their ability to sell it at the appropriate time. Their fundamental hope was that land value would increase once reconstruction programs were in place. This was a highly shared hope in a period of significant economic uncertainty, when many viewed land as an important financial asset and security blanket. However, because land occupied by greenhouses was excluded from consolidation programs, it was widely perceived that this exclusion would hamper the appreciation of land values. Moreover, tying land to lengthy leasing contracts was seen as limiting farmers' freedom to sell as the market improved.

According to the cooperative and the Land Improvement District of Eastern Sendai, local farmers' strong opposition to the expansion of the Michisaki Farm project in Yotsuya increased tension in the community.[22] This climate was considered counterproductive for the establishment of an efficient and effective reconstruction project.

Michisaki Farm's Reaction

Facing this opposition, Michisaki Farm management responded by seeking an alternative location to Yotsuya and implementing moves that would curb future resistance. The alternative to Yotsuya was identified in the community of Southern Gamo in the District of Rokugo (Interview 2013b, 2013c). One of the reasons for the selection of this area was due to the possible use of inexpensive energy for the heating of greenhouses generated by a Sendai City–owned sewage plant (Interview 2013b; Sekine 2013). Moreover, Michisaki Farm intended to use solar energy for its greenhouses and processing plant (Interview 2013b; Sekine 2013). These options never came to fruition;[23] however, the same conditions that made Yotsuya a less than desirable location also affected Southern Gamo. Similar to the case of Yotsuya, farmland was highly fragmented, and its consolidation was difficult because only a relatively small number of farmers agreed to lease their land to the farm. Because farmers were concerned about the presence of such a large corporate-supported farm, only 4 of the 23 ha originally planned for use were obtained. This land was leased from twelve local farmers whose houses and land were seriously damaged by the tsunami.

In Southern Gamo, the quake and tsunami severely affected the local agriculture, and some of the area's prominent farmers were killed, leaving the community in disarray (Interview 2013c). In this context, reconstruction was a highly desirable objective, and Akinori,[24] an influential member of the Southern Gamo Neighborhood Association, actively began persuading local farmers to support the founding of Michisaki Farm. Akinori was a schoolmate of Kiyoshi (Butai Farm) and Saburo (Rokugo Azzurri Farm) and a former member of the Miyagi Prefecture Agricultural Cooperative. He also assisted in some of the deals between the Sendai Agricultural Cooperative and Michisaki Farm. As the example of Yotsuya demonstrated, the involvement of the local agricultural cooperative in decisionmaking was quite important.

While the dire economic situation and the attitude of the Southern Gamo local leadership favored its establishment, Michisaki Farm further opted to launch a program to promote support among local farmers and residents. This program to legitimize the farm's presence consisted of three primary actions. First, local victims of the disasters were supported through in kind donations. Second, the farm participated in community discussions about, and planning for, reconstruction. Third, it sponsored local community festivals to boost morale, support tradition, and display community attachment.

Business Activities of Michisaki Farm

Michisaki Farm leased land at 500,000 yen/ha (5,000 U.S. dollars/ha). This price was more than three times higher than the local standard price of 150,000 yen/ha (1,500 U.S. dollars/ha) (Interview 2013b; Sekine 2013). It also paid additional fees for land improvement. Contracts were signed for 20-year terms with the option to revise after 10 years. These terms significantly exceeded the commonly employed 3-year terms, such as those used by Dole Japan's I LOVE Farms (see chapter 5).

The farm established three greenhouses on 2.8 ha instead of the planned 10 ha. The first produced lettuce on 1.1 ha, the second tomatoes on 1.2 ha, and the third strawberries on 0.5 ha (Interview 2013b; Sekine 2013). These high-tech greenhouses used computers to control temperature, humidity, concentration of carbon dioxide, and sunlight. Additionally, plant growth and diseases were regulated through tablet-type computers, and data were collected and analyzed on a cloud computing system provided by IBM Japan. The local energy corporation, Kamei, provided LPG (liquefied petroleum gas) for the greenhouse heating system. The total cost of the greenhouse was 1.3 billion yen (13 million U.S. dollars) of which 1 billion yen (10 million U.S. dollars) was covered through funds from the government disaster reconstruction program and from programs from the Miyagi Prefecture and Sendai City. The rest was covered by a donation from the Mitsubishi Foundation and low-cost loans provided by Japan Finance Corporation and the local bank, Sendai Bank.

Michisaki Farm planned to produce and sell vegetables year round and also process the produce as prepared salads. Processing took place in one of Butai Farm Group's facilities: E-fresh. E-fresh was originally scheduled to be located near Michisaki Farm, but it was finally located next to Butai Farm. For the reasons mentioned above, Michisaki Farm was not able to lease the necessary land for this facility in Southern Gamo. The fresh vegetables and processed salads were sold to retail chains, such as Aeon and Seven Eleven Japan, the restaurant chain Saizeriya, and local shops managed by the Sendai Agricultural Cooperative.[25] The market for these products was confined to the Tohoku region in eastern Japan and the Tokyo metropolitan area. The farm's marketing and production plans included certifications from GlobalGap, less use of chemicals, the production of halal food[26] and the establishment of its own brand.

By the end of 2013, the farm employed 20 full-time and 25 part-time workers who were all victims of the disasters. This number was less than the 60 workers that were originally planned and announced (Michisaki Farm 2013). Additionally, the farm admitted that in case of a reduction of subsidies, increased expenses would be addressed through labor-saving actions. In effect, Michisaki Farm representatives indicated that the farm would "produce vegetables with high quality, a stable volume and industrial precision. It wishes to find more profitable markets, and contain production costs by restructuring key areas such as personnel and energy use" (Interview 2013b).

Resistance to and Contradictions of the SZR Project

The cases illustrated above are not the only episodes that involved problems with the implementation of the SZR program. As Michisaki and the other corporate farms expanded their presence in the area, Saizeriya also established a 1.2 ha greenhouse that employed ten local farmers. These were farmers whose land was damaged by the tsunami (Interview 2012c). Saburo was appointed president of this farm. He retained ownership of Rokugo Azzurri Farm and the presidency of Michisaki Farm, making the interconnection among these corporate farm projects evident. This overt control of SZR projects by a small group of individuals and corporate entities provoked strong local opposition. Contrary to a tradition of peaceful expression of dissent, this greenhouse was set on fire. Although no one took responsibility for the fire, and no arrest was made, it was clear in the mind of all stakeholders that this was a serious act of local dissent. Simultaneously, four out of the ten local farmers hired by the project resigned. They expressed dissatisfaction with the low wages paid and the unattractive work tasks. These farmers felt that their talents and skills were underutilized and that the overall experience was unrewarding (Interview 2012d). A farmer employed by Butai Farm also resigned. In this case, dissatisfaction was linked to this farm's increased involvement in agri-food wholesaling rather than production. This individual wanted to continue to be a farmer rather than becoming a clerk in the new company (Interview 2012d). After resigning, he returned to his farm and later opened a restaurant, where he sold his farm's products. The restaurant was located in Sendai City.

To be sure, these episodes of opposition did not actually translate into organized political initiatives and critiques of the SZR initiative. They simply remained numerous yet disconnected acts of protest. Some of the key informants that we interviewed explained this outcome by contending that, because their everyday lives were significantly disrupted by the disasters, farmers lacked the necessary intellectual and physical energy to mobilize politically. As conditions remained harsh and dissatisfaction emerged, they maintained, protest could not go beyond discrete episodes of opposition. While plausible, this explanation cannot account for the fact that political mobilization occurred among equally affected fishermen (see chapter 7). An alternative explanation rests on the lack of institutional leadership that characterized the local situation. Existing farmer and local organizations, such as the Sendai Agricultural Cooperative, the Land Improvement District of Eastern Sendai, and also the administration of Sendai City, maintained a contradictory position that did little to channel farmers' dissatisfaction into a coherent critique of, and effective opposition to, the SZR project.

More specifically, in the case of Michisaki Farm, by following their mandates, these institutions should have played an active mediating role between local farmers and this farm and addressed the emerging unwanted consequences of the project. Conversely, the Sendai City administration confined its actions strictly to the bureaucratic tasks related to the establishing of the SZR. It did not address any of the substantive issues that emerged from the conflicting demands of the parties (Interview 2013b). Some individuals in positions of leadership in the Sendai Agricultural Cooperative were personally critical of the SZR project. They spoke against the project and underscored its limitations

(Interview 2013a). At least at this level, they represented the mood of farmers and residents. Yet at the formal level, when forming the official position of the cooperative, they acted differently. Setting aside their personal opinions, they favored the classical institutional posture that views local public organizations as consistently siding with the governing institutions. While contradictory, this position is the outcome of the culture of loyalty (conservatism) to the government that has traditionally dominated Japanese agricultural cooperatives (Ogino 2002). Acceptance of the government's position also characterized the posture of the Land Improvement District of Eastern Sendai, which remained silent on the concerns that local residents voiced about Michisaki Farm (Interview 2012a, 2012e, 2013a).

In effect, the mediating role that these institutions were called on to play was difficult to execute. The representation of the interests of local farmers and their dissatisfaction could hardly be harmonized with the government's agricultural reconstruction policy. Ultimately it required skills and visions that were not found among institutional cadres. Accordingly, siding with the government appeared as a much more practicable course of action. As partial justification for this position, these institutions' leadership cited concerns about preventing the negative consequences of a possible termination of SZR programs and funding. They wanted to avoid the situation in which Michisaki Farm had to shut down and the area experienced loss of income and land value. From this point of view, they viewed their support of the SZR as beneficial to all parties, as it promoted the SZR while safeguarding the economic interests of local farmers (Interview 2012a, 2012e, 2013a).

The leadership of the Sendai Agricultural Cooperative was aware of the loss of legitimacy that support of the government-proposed SZR entailed. In this context, the cooperative promoted its own plan for reconstruction. Defined as alternative to the SZR, it called for the inclusion of the large number of politically marginal and economically fragile small farm holders in a scheme that would simultaneously provide incentives for large and corporate farms and for part-time, subsistence, aged, hobby, and urban farmers (Interview 2013a). Christened "Challenge Plan for the 21st Century," it included a multistakeholder rezoning of available farmland; the shared availability of infrastructure and facilities, such as country elevators and agri-food processing plants; and actions allowing small marginal farms to remain in operation (Interview 2013a). Despite its all-inclusive claims, this plan paid mostly lip service to the interests of local farmers, as it did not address farmers' concerns about the institutional support for, and presence of, larger or corporate farms. In essence, this plan remained silent on the implementation of the contradictory objectives of promoting the simultaneous growth of large corporate farms and small, part-time, and subsistence family holdings. It did not elaborate on ways to protect family farms from the competition and growth of corporate farms that local farmers feared and opposed. This plan remains a complement of the national SZR program.

Additional local farmer- and resident-based initiatives also emerged. In the community of Sanbonzuka in the District of Rokugo, part-time farmers organized to reaffirm their willingness to continue farming and proposed a plan for the future development of the community (Interview 2012d). In August 2013, a group of Sendai City residents formed the Sendai City's Citizens Council to promote a bottom-up reconstruction plan for the District of Eastern Sendai City (Interview 2013e). The council's objectives included a critical review of the existing reconstruction plan and the organization of those farmers and residents who opposed it.

Conclusions

The Sendai City's plan to reconstruct its agri-food sector after the Great Earthquake and tsunami followed the central government's proposed Creative Reconstruction approach that relied on market forces and corporate initiatives to promote socioeconomic growth. The adopted plan called for virtually unconstrained yet publically supported private initiatives centered on the promotion of corporate investment. In line with established neoliberal theories, the generation of greater economic benefits not only for corporations but also for local farmers was anticipated. Employment was also expected to increase, along with the use of advanced technology and expertise resulting in improved skills for the local labor force. This corporate involvement would be instrumental to the establishment of a more productive and efficient agri-food sector.

The application of this policy produced the establishment of the Sendai City SZR. In this SZR program, various corporations were invited to invest, attracted by the availability of public funds and tax abatements. The establishment of Michisaki Farm represents the most relevant case of the implementation of the SZR program locally. The farm and its supporters initiated an investment process that took advantage of the generous public program set up as a part of the reconstruction project. This corporate-state partnership was viewed not only as positive but also as necessary for the successful conclusion of this initiative. Accordingly, the Sendai City SZR made ample funds available for the Michisaki Farm project and was also instrumental in the involvement of large corporations, such as IBM Japan, Kamei, and Mitsubishi in local agri-food production. Despite the large subsidies, the project's generated benefits for the community remained well below expectations. Moreover, the financial commitment of the state came with reduced public oversight, as the neoliberal-inspired SZR program and the Creative Reconstruction framework that inspired it advocated deregulation.

The Michisaki Farm program engendered opposition from local farmers and residents. While episodes of local resistance emerged—including opposition to Kagome's involvement in Michisaki Farm—this dissent materialized mostly through farmers' and landowners' refusal to rent land to the farm. This response emerged as the most readily available and practicable for these actors, and it achieved some results, as it altered the original plans of the farm. Yet it did not translate into a more organized and systematic opposition to the overall political designs that inspired the reconstruction. Paradoxically, it engendered some negative consequences to local residents, because the unavailability of land motivated Michisaki Farm to scale back its original plans, employ fewer workers, and rent less land.

The inability of local residents to generate an opposition movement remains an open question. Yet the lack of institutional leadership can be seen as a relevant reason for this outcome. Existing farmer organizations, such as the local agricultural cooperative, and territorial organizations, such as the Land Improvement District, did not act on the discontent of their constituencies. They had good knowledge of farmers' concerns and yet opted to side with the government. In this environment, alternative grassroots movements gradually emerged, offering possible alternatives to the existing situation.

Ultimately, the Sendai City case is indicative of the crucial contradiction of this reconstruction process. Mechanisms that call for an expanded corporate presence and reliance on the market entail strong state intervention at the financial, structural, and political levels. Moreover, this state intervention is accompanied by greater autonomy of private entities, which are supposed to operate with limited restrictions and supervision. While this theoretical ambiguity deserves our analytical attention in the following chapters, it engendered farmers' and residents' concerns and opposition. To a significant extent, the essential aspect of the dissatisfaction of local farmers centers on the perceived one sidedness of both the decisionmaking process and the actual development of the reconstruction process. As open and collective participation in key decisionmaking processes is rooted in Japanese rural culture, the corporate-directed execution of the reconstruction process and the subordination of the public sphere to it proved to be too removed from a course that could be accepted by all stakeholders. Additionally, results—albeit confined to an initial stage of the reconstruction process—have been so modest that they have not mitigated dissatisfaction. The outcome of this contradictory situation is the development of a restructuring of the agri-food that has been partially disappointing for corporate actors and certainly unsatisfactory for many of the other important local stakeholders. The characteristics and implications of this contradiction are further explored in chapters 8 and 9.

NOTES

1.   The name "city" refers to the administrative area rather than the urban space. This administrative space includes rural areas and farms.

2.   A city designated by government ordinance is an administrative denomination introduced in 1956. Such administrative areas must have more than 700,000 inhabitants and must obtain this designation from the cabinet of Japan. Designated cities are assigned many of the functions normally performed by the prefectural governments. There are twenty cities designated by government ordinance in Japan (MIC 2013).

3.   As is common in Japan, in Sendai City, farmland was highly fragmented. To increase productivity, Sendai City and the national authorities hoped to consolidate this land through a land consolidation and exchange program. In some instances, it involved unequal exchanges that caused some small farm holders to lose a part of their land. Accordingly, these and other farmers expressed concerns about the fairness and desirability of this program.

4.   About 20 percent of all farmers attended city-held briefing sessions in 2012. However, as a result of a strong campaign by the local agricultural cooperative, by the end of 2013, the percentage of local farmers who opposed the land consolidation program decreased significantly (Interview 2013a).

5.   Kagome operated one of its tomato farms in Fukushima. After the meltdown of the Fukushima Daiichi nuclear power plant, it halted production on this farm and quickly searched for a new production site in Miyagi. Had Kagome continued involvement in the Michisaki project, this move would have allowed it to avoid radioactive contamination and benefit from SZR funds.

6.   The magnitude of this operation can be appreciated by comparing it to the average size of Japanese greenhouses: 0.3 ha (AFFRC 2005).

7.   This is a fictitious name.

8.   The Japanese word "butai" means stage. Kyoshi named his farm "Butai Farm" in reference to the presence of the ceremonial stage on the farm (Interview 2012c).

9.   More than 80 percent of Japanese farmers operate less than 2 ha of land (MAFF 2010c).

10.   While Butai Farm produced directly, it also maintained production contracts with more than 100 farmers in the Prefectures of Hokkaido, Aomori, Iwate, Yamagata, Miyagi, Fukushima, Saitama, and Shizuoka (Interview 2012c). For rice production, Butai Farm contracted farmers through the network of the transnational trading corporation Marubeni. It purchased 3,200 mt of rice produced on 650 ha of farmland in 2011.

11.   Aeon is the largest supermarket chain in Japan.

12.   This group consisted of Butai Farm for agricultural production, in addition to Butai Agri Innovation for rice milling and marketing, Shun-no-Kaze for restaurant management, Stage Pass for the employment of disabled individuals and socially oriented projects, E-fresh for food processing, and Michisaki for vegetable production in greenhouses (Butai Farm 2013).

13.   Iris Oyama is a multinational corporation with Japanese roots that is headquartered in Sendai City. It produces and sells household goods, such as home appliances, furniture, pet foods, gardening goods, and metal and plastic products (Iris Oyama 2013). In the joint venture, Iris Oyama owned 51 percent of stock in Butai Agri Innovation, while Butai Farm owned 49 percent (Butai Agri Innovation 2013).

14.   This is a fictitious name.

15.   Rokugo is the name of a district where the farm is located, and Azzurri is an Italian word referring to the color sky blue.

16.   Saizeriya manages 1,000 Italian family restaurants in Japan and also has subsidiaries throughout Asia (Saizeriya 2013a). However, it also operates in seed breeding, farm management, and food processing.

17.   *Michisaki* means "end point" or "goal" in Japanese. Saburo and his associates planned to make this farm a model (goal) for Japanese agriculture of the future (Interview 2013b).

18.   Two of the other three investors limited their participation to the financial dimension of the project. They listed their names on the farm deed and contributed corresponding portions of the original capital. But they refrained from any involvement in the management of the operation (Interview 2013b). This was because Michisaki Farm was eventually located away from Yotsuya, which is where these investors resided.

19.   Historically, rice has been the most important crop produced in Japan. Over the centuries, its cultivation has been carried out by relying on the farming communities' collective management of the critically important water resources. This vital cooperation has taken cultural center stage in Japanese rural society, so that the establishment of mutual respect, harmony, and cooperation among community members is considered paramount. Because of this cultural dimension, consensus on pivotal community decisions is required, and unilateral decisions are viewed as destabilizing.

20.   This is a fictitious name.

21.   From Max Weber's classic work, *The Condition of Farm Labor in Eastern Germany* (Die Verhältnisse der Landarbeiter im Oelbischen Deutschland) (Gerth and Mills [1948] 1998) to contemporary works on the persistence of small family farms in North America and Europe (Bonanno 1987; Mooney 1988), farmers' desire for independence has arguably been one of most documented traits of this group of agriculturalists.

22.   The intensity of conflict in Yotsuya is indicated by the fact that we were not allowed to address questions about this episode to community members and local organizations. Representatives of the Sendai Agriculture Cooperatives, the Sendai City Administration, and the Land Improvement District of Eastern Sendai all refused to answer detailed questions about this episode and to allow us to interview farmers about it. One of these representatives explicitly stated: "This matter cannot be discussed again." It is very usual to forbid people to speak about sensitive issues in rural communities (Interview 2012a, 2012e, 2013a).

23.   According to Sendai City's officials, the city never agreed to any deal about the use of the energy generated by the sewage plant (Interview 2013d). Moreover, the farm was not allowed to install its solar panels for legal reasons. The installation of solar panels was restricted to preserve the quantity of land devoted to farming. In March 2013, the installation of solar panels

on farmland was permitted by the MAFF. But this policy change did not occur early enough to affect Michisaki Farm's plans (*Nikkei Newspaper* 2013c).

24.   This is a fictitious name.

25.   As far as lettuce production was concerned, 50 percent was sold to Aeon, 30 percent to Seven Eleven Japan, and 20 percent to Saizeriya (Interview 2013b). Smaller quantities were supplied to outlets of the local agricultural cooperative.

26.   Since the late 2000s, an increasing number of tourists from Muslim countries have visited Japan. Because of this flow of tourists, halal food items have appeared in Japanese stores. Michisaki Farm began to produce hydroponic vegetables employing fish-based fertilizer, as Muslim consumers do not purchase vegetables grown using fertilizers that include components prohibited by halal.

CHAPTER 7

Fisheries and the Special Zone for Reconstruction

Introduction

This chapter examines the liberalization of fishing rights and the post-disaster reorganization of the fishing sector in the Tohoku region, the coastal area adjacent to the epicenter of the earthquake that was virtually destroyed in 2011. The chapter also illustrates the resistance triggered by reconstruction plans. As indicated in chapter 2, the fishing sector, particularly coastal fishing, is characterized by small, family-owned operations that suffered from a crisis because of globalization and experienced the same economic and structural problems as did farming.

In the Tohoku region, many fishermen lost their lives, boats, and homes, while fishing ports and grounds became unusable as structural damage, debris, and radioactivity affected operations. National and local governments solicited corporate investment to reconstruct and restructure. Following this policy, Yoshihiro Murai, the governor of the Prefecture of Miyagi, established a SZR for one of the fishing communities of Ishinomaki City in the Prefecture of Miyagi. Promoting economic restructuring and profitability, government reconstruction plans included the granting of fishing rights to corporations and the elimination of small fishing ports used by family-owned boats. Fishermen, cooperatives (Japan Fisheries Cooperatives, JFs) as well as residents' groups denounced this plan as a way to use public funds to promote private interests, to eliminate small and family-owned fishing operations and fishing cooperatives, and, ultimately, to avoid addressing the economic and social needs of the local population.

In this chapter, we first review the conditions of fisheries in Ishinomaki City in the Tohoku region. In the second section, we illustrate the process that led to the establishment of a SZR in this area, and in the section after that, we present the case of the establishment of a SZR in the community of Momonoura in Ishinomaki City. This SZR program was strongly promoted by Governor Yoshihiro Murai. The fourth section highlights local opposition to the establishment of SZR programs. Prior to the concluding section, we discuss the case of an alternative reconstruction project that was carried out in the area.

Fishery and Disaster in Ishinomaki City, Miyagi Prefecture

The 2011 disasters severely damaged the coastal areas not only in the Tohoku region but also along the entire northeastern Pacific coast, including the Prefectures of Aomori, Iwate, Miyagi, Fukushima, Ibaraki, and Chiba (Fisheries Agency 2011a). According to the Japan Fisheries Agency, more than 28,000 fishing boats, 319 ports, and 1,725 facilities were destroyed (Fisheries Agency 2011b). The total amount of damage was estimated at 1.3 trillion yen (13 billion U.S. dollars), which constitutes more than half of the total damage of the agri-food sector as a whole. The six prefectures mentioned above compose one of world richest fishing grounds, Sanriku, that, prior to the 2011 earthquake, provided approximately 20 percent of the volume and value of all domestic catches and aquaculture production. It also included 20 percent of all fishing boats and active fishermen in the country. In 2009, these prefectures produced 40 percent of the volume of pike and mackerel caught, 30 percent of farmed oysters, and 80 percent of the farmed seaweed *wakame* (Toho Area Research Institute 2011). This region was also the primary domestic supplier of oyster (80 percent, with 77 percent from Miyagi alone) and *wakame* seeds (30 percent).

Among these prefectures, Miyagi was damaged the most with its saw-toothed northern coastline that heightened the tsunamis' violence and its southern wide plains that allowed the tsunamis' water easy access inland (Sakai 2012). More than 12,000 fishing boats, or 89 percent of all fishing boats, were damaged or washed away; all fishing ports (142), all wholesale markets (ten), and more than half of the 439 fish-processing factories were destroyed (Fisheries Agency 2011b; Sakai 2012). Facilities for some aquacultures, including Coho salmon, scallop, oysters, *hoya* (*Halocynthia roretzi*), and seaweeds (*konbu, wakame,* and *nori*) were also destroyed. And the economically powerful Miyagi oyster seed industry was equally dramatically affected (Demura 2011).

Ishinomaki City in the Prefecture of Miyagi is a large fishing community, being the third largest fishing port (by volume of catches)[1] in 2010 in Japan but also the second most populous city[2] in the prefecture after Sendai City (SME 2012). The present city limits were established in 2005 by the consolidation of seven municipalities. The area economy is dependent on the fishing industry.

Ishinomaki City was the municipality most severely damaged by the earthquake and tsunami, with more than 3,000 fatalities, 400 people missing, 56,000 homes destroyed, and 50,000 evacuated survivors (Ishinomaki City 2014b). All 44 fishing ports in the administrative city, including the large Ishinomaki Fishing Port, were damaged by the disasters, and about 2,800 fishing boats were lost. In November 2013, almost 40 percent of all fish-processing firms were still inoperative, along with more than half of the firms in related industries (Ishinomaki City 2014b). Ishinomaki City also comprises small fishing communities that experienced significant damage. It is in one of these small fishing communities, Momonoura, where the SZR was established.

Special Zone for Reconstruction and the Reconstruction of Fisheries

On May 10, 2011, two months after the earthquake, the idea of an SZR for fisheries was introduced for discussion at the Reconstruction Design Council (see chapter 3). It was proposed by the pro-free-market conservative governor of the Prefecture of Miyagi, Yoshihiro Murai, who quickly and without consulting the fishing community recommended that the creation of an SZR for coastal areas be included in reconstruction legislation. Learning about the initiative from the media, fishermen and their cooperatives, across the country and in the Prefecture of Miyagi in particular, were stunned by the fact that they were not consulted and, more importantly, by what they felt were the significant negative implications of this proposal (Hamada 2013a; *Nikkei Newspaper* 2011c). Soon it was clear that this was an overt attempt to open fishing rights to corporate actors through the ending—albeit with some limits[3]—of the long-established practice of assigning fishing rights exclusively to communities through the mediation and actions of fisheries cooperatives (JFs). In effect, it was an attempt to end the conditions established through the "land reform of fisheries" of the late 1940s that democratized fishing (see chapter 2). From this point of view, it was an attack on the dominance of fishing sector cooperatives and provided a structural barrier to members of local fishing communities, who had expectations of participating in the decisionmaking involving coastal fishing grounds.

With the support of the then-DPJ government and following the recommendations of the Reconstruction Design Council, Parliament eventually passed the Basic Act on Reconstruction on June 24, 2011, yielding to the requests of LDP and its allied party, New Komeito (*Tokyo Newspaper* 2011). As discussed in chapter 3, this act reflected the adoption of the concept of Creative Recon-struction, which called for reduced government spending compensated by the creation of greater profit opportunities for business. The act encouraged recon-struction through the establishment of SZR programs for agriculture and fish-ing, the deregulation of the sectors, and the promotion of private investment in the disaster areas. The following day, on June 25, the Reconstruction Design Council released a document containing the recommendations for the imple-mentation of reconstruction programs (Reconstruction Design Council in Response to the Great East Japan Earthquake 2011). It included measures for the reconstruction of fishing ports that gave priority to large ports and penal-ized those serving small fishing communities (see chapter 3). And, more importantly, it presented the game-changing procedures that created the pos-sibility of direct acquisition of fishing rights by private corporations.[4]

The behavior of the LDP, which supported pro-corporate SZRs, deserves to be further clarified, as this party has been supportive of such rural voters as small fishermen and farmers in the postwar period. Despite political campaigns which had targeted rural voters, the LDP neoliberal promotion of market liber-alization and acquiescence to corporate plans for the relocation of factories from rural areas to overseas locations engendered great dissatisfaction among local residents. Unfortunately for rural voters, however, the long-term decline of the rural economy and the consequent loss of population and the popula-tion's importance in national elections motivated the LDP to gradually shift its electoral strategies to focus on urban voters. Initiated in the 1980s, this strategy has continued more vigorously since the 2000s (Tashiro 2005). However, this strategy cost the LDP the national elections in 2007 and 2009 when it lost its long-term position of ruling party.

The timing of this pro-corporate move was favorable to its proponents. Local JFs were experiencing organizational problems as the loss of lives, struc-tures, and equipment generated by the disasters limited their ability to func-tion and to mount opposition. Simultaneously, JF members were discouraged by the seriousness of the passage of the Basic Act of Reconstruction, but they also felt the consequences of the desperate physical and emotional conditions that accompanied the disasters. The proposal instituting SZR programs was viewed by many as an unfair move in a situation in which unity, solidarity, and mutual help were considered not only just, but above all, fundamental to the recovery of communities along the coastal areas. Despite these problems, oppo-sition was voiced (see below). Yet it was insufficient to prevent the establish-ment of coastal SZR programs from inclusion in the text of the Basic Act on Reconstruction. Accordingly, on June 28, the Fisheries Agency[5] presented its

"Master Plan for Fisheries Reconstruction," which followed the Reconstruction Design Council's recommendations for the implementation of the Act (Fisheries Agency 2011a). On December 26, 2011, the act for the creation of SZR programs became operational (Reconstruction Agency 2012). In the end, this fundamental piece of deregulating legislation was approved in the midst of the chaotic emergency conditions that followed the disasters. It was passed without the traditionally sought consensus of fishermen. In addition, as it engendered resistance and concerns among the fishing communities, its approval made it a symbol of Creative Reconstruction and an approach that elicited the definition of "Shock Doctrine" reform (Hamada 2013a; Okada 2012a; Yokoyama 2011) (see chapter 1).

To be sure, prior to the passage of the Basic Act on Reconstruction, private corporations had some access to fishing rights. They could become members of a JF or could acquire fishing rights voluntarily relinquished by a JF. They also had to meet a number of requirements that remained in force after the enactment of the Basic Act on Reconstruction[6] (Hamada 2013a). Because becoming a member of a JF or waiting for a JF to relinquish its fishing rights have been hardly practicable for them, corporations have persistently demanded changes in the legislation[7] and the ability to acquire fishing rights without any involvement of JFs. From this point of view and in the case of fisheries, the Basic Act of Reconstruction was a fundamental success for corporate forces and their neoliberal political allies. This success was in part possible because of a negative campaign to discredit JFs promoted by business circles, politicians, the media, and even by some of their dissatisfied members (Hamada 2012, 2013a).[8] This poor image consists of charges that JFs, enjoying undeserved privileges, are ineffective, interested in simply reproducing their political and economic power, and dominated by excessive bureaucratization that translates into inefficiency. Because of this unwarranted position, some argue that better performing private firms are not allowed to compete on an equal footing with the JFs and thus are prevented from delivering better services.

The Governor's Project: The Case of the Momonoura Oyster Producers

The name of Yoshihiro Murai, the neoliberal conservative governor of the Prefecture of Miyagi, appears prominently in the narration of the events highlighted in this chapter. A graduate of the Matsushita Institute of Government and Management,[9] he has championed the cause of neoliberalism and has argued in favor of economic rationalization, free market measures, and profit enhancing as remedies to revitalize the local economy and fishing sector. He has also been instrumental in the creation of SZR legislation for fisheries and the establishment of corporate-dominated public committees, such as the Miyagi Prefecture Reconstruction Design Council;[10] he has combatively opposed projects that represented alternatives to his neoliberal creed (Hamada 2013a). Governor Murai included the establishment of SZR programs for fisheries in the Basic Policies of Reconstruction of the Prefecture of Miyagi (Hamada 2013a). On December 8, 2011, the prefecture announced that it would prioritize the reconstruction of sixty major fishing ports to be completed by 2013. Conversely, the reconstructions of other smaller fishing ports and related facilities would be postponed. Both policies were enacted without consulting local fishermen and JFs and lacked their support. Above all, Murai's May 10, 2011, proposal to create local SZR programs for fisheries was also opposed by these groups.

Individual fishermen and cooperatives challenged this move almost instantaneously (Hamada 2013a, 2013b; Tsunashima and Ogawa 2013). The unilateralism of the governor's move was considered too excessive in a situation in which the establishment of consensus among stakeholders and their involvement in decisionmaking not only represented a tradition to be respected, but more importantly, a set of necessary steps to be followed, given the difficult situation. Three days after Murai proposed the SZR plan at the national Reconstruction Design Council, members of the prefectural level cooperative, JF-Miyagi, manifested in front of the prefectural building and submitted a request for the retraction of the governor's SZR plan. Additionally, on May 13, 2011, JF-Miyagi submitted a petition to the Prefecture Assembly to repeal the SZR project. On June 21, the leaders of JF-Miyagi met Governor Murai and handed him a document with more than 14,000 signatures opposing his initiative. Fueling this strong opposition were concerns that, rather than promoting business, this measure would generate capital flight and debts[11] (Interview 2013a). Local protests escalated to the national level. The national organization of fishing sector cooperatives, JF Zengyoren, organized an emergency national meeting of cooperatives on July 6, 2011. Some members of Parliament were also invited (Hamada 2013a, 2013b; Tsunashima and Ogawa 2013). At the end of the meeting, JF Zengyoren submitted a petition to the MAFF opposing the SZR project.

The cooperative's petition to halt the SZR project was also submitted to the Prefectural Assembly on May 13, 2011. Although this petition was adopted by the assembly's Industries and Economy Committee by a 6 to 3 vote, it was eventually rejected by the full assembly by a resounding 37 to 20 vote in October (Tsunashima 2012). Hamada (2013b) in his analysis of these events lists three reasons for the LDP-dominated assembly's vote in favor of the project. First, because the LDP's prefectural office requested an open vote, members of the assembly voted strictly according to party lines. The LDP had the majority in the assembly, and this majority voted unanimously in favor of the project. Second, the vote came just before the elections for the renewal of the assembly. Eager to enlist the governor's support for reelection, undecided members of the LDP refrained from crossing the party line on this matter. Finally, JF Miyagi leadership acknowledged the support of the Japanese Communist Party. This event further alienated possible LDP support for the petition. This pro-SZR vote was interpreted as providing legitimacy to the program.

Despite the setback, protests continued at the local and national levels. It spread from the fishermen and cooperatives to the intellectual and scientific communities, and to the general public. Governor Murai responded by issuing a moratorium on SZR legislation until late in 2013. In reality, this action was simply a ploy to weaken opposition and gain time to further the establishment of the SZR project (Hamada 2013a, 2013b). In June 2012 while the moratorium was in effect, Murai actively intervened to establish a corporation, Momonoura Oyster Producers (MOP), which counted on the investment of 15 fishermen from the Momonoura District in Ishinomaki City and funds from Sendai Suisan, a leading corporation in the fishing sector (see chapter 4). For the original investment, the 15 fishermen contributed a modest sum, 4.5 million yen (450,000 U.S. dollars),[12] and established MOP in August 2012. In October 2012, Sendai Suisan invested 4.4 million yen (440,000 U.S. dollars) in MOP and became involved in its management (MOP 2014). Initially, plans included the involvement of Western Japan, a corporation with headquarters in Kobe. Western Japan's participation, however, was eventually dropped because of local opposition claiming that nonlocal corporations do not circulate their profits in local communities (Furukawa 2014), and Sendai Suisan was invited to participate in the initiative by the Prefecture of Miyagi (Interview 2013a).

The involvement of the 15 local fishermen and their original investment deserves clarification. Prior to the 2011 disasters, in the district of Momonoura there were only 19 oyster fishermen. Their production was primarily generated through aquaculture (Interview 2013a). Farmed oysters from Momonoura are known for their high quality and command high prices. Accordingly, oyster farmers had an average annual income that exceeded 10 million yen (100,000 U.S. dollars). Eighteen of these 19 local fishermen were senior citizens who were more than 70 years old. The only exception was one fisherman, Keisuke,[13] who was in his 50s. These individuals faced the typical problems of aging farmers and fishermen in Japan: primarily, they could not count on younger family members for the continuation of their businesses. Accordingly, their goal was to gradually disengage from oyster farming and soon retire. In this context, after the earthquake and tsunami almost completely destroyed their homes, boats, and aquaculture facilities, it was relatively easy for them to decide to migrate to either the prefectural capital, Sendai City, or to Ishinomaki City. They wanted eventually to rebuild their homes, but in locations that would guarantee better protection against future tsunamis.[14]

Following his plans to restructure the local economy, Governor Murai considered Momonoura among the most appropriate sites where private capital could most effectively be employed for the reconstruction and revitalization of local fisheries. He convinced the 15 local aging oyster fishermen to postpone retirement and participate in the establishment of MOP. They eventually agreed. The projected income from MOP was 150,000–200,000 yen per month (1,500–2,000 U.S. dollars), which was sufficient only for semi-retired workers[15] (Interview 2013a). The situation was different for the younger fisherman. Because of the low returns that MOP implementation entailed, he did not participate. Governor Murai's insistence that semi-retired elderly fishermen be involved in this project was neither about employment nor about the—otherwise insufficient—income generated. It was about meeting the requirements of the Fisheries Act for the granting of fishing rights to a corporation. As indicated above (see note 6), this act regulates the assignments of fishing rights and establishes that they can be granted to a corporation only through the involvement and actual participation of local fishermen. In reality, MOP was controlled by the economically large and politically powerful Sendai Suisan.

On August 30, 2012, MOP was officially registered. In October of the same year, the Sendai Suisan participation in MOP was defined, and one of its associates became the company's acting CEO (Interview 2013b). As these events unfolded, once more cooperatives and fishermen were taken by surprise by the rapidity and success of this operation. They lamented the perceived unjust timing of this action that unfolded when their physical and economic conditions were still quite precarious (Tsunashima and Ogawa 2013).

In September 2012, the governor's office announced the establishment of a SZR program in Momonoura, Ishinomaki City. This initiative included the availability of public funds for the creation of new business activities in the fishing sector (Hamada 2013a, 2013b; Tsunashima 2014). Not surprisingly, the public funds made available for the initiative were much higher than the initial investment for the creation of MOP. That original sum was set at a low amount to allow the fifteen local fishermen to gain the majority of shares of the original enterprise, as required by the Fisheries Act. For the actual implantation of MOP, the local government made available 550 million yen (5.5 million U.S. dollars) from a total SZR budget of 650 million yen. Ultimately, the total investment for MOP was 1.1 billion yen (11 million U.S. dollars) with Sendai Suisan investing the remaining 550 million yen (Interview 2013a). Despite numerous objections,[16] the budget was approved by the Prefectural Assembly in October 2012.

As MOP was constituted, it appeared that Sendai Suisan was positioned to benefit from the opening of fishing rights to corporations. However, public opposition to Governor Murai required a different and more prudent political strategy that addressed the dissatisfaction of the local fishing community. Thus, following the disasters, Sendai Suisan initiated an aid program designed to rebuild the local fishing fleet. It purchased fishing boats countrywide for redistribution to local fishermen (Sendai Suisan 2012). This action was congruent with Governor Murai's appeal to invest in MOP. Accordingly, the façade of Sendai Suisan's involvement in the reconstruction became transparent as the company showed support to local fishermen in reviving their oyster farming and economy while providing backing for Murai's actions. Substantively, Sendai Suisan's actual goal was instrumental in nature and aimed at gaining a favorable position in the lucrative oyster market in Momonoura (Interview 2013a). It wanted privileged access to the area's high-quality production. Yet maintaining good relations with the local fishing community was evidently strategically important for this corporation (Interview 2012, 2013a). Accordingly, and departing from the governor's expectations, Sendai Suisan forfeited its privilege to gain fishing rights through MOP and, instead, asked MOP to apply for membership in the local cooperative. Eventually, MOP was granted fishing rights on October 30, 2012 (Hamada 2013a, 2013b; Tsunashima and Ogawa 2013). This move made clear to many observers that Murai's project to allow corporations to directly acquire fishing rights had failed; the alternative strategy to obtain fishing rights through cooperative membership appeared to be more palatable. According to Hamada (2013a, 2013b), however, the MOP strategy to join the cooperative was primarily designed to access this cooperative's facilities—such as the oyster shell–removing house—and minimize production costs. On March 6, 2013, MOP's first shipment of farmed oysters reached local supermarkets (Tsunashima and Ogawa 2013). On August 30, 2013, MOP was granted fishing rights by the SZR, a move that was previously approved by the government on April 23 of the same year.[17]

Ironically, MOP received fishing rights in three different ways: (1) through the governor's office via the SZR on August 30, 2013; (2) through membership in the local cooperative; and (3) through the fishermen co-owners of MOP, who were also individual members of the cooperative. This unique situation emerged despite the strong opposition of fishermen, cooperatives, citizens, and scientists at local and national levels. MOP, however, recorded a 79 million yen deficit (790,000 U.S. dollars) in 2013 (Tsunashima 2014).

Opposition

The opposition discussed above was accompanied by criticisms and actions by citizens. The Miyagi Prefecture Citizens' Center for Support of Recovery and Reconstruction from the Great East Japan Earthquake, a citizens' group established in Sendai City after the 2011 disasters, collected signatures to oppose the SZR project and organized a symposium, at which stakeholders were invited to express their opposition to SZR programs. A committee of the National Reconstruction Design Council stressed the negative consequences that changes to the existing fishing rights regime generated by the implementation of SZR projects could cause to resource management and conflict mediation traditionally carried out by cooperatives. The full council set these comments aside when it voted to approve the SZR program on June 25, 2011 (Hamada 2013a, 2013b).

Additional public political bodies, such as the Area Fishery Adjustment Committee, also expressed opposition to SZR. The Area Fishery Adjustment Committee is assigned to play an important mediating role between fishermen and cooperatives and is a consultative body for the governor. It is an administrative body present in every prefecture with members elected by fishermen. As the governor's office reviews applications for fishing rights by fishing sector cooperatives and fishery corporations, it must consult with the Area Fishery Adjustment Committee on important matters, such as the safeguards of local interests and the preparation of sea area maps to adjudicate the specific rights of each stakeholder. However, Governor Murai bypassed this process and promoted his SZR proposal without the opinion or consent of the Miyagi Area Fishery Adjustment Committee (Hamada 2013a, 2013b; Tsunashima and Ogawa 2013). Governor Murai consulted the committee about the Momonoura SZR project only on March 25, 2013, almost two years after he proposed the program and six months after it was approved. This behavior outraged many committee members, who resigned (Interview 2013a). Because of the governor's political support, the opposing members on the committee could not muster the two-thirds of all votes necessary to overrule the establishment of a SZR in Momonoura (Tsunashima and Ogawa 2013). Commenting on the political differences between the committee and its constituency, Tsunashima and Ogawa (2013) pointed out that such differences should be addressed through reforming the committee.

The issue of the SZR for fisheries created problems in the community of Momonoura. Prior to the 2011 disasters, all oyster fishermen worked harmoniously as members of the local cooperative. Their work was guided by the established cultural norms of cooperation and harmony that, as in the case of the management of farming resources (see chapter 6), required the consensual management of natural resources. The establishment of MOP and the SZR divided the community and affected cooperation among fishermen, although those who joined MOP continued to work together (Interview 2013a). Nevertheless, Keisuke was isolated, and his operation was affected. Keisuke eventually asked the local cooperative to be allowed to move his oyster farm to another fishery away from the area operated by MOP. He also petitioned for the use of another oyster shell–removing house. According to members of the local cooperative, the quality of the work of those who joined MOP suffered. When they worked as independent fishermen, their commitment to their work was higher. They frequently went to sea to check their aquaculture facilities. However, once they became employees of MOP and lost control of their facilities and boats, their work habits deteriorated. The frequency of their trips to the aquaculture facilities diminished, and even in emergencies—such as when a large typhoon affected the bay—their actions demonstrated they were not as concerned for the well-being of the oyster business as previously. Ultimately, local cooperative members were afraid that this would result in a decrease of the region's product quality. The establishment of MOP and the SZR also created strong and multilevel tensions between MOP members and the other fishermen, between MOP and the local cooperative, between the governor and cooperative at the local and national levels, and among members of the Area Fishery Adjustment Committee.

In the case of the latter, additional problems emerged after the approval of the SZR. Controversy erupted on issues related to the extent of the area of operation of MOP. In particular, the escape route for fishing boats was altered, and the required "straight line" of evacuation was not maintained (Interview 2013a). As demonstrated by the 2011 tsunami, this is a very sensitive matter, because it is essential for fishermen to move their boats quickly from port to offshore to avoid dangerous weather conditions. Moreover, this issue is of additional importance in Momonoura, as the bay serves as the marina for boats from adjacent areas. Conversely, the controversy led to negotiations between the local cooperative and MOP that actually resulted in a mutually satisfactory agreement. It was agreed to maintain the straight-line evacuation route, and the accord was ratified on May 20, 2013 (Tsunashima and Ogawa 2013). However, Governor Murai overruled the decision and reinstated the original plan with an "arched" evacuation route on June 18, 2013. The governor's decision jeopardized the safety of local fishermen and fueled their sense of betrayal, resulting in more confrontations and conflict. This confrontational mood replaced the traditionally dominant community posture that stressed working together to promote consensus and harmony. This posture has been traditionally employed to regulate social relations among community members. Questioning the legality and merit of Murai's actions, the local cooperative is working to develop legal challenges to the governor's actions.

An Alternative to Reconstruction: The Case of the Prefecture of Iwate

Diverging from the reconstruction policy adopted in Miyagi Prefecture, the Prefecture of Iwate pursued a strategy that prioritized the recovery of traditional systems of fishing. Iwate Prefecture is located to the north of the Prefecture of Miyagi and, together with Miyagi and Fukushima, is among the areas most severely affected by the 2011 disasters. Its fishing industry was nearly wiped out, with about 10,522 fishing boats, 108 of its 111 ports, and 81 percent of its fish-processing plants damaged by the earthquake and tsunami (Fisheries Agency 2011a, 2012). In monetary terms, the damage suffered by the local fishing industry reached 359 trillion yen, which was equivalent to 59 percent of the losses experienced by the entire local industrial apparatus (Prefecture of Iwate 2011). Three hundred and seventy-five members of the fishing sector cooperatives were either killed or missing. The number of fatalities is equal to 3 percent of the total number of cooperative members in the prefecture (Hamada 2012, 2013a).

On April 11, 2011, the Prefecture of Iwate established the Great East Japan Earthquake and Tsunami Reconstruction Committee, formed exclusively of local residents (Hamada 2013a). This is in contrast to the Prefecture of Miyagi, where advisors linked to national business circles and not necessarily tied to the area were appointed to the committee. The driving principle that inspired the actions of the Prefecture of Iwate was that local members were best suited to express and critically evaluate local needs during the processes of recovery and reconstruction.

Distancing itself from the idea of reconstruction as a proxy for restructuring, the Prefecture of Iwate interpreted this strategy in terms of recovering the methods that had historically defined local social and economic relations by prioritizing the restoration of local jobs and economic relations that included local fishing and the fishing industry in general. The objective of restoring communities' economic livelihoods and social functions was articulated in the Basic Plan of Reconstruction (Prefecture of Iwate 2011). Rejecting views that reconstruction be primarily directed to the enhancement of business activities and profit, the plan stated that people and their needs should take center stage in the definition and implementation of policies of reconstruction.[18] Moreover, rejecting extant criticisms and stressing the historical role and contributions of the fishing sector cooperatives, the Basic Plan of Reconstruction gave cooperatives and wholesale markets priority in the rebuilding effort (Hamada 2012, 2013a). In this context, the reconstruction of all fishing ports, including small ports, was given priority in the plan (Okada 2012a). The Prefecture of Iwate also provided local funds to be added to national government subsidies to fishermen for the replacement of lost boats. The collective use of boats was incentivized, a measure that responded to the need of further reducing the cost that fishermen had to bear to reconstruct their fishing activities (Hamada 2013a). Local municipalities also followed prefecture policy and introduced subsidies for the collective use of fishing boats, providing substantive economic relief to area fishermen's efforts to replace their boats. As a result, a more socially equitable system of reconstruction was established that promoted community consensus rather than the conflict characterizing the process in Miyagi Prefecture. All these initiatives supported successful recovery of fishing ports, cooperatives, and communities. For instance, the fishing cooperative Omoe in Miyako City, Iwate, quickly resumed its operation in May 2011 (Furukawa 2014).

Sociohistorical and political factors explain a substantial part of the rationale that provided a more balanced reconstruction plan in this prefecture. At the sociohistorical level, the Prefecture of Iwate is not part of the economic networks that support major markets, such as those found in the metropolitan Tokyo region. Because of their economic marginality, small fishery communities have successfully remained relatively autonomous. Geographically, the saw-toothed contour of the coastline discouraged outside investment and the application of modernist strategies of development. Consequently, the area was able to grow through alternative production strategies that relied on fishery cooperatives and the fishing industry's traditional wholesale market system. At the political level, the posture of the DPJ local governor, Takuya Tasso, stood in sharp opposition to that of Governor Murai. Governor Tasso took a critical stand on neoliberal initiatives, which promoted the possibility of implementing alternative reconstruction policies.

Conclusions

The establishment of SZR projects relied on the principles that the liberalization of fishing rights, the deregulation of existing legislation, and the promotion of corporate investment would accelerate the post-disaster reconstruction process and prove beneficial to the revitalization of coastal regions. This neoliberal posture is supported by the discourse that sees reconstruction as founded on private intervention and the enhanced search for profit as a strategy to effectively rationalize the use of socioeconomic resources. Reconstruction, therefore, became synonymous with restructuring. It stands in contrast to the concept of recovery, which views post-disaster intervention as a process that allows local stakeholders to regain control of their socioeconomic activities through a process involving their participation in decisionmaking, respect for local economic relations, and cultural sensitivity linked to the traditional methods that promote harmony and consensus in the region's various communities. The cases presented in this chapter demonstrate the vastly different conditions and results of reconstruction efforts in the disaster-affected fisheries of the Prefectures of Miyagi and Iwate.

The reconstruction approach promoted in the Prefecture of Miyagi was resisted by local fishermen and their cooperatives. Despite the harsh reality of a difficult recovery process, the fisheries mobilized protests against the SZR project and the liberalization of fishing rights. Governor Murai's SZR plan was seen as an unexpected and unfair attack on the traditional manner by which fishing rights were assigned and also on cooperatives and their members. Feelings of unfairness were strengthened by perceptions that reconstruction proposals came at a time when the fishing community could not adequately respond because of the total economic devastation that area residents faced. Additionally, these cooperatives and their members' opposition to the SZR proposal focused on Governor Murai's one-sided approach that favored private companies and his obvious lack of concern for the traditional consensus that affected stakeholders' participation in reconstruction. Murai's decision to exclude local communities from decisionmaking processes appeared to belittle their fundamental rights as Japanese citizens. Violating established local cultural patterns, Governor Murai's unilateral decisions fueled their understanding that the local political leadership had selected to stand with corporations in opposition to the local communities.

Moreover, community members feared that the liberalization of fishing rights would significantly weaken their conflict-mediation protocols and collective resource management, which historically had been carried out by the cooperative. Finally, the SZR proposal was accompanied by discussions of a possible radical reform of local cooperatives. The need to change the organization of cooperatives was based on a negative assessment that fishing sector cooperatives were economically ineffective, inefficient, and lacked competitiveness. Additionally, they were viewed as enjoying unwarranted protection from outdated national legislation that prevented the more desirable expansion of private corporations into the rural market in general and the lucrative rural financial market in particular.

In the case of the establishment of MOP, the implications of the split between the governor and the local community were clearly perceived by business actors. In effect, MOP leadership preferred a less controversial course of action than the one proposed by Murai. It can be maintained, therefore, that the granting of fishing rights through the SZR program was designed more to make a political statement about the liberalization of fishing rights rather than to promote the area's recovery. The latter was simply an act to legitimize liberalization at a time when the SZR was strongly resisted and was losing support. The controversial evolution of the recovery effort was further illustrated by the modalities through which evacuation routes for MOP operations was established. In this instance, the local stakeholders not only saw their efforts to negotiate a mutually satisfactory solution nullified, but also viewed their safety as being jeopardized.

In contrast to the events in the Prefecture of Miyagi, the Prefecture of Iwate, one of the most severely damaged prefectures, promoted an alternative model centered on recovery rather than reconstruction. This model was based on the prioritization of the needs of local residents rather than on the expansion of private sector business opportunities. Moreover, it entailed the reconstruction of all damaged fishing ports and the reactivation of traditional support structures, such as fishing cooperatives and wholesale markets. Additional initiatives supporting local needs included subsidies for the acquisition of new fishing boats and incentives to use the boats collectively.

The case of Momonoura and its alternative in the Prefecture of Iwate show at least two methods for addressing the consequences of disasters. For our purposes, it is important to underscore the contradictory proposal of the neoliberal reconstruction model supported by Governor Murai. It places restructuring in stark contrast to the culturally established dimensions of cooperation and consensus and the expansion of the economy as an alternative to strategies that prioritize the economic and physical safety of local residents. Affected by the consequences of the disasters, local fishermen and residents called for economic and physical security as basic principles to guide the regions' recovery efforts.

As proposed, these priorities are incompatible with the ideology supporting the SZR project. For Governor Murai, the achievement of economic profitability is the precondition that determines the achievement of social and physical well-being. In this context, the contradictory dimension of Murai's proposal rests not only on the overt bypassing of the vitally important involvement of local stakeholders in decisionmaking but also on its lack of social instruments to generate such involvement. By rejecting established forms of decisionmaking and replacing them with unilateral decisions, the governor's action inspired irreconcilable opposition. Characterized by these diverging demands, the post-disaster evolution of coastal fisheries was transformed into an unstable and contested setting.

NOTES

1. In Japanese scientific circles, three types of fishing communities are generally identified to illustrate the status of the sector: large, medium-sized, and small (Hamada 2013a). Heuristically, and given the limited presence of medium-sized communities, we use a simplified typology that excludes the latter and focuses on the two remaining types: large and small communities. These communities are typical of the Prefecture of Miyagi and the other damaged areas. Large fishing communities are defined as those counting on large fishing ports and working with large deep-sea fishing boats operating in domestic or international waters. Communities in this category contain large fishing industry clusters that integrate firms in seafood processing, refrigeration, wholesaling, transportation, trading, shipbuilding, energy, and other subsectors. Small fishing communities are defined as those operating small fishing ports, serving a limited number of small boats, and practicing coastal fishing and aquaculture. While this type consists of communities that are less populous and economically much smaller than those in the large category, it contains the vast majority of the existing fishing communities.

2. Prior the 2011 earthquake, the population of Ishinomaki City was about 163,000 (Ishinomaki City 2014a), but it had decreased to about 150,000 inhabitants by 2014 (Ishinomaki City 2014b).

3. According to the Fisheries Act, which has been regulating fisheries since the 1940s (see chapter 2), fishing rights are divided into four categories according to fish species and fishing methods (Demura 2012). There is a type of fishing rights that is exclusively granted to JFs. For the other three, JFs have priority access. The new legislation involves only one of these three other types of fishing rights, which is called "Fishing Rights of a Specific District" (*Tokutei Kukaku Gyogyouken*). It allows the granting of equal status between cooperatives and corporations, allowing corporations to apply and obtain fishing rights and bypassing any possible opposition by cooperatives.

4. In the establishment of the Fisheries Act, the selection of JFs as the entities in charge of handling fishing rights was based on the understanding that they were best suited to manage and protect human, natural, and economic resources and mediate and resolve disagreements among cooperatives' members (Hamada 2012). This assumption was confirmed over the decades, as cooperatives were able not only to foster the voicing of their members' opinions in the collective management of resources and investment but also to control the overdevelopment of coastal areas by curbing the construction of industrial complexes, nuclear power plants, and military bases.

5. This is an agency of the MAFF that supervises the administration of fisheries in Japan.

6. According to the 1949 Fisheries Act (revised in 1962; see chapter 2), which regulates fishing rights, a number of conditions must be met by corporations to obtain fishing rights. (1) The primary business objective of the corporation must to be to operate fisheries. (2) More than seven local fishermen or 70 percent of all local fishermen must be employees or must be shareholders of the corporation. (3) More than half of all employees or shareholders must have worked in fisheries in the corresponding fishing grounds. (4) More than half of the stock of the applying corporation must be held by individuals who have a full-time job with the corporation (Demura 2012; Kawai 2011).

7. The goal of altering the principles that guided the establishment of the Fisheries Act and the consequent power of JFs has been a longstanding objective of business circles and neoliberals. As early as 2007, a committee established by the Japan Economic Research Institute, a think tank created by four major business groups, including *Keidanren* and the Japanese Association of Corporate Executives, suggested that the improvement of Japanese fisheries should be based on a reform that would allow private corporations to gain direct access to fishing rights (Japan Economic Research Institute 2007). The so-called Takagi Report (from the name of the committee chair Yuki Takagi) became one of the fundamental documents that informed discussion in the Japanese Administration on deregulations and economic change (Hamada 2013a; Kawai 2011).

8. Aside from the attempt to acquire direct access to fishing rights, another reason behind this negative campaign was the corporate design to capture some of the cooperatives' significant share of the lucrative rural financial market and, in particular, rural banking, savings, and insurance. Responding to criticisms from business circles and the liberalization of the financial sector, since the 1990s, agricultural and fisheries cooperatives have undergone a series of mergers that ultimately strengthened their position in financial markets (Agricultural Policy Council 1996; Ishida 2008). As cooperatives expanded their financial activities, banks and their political supporters asked that they meet some of the same requirements that government regulations imposed on banks. In this context, banks and neoliberals proposed greater liberalization of the sector, yet they also requested the imposition of restrictions on the financial activities of cooperatives (Agricultural Policy Council 1996).

9. This institution was established in 1979 by the founder of Panasonic, Mr. Konosuke Matsushita, to educate young people in politics and the management of local resources and governments (Matsushita Institute of Government and Management 2014). Graduates of this institute include many neoliberal politicians, such as former Prime Minister Noda.

10. The members of this council, appointed by Governor Murai, were predominantly members of transnational corporations' think tanks, such as Mitsubishi, Nomura, and Mitsui, as well as members of the Development Bank of Japan (Miyagi Prefecture Disaster Reconstruction Council 2011).

11. Concerns were also fueled by the recent failure of aquaculture initiatives of Coho salmon production in the district of Ayukawa, Ishinomaki City. Over the past few years, corporations have invested in the lucrative business of salmon farming, convincing local fishermen to enter into partnerships with them. However, these corporations quickly disinvested once negative market trends emerged, leaving local fishermen with significant debts.

12. Each of the fifteen fishermen had to invest only 300,000 yen (3,000 U.S. dollars) instead of the 5–10 million yen needed if they wanted to resume their business outside the SZR scheme (MOP 2014).

13. This is a fictitious name.

14. Plans to rebuild destroyed homes on higher grounds have been proposed for many disaster areas. However, the cost of these much more expensive lots, their limited availability, and relocation problems associated with the unwillingness of residents to leave their original communities and jobs complicated these plans' implementation.

15.   According to JF of the Prefecture of Miyagi, average annual sale of farming oyster per fishermen in Momonoura was 19 million yen (190,000 U.S. dollars) before the disaster.

16.   The primary set of objections concerned how MOP was funded. This company was created after the March 2011 disasters. Therefore, it was not entitled to receive funds from the national government reconstruction programs. To address this situation, the Prefecture of Miyagi established a new program that, while formally available to all affected fishing and farming operations, went almost entirely to MOP. Also questioned was the original statement of the governor that the SZR for fisheries should be established to reduce public expenditures and increase private investment. In the case of MOP, the public money invested was as large as private contributions.

17.   In January 2014, MOP opened a new oyster shell–removing and packing facility and ceased using facilities belonging to the local cooperative. It also heralded the creation of new jobs, stressing that the total number of workers increased to twenty-one and that number included some young employees in their twenties (MOP 2014). In August 2014, MOP began online retailing of farmed oysters for the domestic market (*Nikkei Newspaper* 2014). The price of these oysters was 11,700 yen/kg (117 U.S. dollars/kg), which was higher than that for oysters from Hiroshima (3,000 yen/kg or 30 U.S. dollars/kg in August 2014) (Kakaku.com 2014). The oyster produced by MOP commanded higher prices than those from Hiroshima, one of the most highly regarded providers of oysters in Japan.

18.   This reconstruction centered on human needs was recommended in 1924 by Fukuda (1924) in the aftermath of the Great Kanto Earthquake of 1923. He wrote that reconstruction should be centered on human needs and the reconstruction of survival chances of people rather than on the reconstruction of "Imperial Capital" (meaning the accumulation of capital) that was promoted by the state (Okada 2012a). The reconstruction approach based on the concept of human needs should not be simply equated with an anthropocentric posture that places humans in a privileged position vis-à-vis the rest of nature. Rather, it should be viewed as an approach stressing the harmonious interdependence of all components of nature and an attitude that privileges life over profits.

CHAPTER 8

Agri-Food Corporations, the State, Resistance, and Disaster Reconstruction under Neoliberalism

Introduction

Reflecting on the material presented and the analytical points made in each of the preceding chapters, this chapter outlines and provides specific conclusions that link the book's four central themes. First, we offer observations on the characteristics of Neoliberalism and the consequences of its adoption in Japanese agri-food, stressing its limitations both in terms of the existence of family farming and fishing as systems of production and as ways of life. Additionally, we conclude that limited understanding of the characteristics of Neoliberalism favors alternatives that do not transcend the very parameters of this ideology.

Second, we reflect on the use of Neoliberalism to address the consequences of disasters, such as those that impact Japan's farming and fishing communities. Although the local resistance that Neoliberalism engenders is widespread, it varies, resulting in coordinated and much stronger episodes of opposition in conjunction with atomized and weakly organized resistance. As national and local governments insist on promoting the corporatization of rural areas, the solutions to the problems created by the application of Neoliberalism amid disasters are constrained further by the creation of additional market solutions that simply uphold neoliberalization.

Third, we propose that the state-sponsored neoliberal discourse promotes a greater corporate presence in the sector today than in the past as the primary effective strategy to address economic stagnation. This view is legitimized by claims that describe family farming and fishing as ineffective and inefficient and run by aging operators offering dismal opportunities for the enhancing of market competitiveness. In this context, public institutions operating in the sector have difficulty performing those important roles that they have played since the early postwar years. As resistance to corporatization increases, corporations have focused on eliminating opposition by reducing transaction costs and securing a stable and steady supply of commodities for food processing and retailing at the expense of rural communities. For example, state and corporate actions depart from publicly announced claims. We illustrate this point by showing disparities between state and corporate pronouncements and the actual conditions concerning labor relations, outcomes, the amounts of investment, the mobility of capital, and the fiscal soundness of neoliberal policies.

Finally, we probe the reasons, conditions, and forms of resistance that developed in opposition to neoliberal policies and corporate involvement in Japan's agri-food production. By underscoring the differences between more successful forms of resistance in fishing and instances of individualized and overall weaker resistance in farming, we argue that these differences can be explained by four observations. First, the introduction of SZR programs created a new and unprecedented context that allowed corporations to acquire fishing rights and increase their presence in the sector. The extent of the game-changing nature of this move and the rapidity with which it occurred triggered a strong opposition from fishermen. These changes occurred gradually in farming and were accompanied by limited discussion in political arenas, resulting in a much less contested social environment.

Second, opposition occurred in the presence of strong institutional leadership within the fishing cooperative structure. However, this situation did not materialize for the farming sector. Farmer organizations' traditional loyalty to the government constrained them from mobilizing opposition. Third, the fishing sector opposition enjoyed external political support and significant press coverage. These circumstances did not occur in farming. And fourth, fishermen and their cooperatives enjoyed the powerful support of nongovernmental organizations, consumer cooperatives, residents, and intellectuals who joined in the opposition. Resistance in the farming sector was not supported to the same extent.

Neoliberalism in Agri-Food

In the 1980s, Prime Minister Nakasone (LDP) embraced Neoliberalism and declared that the political and economic theory was necessary to address the socioeconomic problems that halted Japan's formidable post–World War II economic and social expansion. In the case of agri-food, Neoliberalism undermined the three pillars that framed the postwar agri-food policy (see chapter 2). The first pillar consists of the establishment of modern and democratic social relations and institutions designed to overcome the semifeudal and authoritarian social arrangements of prewar agri-food. The second refers to the construction of a sector based on family ownership of productive units, whereby land and fishing rights were to remain under the control of family-run operations. The third consists of the centrality of the collective management of natural resources and the establishment of consensus in relevant community decisions and decisionmaking processes.

Standing counter to these established dimensions of agri-food, the implementation of Neoliberalism resulted in the sector's economic decline and the emergence of social tensions, local dissatisfaction, and opposition. To be sure, pressure to liberalize Japanese agri-food markets and production predated the full adoption of Neoliberalism. The success of the export-oriented economic model motivated many developed countries, and above all the United States, to respond by requiring access to some Japanese markets, such as agri-food. Despite this pressure and additional concessions associated with Japan's membership in the GATT, successful protectionist policies continued to characterize the sector. As indicated in chapter 2, the social and structural importance of agri-food was significant, as it played the role of reservoir of surplus labor and contributed to the buffering of some of the negative consequences associated with rapid social change. In this respect, the "backwardness" of the farming sector was one of the conditions that propelled the expansion of manufacturing and the economy (see chapters 2 and 9).

Eventually, the implementation of Neoliberalism translated into the deregulation of land and commodity markets with the virtual elimination of protectionist and commodity support programs and policies. The concomitant appreciation of the yen further decreased the already very limited competitiveness of local farmers and promoted an increase in imports. The ensuing decline of the price of agricultural products constituted an advantage for dominant urban industrial groups. The latter benefited from the availability of affordable food that decreased the cost of employing the industrial working class and contributed to the pacification of social relations.

This initial phase of market deregulation was followed by a second period, consisting of the corporatization of agri-food. The beginning of this period coincided with the start of the new century and justifies increasing corporate presence in agriculture and food. The result is the substitution of independent farmers with corporations as a legitimate tool to revitalize the rural economy and enhance the international competitiveness of the sector. Some state-sponsored incentives, including cash subsidies, tax abatements, and administrative support, render this shift highly favorable to corporate efforts.

As demonstrated throughout this book, corporatization and market liberalization signified the deterioration of the economic status of farmers and the overall socioeconomic conditions of rural areas. It is relevant that currently, Japan's food self-sufficiency ratio[1] is declining sharply and stands at a level whereby only 39 percent of the per capita daily calories are locally produced. Additionally, most farmers and fishermen are above retirement age, which creates the problem of the economic and social costs associated with supporting this aging rural population. Above all, the poor economic condition of farmers prevents an adequate generational replacement, as younger rural residents prefer to migrate to urban areas or find employment in other sectors. This situation is a major obstacle to the continuation of the tradition of family farmers and fishermen and of an established way of life in rural Japan. Moreover, the decline of family farming is often associated with a number of negative consequences. The degradation of the rural environment is among the most cited of these effects. The waves of floods and landslides that recently affected rural areas is, according to many, the result of the declining stewardship of the land traditionally associated with family agriculture.

However, it is not surprising that the Japanese government promoted corporatization and accelerated the implementation of neoliberal policies. It follows the basic tenets of this theory as reviewed in the Introduction to this book (see also chapter 9). In those pages, we underscored that according to Neoliberalism, economic and social problems are addressed through the creation of markets. Therefore, the optimal solution to the crisis in agricultural production and rural areas is to be found in the creation of more markets. The role of the state, in this context, is to create all the necessary conditions for the establishment of these markets. The state, in other words, is an actor in the establishment of new market relations. Additionally, unlike classical laissez-faire postures, Neoliberalism defines the presence of large corporations and their power in the market as benign. While justifying the existence of monopolies and equating them to a competitive market, Milton Friedman ([1962] 1982, 119–120) considers it erroneous to view the large size of companies as a problem for the economy. Abenomics, which stresses the intervention of the state to create markets and expand the presence of large firms, is perfectly in line with these tenets.

The deregulation and liberalization of Japanese agri-food and its consequences are widely documented in the literature (see chapter 1). The analysis presented in this book shows the explicit association of these changes with Neoliberalism. It, therefore, differs from a common argument presented in the literature that sees these changes as part of globalization. While corporatization is linked to globalization, the most decisive aspects of this phenomenon are associated with deregulation and state intervention to that effect. These are features of Neoliberalism. Additionally, our conclusions also contribute to the literature by stressing the active role of the state in the neoliberalization of agri-food. This emphasis supports arguments that confine the withdrawing of the state to the social sphere (social welfare and support of lower and middle classes) and stresses the interventionist dimension of the state in processes of deregulation and marketization.

Disasters and Reconstruction Processes

Pertinent literature shows that both natural disasters and reconstruction processes are socially created. As such, they can be viewed as contested terrains where the interests of conflicting groups and established power relations motivate actions and explain consequences. In this context, the weakest components of society often suffer from the most negative of these consequences (see chapter 1). The case studies presented in this book show that Neoliberalism characterized reconstruction following recent disasters, such as the Southern Hyogo Prefecture Earthquake in 1995 and the Mid-Niigata Prefecture Earthquake in 2004 (see chapter 3). The Creative Reconstruction strategy that was adopted under these circumstances prioritized private sector investment, interests, and leadership.

Despite the less than desirable outcomes of these past experiences (see chapter 3), the application of neoliberal measures continued to characterize reconstruction following the triple disaster of March 2011. Both the DPJ and the LDP employed Neoliberalism as their guiding policy and promoted such measures as the creation of Special Zones for Reconstruction, pro-corporate changes in the tax code, and public funding of corporate projects. Additionally, major pro-corporate political actors, think tanks, and corporate associations quickly sprang into action and remained actively involved in the determination of reconstruction policies and programs. As in the case of the creation of agri-food policy, the Japanese neoliberalization of disaster reconstruction is based on the tenet that solutions to extant problems should be found in the creation of markets, not in state-funded, publicly controlled resources. State intervention to address the consequences of disasters and provide conditions that would mitigate future occurrences is redirected toward the empowerment of private actors and the strengthening of market relations. From this point of view, the Japanese disaster reconstruction experience is an example of advanced neoliberalization.

As indicated in the previous chapters, neoliberal efforts engender contradictions, with farmers, fishermen, and local residents resisting these strategies. Local residents remain unconvinced of the ability of corporate actors to address their needs, are worried about the growth of corporate power in rural communities, and remain uncertain about the degree to which they would be allowed to participate in decisionmaking processes. Moreover, they see the severity of the disasters as adding to the preexisting serious socioeconomic conditions experienced by rural communities, family farmers, and fishermen. Opposition to the establishment of SZR programs in Sendai City (see chapter 6) and Ishinomaki City (see chapter 7) are all instances of this resistance. However, the degree of opposition varies. Farmers' refusal to rent land to the Michisaki Farm in Sendai City registers on the weak side of this spectrum, while the resistance of Ishinomaki City's fishermen to the liberalization of fishing rights in the SZR in Momonoura is an instance of much stronger opposition (chapter 7). The contradictions and limits of neoliberal reconstruction policies are obvious to farmers and fishermen. They are aware that there is a significant gap between local stakeholders' needs and the solutions proposed by central and local governments. Following Neoliberal tenets, government strategies prescribe more liberalization to address the very limits of market-based strategies, opening up the possibility of a furthering of the crisis (see Chapter 9).

Following these findings and considerations, our analysis supports existing literature that sees disasters as instruments for the further neoliberalization of social relations (the so-called Shock Doctrine). The lack of involvement of local farmers and fishermen and their opposition to Creative Reconstruction are elements that indicate the limited consideration of democracy by Neoliberalism. Defined as "Neoliberal Totalitarianism" by Hashimoto (2014), this type of reconstruction is a process of restructuring social relations that translates into an attack on established rights (ownership of farm land and fishing rights) of local residents. Moreover, it is a process that—following classical neoliberal tenets—stresses the freedom of pursuing profit over people's goals and aspirations.

Government and Corporations in Agri-Food

The implementation of neoliberal policies is accompanied by an increase in the presence of corporations in agri-food. Departing from past views that gave primacy to the notion of "land to the real farmers," the government proposes a discourse that welcomes corporate growth and sees it as an effective strategy to address economic stagnation and revitalize rural areas. Additionally, corporations are considered preferable to independent farmers and fishermen whose age and declining number are deemed detrimental to the enhancing of market competitiveness. The fact that independent operations are small, run by the family, often part-time, and reduce the amount of land cultivated further legitimizes this discourse.

The government's support for corporate presence in agri-food has implications for established institutions operating in the sector. The activities of farming and fishing cooperatives (see chapters 5 and 7), Area Fishery Adjustment Committees (chapter 7), and agricultural committees (chapter 9) are all affected by the neoliberal posture of the government. As indicated above, these were entities created in the post–World War II years to promote collective resource management, give voice to family farmers and fishermen, and promote these groups' interests. As a result, these institutions played a pivotal role in the economic evolution and social stability of agri-food. In the current climate, however, while opposition to corporations is not necessarily one of these institutions' objectives (see chapter 5), doing business with corporations is problematic, and cooperatives remain penalized by recent structural reforms promoted by Prime Minister Abe. These reforms also reduce the power and role of agricultural committees.

Constituted and elected by local farmers, agricultural committees are viewed as adversarial by political groups that promote a corporate presence in agriculture. In this context, their roles as regulators of farmland transactions and promoters of land redistribution to farmers are to be transferred to other agencies. The newly created Farmland Redistribution Program has begun to control the acquisition of land made available through farmers' retirement. The redistribution of this land is no longer exclusively directed to existing farmers but is now open to corporations (see chapter 9). Moreover, this pro-corporate climate allows restrictive interpretation of the role of these agencies. The events discussed in chapter 7 show that the governor of the Prefecture of Miyagi, Yoshihiro Murai, restricted the role of the Area Fishery Adjustment Committee in the process of approving MOP's activities in Momonoura Bay.

As rural residents' dissatisfaction persists, opposition to market liberalization continues, and the economic expansion of the sector stagnates, the government is called on to legitimize its use of neoliberal measures. This is particularly the case because plans to address current issues do not depart from the introduction of more pro-market measures, such as the proposed signing of the Trans-Pacific Partnership Agreement. As indicated in chapters 5, 6, and 7, the view promoted by Abenomics proposes new doses of Neoliberalism for the agri-food sector and rural communities. In this context, the government's pro-corporate efforts are—albeit in part—likely linked to expectations that corporations and their political backers would be more effective supporters of government-sponsored political candidates and policies than the diminishing ranks of aging farmers and fishermen. Disregarding the social and systemic importance of family farmers and fishermen (see chapter 9), recent Japanese administrations have squarely placed all their bets on a corporate-led revitalization of the rural economy and society. In December 2014, national elections were called to eliminate obstacles to the further implementation of Prime Minister Abe's neoliberal policy. As Abe and his LDP won the elections, plans to continue the neoliberalization of the rural economy, such as the introduction of Special Zones for Regional Revitalization, intensified (*Asahi Newspaper* 2014).

For their part, agri-food corporations, such as Dole Japan, Kagome, and Sendai Suisan are actively involved in the execution of restructuring programs centered on the reducing transaction costs and securing a stable and steady supply of commodities for food processing (Kagome) and retailing (Dole Japan and Sendai Suisan). While these corporations establish contract schemes with independent farmers and access spot trading for supply, their control of these systems remains problematic. As indicated in chapter 4, Dole Japan's problems with contract farming motivated this and similar corporations to pursue vertical integration strategies. Their objective is to limit opposition of local farmers and cooperatives and, to that end, establish direct control of the entire production chain. This situation indicates the limits to the theory that contract farming is the most desirable form of corporate positioning in supply chains (e.g., Boyd and Watts 1997; Martinez, Aboites, and Constance 2013).

In many countries, agri-food corporations' focus on enhancing profit opportunities is pursued through new and innovative investment. Encouraged by state deregulation, this posture dovetails with the process of financialization whereby returns are sought through investments in stock and securities markets rather than through investments in production (Bonanno 2014b; Bonanno and Bush 2015; Wolf and Bonanno 2014). Financialization not only involves agri-food commodities but also farmland and fishing rights. Accordingly, these entities are treated as financial assets, and as such, they are no longer viewed exclusively as factors of production but are transformed into items whose short-term trade value in primary and secondary stock markets is of paramount importance. As indicated in previous chapters (see chapters 2 and 7), publicly traded corporations cannot directly own farmland and cannot hold fishing rights in Japan. However, they can lease farmland for agricultural production and obtain fishing rights under specific conditions. And the major business circles persistently request the liberalization of property rights on farmland and securitization of fishing rights (Yukitomo 2013).

Non-agri-food corporations, such as IBM Japan (see chapter 4), also seek to diversify by investing in the sector. In the case of IBM, excessive international competition and loss of markets prompted the search for new business opportunities. In this context, agri-food was deemed appealing not only because of government-supported deregulations and pro-corporate policies, but also due to forecasts predicting future world food and land shortages, climate change, and geopolitical instability. All of these considerations indicate preferences for enhanced involvement in strategic commodities, such as agricultural products and food. Despite these positive expectations, however, only a handful of corporations report earnings in agricultural production. Most agri-food companies operating in Japan show negative balance sheets despite receiving public subsidies (Sadakiyo 2012). Still optimistic about future growth and continuous state support, these negative returns do not discourage further corporate involvement in the sector, backed by calls for more deregulation and the implementation of neoliberal policies. Far from being a success story, the corporatization of agri-food remains a strong government-sponsored political project contested at the local level (see chapter 7).

The limits of the neoliberal project in Japanese agri-food can be also seen through the discrepancies between claims made by the government and corporations and the actual events characterizing the sector. Four instances can best illustrate these gaps. The first refers to labor relations. Government pronouncements and corporate plans call for the creation of new, stable, and adequately remunerated jobs that would make full use of the application of advanced technology and produce better socioeconomic conditions for rural areas. However, the number of jobs created does not meet local expectations or publicized corporate estimates. Following established trends in which stable and well-remunerated jobs are replaced with unstable, part-time, and poorly paid employment, the workers hired are unskilled members of marginal labor pools, such as women, students, and the elderly. Clashing with pronouncements about community development and revitalization, virtually all these workers are commuting urban dwellers with no connections to, nor membership in, the local agri-food labor force (for example, the case of Nittan Farm discussed in chapter 5). Moreover, reliance on strictly supervised unskilled labor is telling of the real corporate intentions about the use of advanced technology and the desire to upgrade the skills of the existing local labor force. Blaming global economic downturns, global competition, and other negative circumstances, corporations also remain strategically silent on their labor-saving efforts and intentions to create precarious and part-time jobs. In effect, corporations present a discourse that exonerates them from the lack of job creation. In this discourse, references to the impartiality of market trends are used to justify the implementation of industrial plans based on the use of precarious and low-paid jobs (see chapters 5 and 6).

In chapter 5, we document the manner in which part-time workers employed by Izumi Farm, one of Dole Japan's franchise farms in the Prefecture of Kagoshima, were all paid at the local minimum wage level (5.56 U.S. dollars/hour). This is a wage level that is well below those paid in the United States and the EU. The situation is worsened by the economic fact that the cost of basic items, such as housing, food, and transportation, is much higher in Japan than in North America and Europe. And in the case of the fishing corporation MOP, independent fishermen were transformed into wage workers and their incomes drastically reduced (see chapter 7). The establishment of low-paid, precarious jobs is enforced through the quite common threat of layoffs. When Izumi Farm was relocated to another prefecture, local part-time wage workers lost their jobs (chapter 5). As indicated by the president of Michisaki Farm in the SZR of Sendai City, a preferred industrial strategy is to contain costs of production through the reduction of personnel (chapter 6). In addition, labor conditions are also threatened (chapter 7). The open violation of safety norms for evacuation routes by MOP is a case in point. In this instance, corporate control of decisionmaking processes increases benefits for the company to the detriment of the safety of local fishermen.

The second instance refers to the negative consequences of limited investment in land and fishing grounds (see chapters 5, 6, and 7). Neoliberal statements identify the growing involvement of corporations in agri-food as one of the primary conditions for the economic growth of the sector and of rural areas. In reality, corporate industrial policies contemplate a limited involvement in the socioeconomic development of local communities. They promote strategies that prioritize cost-saving moves, capital hypermobility, and the flexible use of labor and other factors of production. In this context, rather than promoting local socioeconomic growth, corporate strategies center on the accelerated exploitation of local resources backed by plans to relocate to areas that are more convenient in the event that local conditions become difficult to manage. Agro-ecological differences add to this situation, as locally held views about good agricultural practices clash with corporate preferences. Ultimately, these corporate policies engender poorer economic conditions, dissatisfaction among farmers, and acts of opposition (chapter 5). Exceptions exist, however. Employing a community-oriented approach, Nittan Farm, a Dole Japan's franchise farm in Hokkaido, was able to enlist the collaboration of local farmers and rapidly increased the quantity of land it leased from them (chapter 5). In this case, Nittan Farm respected locally adopted crop rotation systems and invested in soil improvement. However, this policy did not prevent the company from threatening to relocate when its requests to local authorities were challenged.

Third, in the corporate arsenal, hypermobility remains a fundamental tool against rural communities' actions for the promotion of economic growth and social stability. Supporters list job creation, economic growth, increased tax revenue, and the diffusion of technological innovations as salient positive consequences of neoliberal policies. Yet these results hardly materialize, and as communities express their dissatisfaction, corporations either threaten to or actually move their operations (see chapter 5). Farmers, fishermen, cooperatives, landowners, wage workers, and members of local communities are all aware of the possibility of, and remain vulnerable to, the consequences of corporate hypermobility (chapters 5, 6, and 7). This awareness and the loss of participation in decisionmaking processes and control of the management of local communities emerge as precipitating factors in the crisis of legitimation of neoliberalism (chapter 9).

Finally, claims that corporatizations reduce public expenditure and positively affect the state budget are contradicted by the existence of large public subsidies to corporations (see chapters 5, 6, and 7). According to classical neoliberal theory, companies should not be subsidized. Financial support from the state alters the functioning of the market and, ultimately, discourages companies from innovating and becoming more efficient. Despite these claims, corporations request funding, and corporate economic activities receive public financial assistance, as they enjoy support within Japanese political circles. The rationale for this position rests on the need to create exceptional economic stimuli to reignite the economy, a strategy that has been adopted by public authorities in Japan, the United States, and the EU. The theory is to eventually eliminate these stimuli and return to the free functioning of the market.[2] Yet in the case of Japanese agri-food, these financial support measures are continued and remain too expensive and too important to be simply viewed as stimuli to corporations (chapter 7). More significantly, the injection of public money into corporate coffers does not necessarily result in local socioeconomic development, nor does it halt corporate hypermobility (chapter 5).

Resistance

Dissatisfaction with the recent corporation-dominated evolution of Japanese agri-food engendered opposition from farmers, fishermen, cooperatives, local authorities, and residents. The material presented in the previous chapters shows that dissatisfaction and the resultant opposition are motivated by economic, political, and cultural considerations. Economically, farmers and fishermen are overtly worried about the possible loss or devaluation of their farmland and fishing grounds and their inability to maintain their status as independent producers as the growing presence of corporations, the corporations' equally relevant hypermobility, and the implementation of leasing schemes character- ize production. Similarly, the growing presence of corporations is viewed as a factor that worsens the status of labor relations, as workers face job precarious- ness, enhanced control, layoffs, and safety issues. Perception of the worsening of local conditions is also fueled by fears of contamination of local natural resources and inadequate management of farmland and fishing grounds (see chapters 5, 6, and 7).

Politically, the concentration of corporate power translates into local groups' lack of participation in the decisionmaking processes (see chapters 5, 6, and 7). Farmers and fishermen also lament the lack of alternatives that the present situation and dominant political view entail. Justified by calls about the impar- tiality and, therefore, neutrality of market mechanisms, corporate decisions are experienced as forceful unilateral actions.

Culturally, the incompatibility between corporate behavior and traditional cultural patterns delegitimizes corporate proposals in the eyes of local residents. They experience the break with traditionally established forms of management of public life as threats to the stability and future development of these com- munities (see chapter 9). In the case of local authorities, dissatisfaction focuses on the unmet promises by corporations about community growth, employment creation, the introduction of new technology, and corporate hypermobility (chapters 5 and 6). In the case of cooperatives, their opposition is fueled by the threat that corporate hypermobility and political power create to their existence and historical role (chapters 5, 6, and 7).

In a significant number of cases, opposition translated into farmers' refusal to lease their farmland to corporations (see chapter 5 and 6) and fishermen's refusal to participate in the creation of new fishing corporations, such as MOP (chapter 7). In other instances, citing low pay, routinized work, and unskilled tasks, wage workers left their jobs with corporate farms and returned to farming their own land (chapter 6). Employing available administrative tools, community authorities joined this local anticorporate campaign. Some administrations opposed corporations by delaying their certification as Certified Agricultural Producers. These delays also prevented corporations from having immediate access to discounted credit (chapter 5). In the case of Nittan Farm in Hokkaido, when the administration of the town of Atsuma delayed certification, Dole Japan responded by relocating Nittan Farm to an adjacent region. Also, lack of administrative support for Izumi Farm in the Prefecture of Kagoshima led to a move to the Prefecture of Nagasaki. These are strategies similar in principle to those pursued in other parts of the world as rural communities oppose the local presence of corporations.

In the case of cooperatives, refusal to do business with corporations emerged as the most frequent form of opposition (see chapters 5 and 7). At the outset, cooperatives worked with corporations and even allowed them to acquire membership in the cooperative. However, episodes of exerting corporate power and unilateralism violated established cultural norms and were interpreted as adversarial. Accordingly, cooperatives began to actively oppose corporations. For instance, in the case of Goto Farm in the Prefecture of Nagasaki (chapter 5), after a period of collaboration, the local cooperative severed all business deals with this firm, including the previously negotiated use of the cooperative's facility and product sorting station (chapter 5). As a result, Goto Farm was forced to build its own facilities. In the case of MOP, the local fishing cooperative allowed this corporation to join the organization, acquire fishing rights through this membership, and use the cooperative facilities (chapter 7). However, as disagreement between the cooperative and MOP and the governor of Murai developed, it asked all its members to halt all business activities with MOP and its parent company, Sendai Suisan.

Finally, a case of overt anticorporate violence was recorded when corporate greenhouses were set on fire (see chapter 6). The perpetrators were never arrested, nor was an official explanation of this act ever provided. It can be assumed, though, that it was the result of intense opposition among some members of the local farming community to the presence of the corporations.

As the discussion provided in the previous chapters indicates, these forms of resistance are numerous, yet they are rather spontaneous, not necessarily well organized, and not part of an established anticorporate movement. In essence, the dissatisfaction that corporate actions engendered created protest that has not yet evolved into a true opposition movement. Simultaneously, however, some more organized resistance developed, such as that illustrated in chapter 7 whereby fishermen, cooperatives, local residents, and members of the intellectual community signed petitions and organized gatherings and demonstrations.

The difference between organized resistance in fishing versus the more unsystematic opposition in farming deserves additional discussion.

Organized and Disorganized Resistance

The differences between the resistance of farmers and fishermen can be explained by four observations. First, the introduction of SZR programs created a new and unprecedented context, as the opening of fishing rights to corporations proposed a new set of rules never before experienced in Japan. To be sure, corporations could access fishing rights before the implementation of SZRs but only under specific conditions (see chapter 7). However, the significance of this new situation rests on the fact that corporations have the same level of access to fishing rights that cooperatives enjoy. This significant and sudden rule change in the aftermath of the 2011 triple disaster encouraged fishermen and their cooperatives to manifest their discontent and opposition at the local, prefectural, and national levels. The ensuing political debate popularized the case and polarized public opinion. In the case of farming, changes that allowed corporations to have direct access to farming occurred gradually and, contrary to the case of fisheries, they were not the subject of political discussion. In short, the corporatization of agricultural production was not as politicized and widely discussed as in the case of fishing.

Second, opposition occurred with the presence of some strong institutional leadership both within the local fishing cooperatives and at the level of the national federation. In the farming sector, conversely, there was a lack of institutional leadership and strength. Agricultural cooperatives and farmers associations (such as the Irrigation Association and the Land Improvement Association) failed to oppose neoliberal measures, primarily due to these organizations' traditional loyalty to the government. For virtually all the leaders of these institutions, opposing the government was not a strategy to be practiced. More radical organizations, such as the Via Campesina–affiliated Japan Family Farmers Movement or (*Nouminren*) expressed dissent in their publications but failed to translate it into broader and organized forms of struggle. Their limited size can be viewed as one of the fundamental explanations for this lack of action. As a result, most of the opposition emerged in terms of individual, atomized actions.

Third, fishing sector opposition enjoyed broader political support. While the national Reconstruction Design Council, the Prefectural Legislative Assembly, and the Area Fishery Adjustment Committee eventually approved Governor Murai's proposal to establish a SZR program for fisheries and liberalize fishing rights, there were members of these institutions who vocally opposed these measures. They strongly voiced their opposition during the discussion phase of the legislative process, making their dissenting points clear and popular.

Additionally, local newspapers (such as *Kahoku Shimpo*) also publicized the debate locally and nationally, giving further voice to dissent. In the case of farming, most political parties and trade unions supported the government and offered only limited criticism to the neoliberalization of farming. Dominant was the discourse that identified in the advanced age of farmers and the related issue of generational replacement as the most decisive obstacles to the development of farming. Following this discourse, the growth of family farming was viewed as a difficult road to follow as opposed to the more promising corporatization of the sector. This discourse was popular not only among politicians but also with the public. Additionally, the media gave limited coverage to farmers' opposition and supported discourses that stressed the desirability of neoliberal reforms.

Finally, fishermen and their cooperatives enjoyed the powerful support of nongovernmental organizations, consumer cooperatives, residents, and intellectuals. They became fishermen and fishing cooperatives' strong allies by assisting in the organization of demonstrations and a host of protest actions. Also, a number of intellectuals published documents in support of these groups. In the case of farming, the popularity of the above-mentioned discourse about the limits of family farming and the gradual pace of the neoliberal reforms explains the lack of support to this struggle.

The overall picture that emerges from this analysis is that family farms and fishing operations are poorly equipped to modernize effectively. Their structural characteristics and those of their operators appear to be insurmountable obstacles to reach adequate market competitiveness. Simultaneously, the corporatization of agri-food also entails limited accomplishments in that direction. This sectorial reading of the situation, however, does not do justice to the systemic relevance of agri-food and the implications that it entails. These are the issues discussed in chapter 9.

NOTES

1. The self-sufficiency ratio (discussed in chapter 2) is a component of the notion of food sovereignty that stresses the right to food for local communities and their ability to control food policies, organize food production, and access the necessary natural resources to produce food. Simultaneously, this ratio is an indicator of the calorization of diets, whereby adequate nutrition is measured in terms of caloric intake. For a critique of calorization and the importance of food security and sovereignty, see Carolan (2013) and Wittman, Desmarais, and Wiebe (2010).

2. The ending of quantitative easing (the financial asset purchase program) in the United States, which occurred in 2014, is an illustration of this economic strategy. Quantitative easing remains in place in Japan through Abenomics and in Europe. Simultaneously, intervention of the state to support corporations has been justified in terms of the neoliberal tenet that the state must preserve the good functioning of the market and support companies whose problems would negatively impact the entire economy.

CHAPTER 9

Neoliberalism in Japanese Agri-Food

A Systemic Crisis

Introduction

In justifying the relevance of their study of neoliberalism in Japanese agri-food, Iba and Sakamoto (2014) stress the limited availability of English language studies on this topic. Their point reflects a broader effort of the Japanese scientific community to overcome two key tendencies of the local academia. The first, and arguably more general, refers to the practice of confining debates about domestic issues almost exclusively to circles of Japanese scholars using Japanese as the language of communication. The second, and more scientific in nature, regards the adoption of approaches in which the evolution of Japanese agri-food is placed not only in the context of discussions about domestic development, but also in terms of a trajectory of development that is supposed to follow a path similar to that of the manufacturing sector based on increased production and productivity. In essence, the conditions of Japanese farming and fishing are observed as, and explained in terms of, the delay in—or lack of—capitalist development that has characterized these sectors.

However, the growing international availability of information and analyses about Japanese agri-food provides countermoves to these tendencies and elements for the scrutiny of interesting and timely subjects concerning this country and society. One of these themes is the introduction of Neoliberalism to a society and a sector (agri-food) that have historically displayed significant differences from the societies and cultures where this way of thinking and the resultant political proposal originated (that is, North America and Western Europe). As the previous chapters illustrated, historically and contingently, Japan lacks the socioeconomic tradition and cultural traits that make the adoption of Neoliberalism and its translation into functional political measures readily available options. In this concluding chapter, it is our objective to illustrate the systemic limits of the adoption of neoliberal measures in the Japanese agri-food sector. The point we wish to underscore is the incompatibility of Neoliberalism with the conditions that define Japanese agri-food.

The broader debate on the Japanese economy and society is characterized by a dominant view that identifies the reasons for existing problems in the unwillingness or inability of actors in the Japanese socioeconomic system to fully embrace Neoliberalism and to adapt to the requirements of globalization. More nuanced analyses, however, underscore positions that, while divergent, escape the monolithic posture that identifies Neoliberalism as the solution to all problems. At one pole of this spectrum is the thesis of "institutional obsolescence" (for example, Garside 2014). This view sees in the very sociocultural and structural elements that characterized Japan's catch-up growth period the primary impediments to the contemporary adoption of effective development strategies. The Japanese postwar plan comprised a unique blueprint centered on solidarity among the social parts, the sharing of common objectives, and consensus on the instruments to achieve them. This was a recipe for growth that departed from the American and European Fordist goal of limiting the unwanted consequences of capitalism and focused on attaining and maintaining a significant presence in the international market of selected consumer goods. The inability of Japanese institutions to abandon attachment to this model, this thesis contends, represents the condition that not only prevented the successful adoption of Neoliberalism but also the implementation of other—and certainly more desirable—models.

At the other end of the spectrum, we can locate positions that identify in the very attempt to introduce neoliberal measures the source of problems for Japan (for example, Lechavalier 2014). According to this view, Neoliberalism not only worsened the socioeconomic conditions of many segments of Japanese society but also made established forms of coordination of the economy and society obsolete. Regulations based on market mechanisms alone proved themselves inadequate to reinvigorate the economy and reorganize society. Simultaneously, they failed to solve those very structural problems—such as the persistence of inefficient firms—that were identified as the issues that Neoliberalism could efficiently address. Denouncing the view that posits neoliberal globalization as a "natural" event, this position calls for the recognition of the negative impacts engendered by this process and its associated policies. According to both these views, however, the problems of contemporary Japan remain, to varying degrees, connected to the social organization of the postwar growth system and the cultural and organizational features that it entailed. These elements not only have become so entrenched in Japanese society, but also enjoy a legitimating power (they are considered naturally fitting to that society), and alternatives are difficult to contemplate.

Clearly, the agri-food sector is only a portion of society. Therefore, discussions about the overall evolution of the economy and society of Japan cannot be directly applied to the sectorial dimension represented by agri-food. Simultaneously, however, the evidence and discussion introduced in the previous chapters allow us to speak to the overall debate on the application of Neoliberalism and its consequences at the level of agri-food. Those observations also allow us to employ agri-food as an example of the types of issues that contemporary Japan is facing. In this context, it is important to recall that in the previous chapters, we documented the introduction of neoliberal measures as an attempt to address the crisis and contradictions of agri-food. We also illustrated the manner in which the introduction of these measures is actually a process of neoliberalization whereby they are resisted and often modified by this resistance. The neoliberalization of agri-food was accelerated after the 2011 tsunami and earthquake disasters, and the devastating events that followed were the catalyst to further neoliberalize the sector. We also illustrated the resistance that Neoliberalism engendered at the local level and its cultural incompatibility with traditional traits dominant in agricultural and fishing communities.

In the remainder of this chapter, we stress the relevance of agri-food in the overall post–World War II growth model. We argue that it was because, rather than in spite of, the less "advanced" status of farming and fishing that the impressive success of the Japanese socioeconomic model was possible. In this context, we offer a reading of the sector that emphasizes the totality of the socioeconomic evolution of the country. In the following section, we approach the theme of the systemic crisis of Japanese agri-food. We briefly state that the conditions that made farming and fishing functional during the postwar growth period turned into contradictions in the following decades. By presenting a succinct review of the basic tenets of Neoliberalism, we illustrate their incompatibility with the more collectivist, cooperative, and communally-based practices and culture of rural Japan. Dwelling on Habermas's concept of crisis of legitimation, we propose a reading of the current situation in terms of crises of social integration and system integration, in which the incompatibility between the local culture and practices based on the neoliberal approach creates contradictions that cannot be addressed through available instruments. In the concluding session, we review recent events that translated the broader dissatisfaction with the implementation of neoliberal measures into the introduction of a new course of economic policy by Prime Minister Shinzo Abe (policy known as

"Abenomics"). However, the economic policy selected for the agri-food sector follows a distinct neoliberal path that reproduces the same problems of recent years. We conclude that while evaluations of Abenomics are premature at best, its problematic nature leaves little optimism for a future in which the aspirations of farmers and fishermen are fulfilled.

Systemic Dimension of Japanese Agri-Food

In our review of the evolution of agri-food (see chapter 2), we documented the position of this sector in the overall Japanese postwar model of development. This model's success was made possible by factors that promoted the effective export of manufacturing goods. Simultaneously, it was also made possible by the contributions of the agri-food sector. In the postwar model, farming and fishing represented reservoirs of affordable labor for the expanding urban export-oriented sectors. Additionally, while investment in, and processes of modernization of, farms and fisheries did not occur at a sustained pace, these sectors provided food and raw material for urban workers, city dwellers, and industry, representing important outlet markets for chemical and mechanical products, and through trade concessions they played an important role in the favorable shaping of international commercial relations (Teruoka 2008). In essence, the limited and, arguably, distorted development of farming and fishing was ultimately functional to the overall expansion of the Japanese economy and society.

To be sure, the contradictory aspect of this type of functionality was evident in the existing literature (see chapter 1). Yet, this way of reasoning is a reminder of the importance of achieving equilibrium in processes that expand social formations. The stable evolution of society requires the maintenance of a normative structure that engenders mass loyalty and the availability of a system of social control that counts on instruments contained within the organizational principles of society (Habermas 1975; Luhmann 2013; Parsons 1968 [1937]).[1] In the case of the rapid postwar economic growth period, mass loyalty and the support for the existing normative system were maintained through a set of measures that were both economic and social. They legitimized the Japanese model of development by engendering popular support and providing effective responses to emerging problems. In other words, as per Habermas, the system could find solutions to extant issues by mobilizing instruments that were accepted as appropriate and considered within the limits of the resources available. At the economic level, one of the most effective of these instruments was the transfer of resources from the manufacturing and urban sectors and regions to rural areas (Garside 2014; Teruoka 2008). This transfer of resources allowed the containment of the negative consequences of slow rates of development in rural regions and the persistence of traditional farms and fishing operations. Additionally, efforts that strengthened the growth of stable jobs in urban areas and sectors on one hand, and established part-time or off-farm employment in rural areas and sectors on the other, represented phenomena that were seen as addressing disequilibria associated with the economic growth of the nation. These were viewed as effective and compensatory factors that explained the declining family income of agriculturalists and fishermen and delayed or limited opportunities for labor to exit these sectors (Lechavalier 2014; Ohkawa, Johnston, and Kaneda 1970). In this context, the rural (farming and fishing) to urban (industrial production and the service sector) migration was understood as a traumatic yet needed and, ultimately, positive step toward the development and economic prominence of the country (Ohkawa, Johnston, and Kaneda 1970).

Socially, stability was strengthened through a management-labor accord that involved a set of fundamental and culturally specific characteristics. These characteristics included the participation of labor in decisionmaking processes and the strengthening of practices that emphasized the creation of consensus. In urban industrial settings, this objective was accomplished through the implementation of "companism"—or the alliance between wage earners and managers that promoted the well-being of firms (see chapter 2). In contrast to the cases of other advanced societies of the time, companism consisted of intrafirm solidarity and collaboration. Its applications were specific to each company and mandated a more direct interaction between managers and workers and solidarity within the firm (Lechavalier 2014). In rural settings, solidarity and collaboration were pursued through the practice of established culturally based behavioral patterns that foster cooperation; reciprocity; and ultimately, consensus in the making of community-relevant decisions (see chapters 6 and 7; Scott 1979). The practice of these culturally based behavioral patterns of community solidarity remained strong throughout the postwar growth years and beyond but was challenged by Neoliberalism.

The importance of local communities and their participation in the process of socioeconomic growth was supported by post–World War II legislation that defined the development of farming and fishing. The various and fundamental legislative measures of the time (Land Reform; Agricultural Land Act; Agricultural Basic Law; Fisheries Law) stressed the centrality of family holdings and limited corporate presence. While recurrent moves attempted to change these arrangements, the desirability of family-run operations and the centering of decisionmaking processes at the community level remained fundamental tenets in the cultural and political panorama of Japan. Moreover, the administration and management of resources through cooperatives reinforced the notion of the desirability of decisions made collectively with the consensus of community members. This situation stands in contrast to conditions that defined the growth of similar sectors in other advanced societies, such as the United States, where neither legislative measures nor cultural characteristics of this type were dominant.

Following Habermas (1975), these characteristics of farming and fishing in the postwar growth period allowed the "subjective" recognition of the validity of the model proposed (social integration) on the part of the members of the Japanese society. Moreover, they gained "objectivity" as unresolved problems were addressed in a manner that allowed the reproduction of the system (system integration). In this respect, the abovementioned view of the evolution of agri-food in terms of its limited capitalist development and preservation of weak productive structures can be contrasted with our interpretation that perceives in the totality of the mechanisms of social stability and reproduction the explanation of the evolution of agri-food.

The contradictions contained in this developmental model, rather than being dismissed as either irrelevant or weak, assume a significant role, as they are indications of the ability of dominant actors to mobilize steering mechanisms that controlled them (Habermas 1975, 7). In this context, it is (partially) "because," rather than "despite," of farming and fishing that the growth period of Japan was possible and that the legitimation of its model of development was achieved. Moreover, it can be proposed that the contemporary crisis of agrifood is not a simply a sectorial crisis. It is, instead, a systemic crisis, because the system of economic growth and social stability proposed through the introduction of neoliberal measures is failing at the levels of social integration (lack of acceptance of the proposed model) and system integration (lack of availability of effective steering mechanisms).

Systemic Crisis of Japanese Agri-Food

Changed Historical Conditions

One of the primary conclusions reached with virtual unanimity by the pertinent literature on the socioeconomic development of Japan since the 1990s is the globalization of the economy and society and the transnational forms of capital accumulation that characterized it and made the nation-state-centered

Japanese postwar model obsolete (Bailey, Coffey, and Tomlinson 2007; Hamada, Kayshap, and Weinstein 2011; Holroyd and Coates 2011). It was not simply the export-led aspect of this model that was made ineffective, but also the cultural patterns that supported it (Garside 2014; Lechavalier 2014). The culture of companism that characterized the Japanese management-labor accord, along with the interplay of the national bureaucracy and corporate leadership, became arrangements that could hardly fit the conditions of globalization. As indicated in chapter 2, these changes reflected a global power struggle in which prominent nation-states (chiefly the United States) and corporations promoted the creation of transnational networks of production and consumption and the adoption of market-opening neoliberal postures (Harvey 2005a; Robinson 2004). In this context, U.S.-led international political moves to curtail the effectiveness of the Japanese export model, combined with Japanese corporate strategies for plant relocations and decentralization of production to foreign countries, contributed to the global reorganization of economic relations (Garside 2014; Holroyd and Coates 2011).

As Japanese firms became transnational corporations and nation-state-based Fordist strategies were replaced by neoliberal policies, farming and fishing ceased to play those important roles that they performed in the postwar growth model. First, the crisis of the 1990s marked the end of the "functionality" of the flow of labor from rural to urban areas. The crisis-induced industrial restructuring involved not only the contraction of employment but also its *contractualization:* stable jobs were replaced by short-term, precarious, and often part-time employment. This had the delegitimizing effect of putting an end to the expectation and practice that rural outmigration would translate into stable and better-paid urban employment. Second, the organization and development of agri-food could no longer be employed as (1) instruments to support the expansion of manufacturing and (2) factors to be employed in international negotiations to benefit the export sector. In the postwar growth model, price-support programs, import restrictions, and the overall protection of the agri-food sector contributed to the creation of stable levels of income for farmers, the availability of locally produced food, and the outflow of labor from the sector. As indicated in chapter 2, these were all conditions that contributed to the postwar socioeconomic expansion. Additionally, with the expansion of the industrial export sector, concessions concerning the agri-food sector were employed to maintain favorable conditions for the manufacturing sector. Under neoliberal globalization and following the liberalization of agri-food production, the sector lost this characteristic.

The question that this analysis logically begs is about the capability of neo-liberal instruments to allow farming and fishing to maintain acceptable levels of social integration and system integration. As the traditional role of agri-food in the context of the overall Japanese social formation is exhausted, can the possibilities of problem solving be found in the principle of Neoliberalism? Using the evidence presented in the previous chapters, the remaining portion of this chapter explores this question through a brief review of the ideological tenets of Neoliberalism and the socioeconomic conditions that emerged for its application.

The Neoliberal Proposal

Ideologically, Neoliberalism is discussed and promoted not only as an effective economic policy but also as a social policy. For the case of agriculture, the tenets and desirability of Neoliberalism have been reviewed by classical proponents of this theory, such as Milton Friedman ([1962] 1982) and F. A. Hayek ([1960] 2011). Colleagues at the University of Chicago in the 1950s[2] and advisors of major neoliberal political leaders,[3] Friedman and Hayek illustrated the superiority of Neoliberalism,[4] the desirability of individualism,[5] and the limits of state intervention and any form of collectivism in agriculture. In his *Capitalism and Freedom*, Friedman ([1962] 1982, 177) criticizes what he terms "social welfare measures" to demonstrate the ineffectiveness of policies inspired by humanitarian and equalitarian sentiments and attempts to control undesirable consequences of the functioning of the market. He considers farm price-support programs among the clearer examples of the distortions induced by state intervention. Stressing the importance of the impersonality of the market, he portrays state intervention as the outcome of the working of special interests and, accordingly, an inherently unequal and discriminatory process. In his view of the case of agriculture in the United States, state intervention is the result of the overrepresentation of rural districts in the electoral system and Congress and the mistaken belief that farmers have a lower than average income (Freidman [1962] 1982, 181).

His argument goes like this. First, small farms sell less than large farms do. Additionally, this difference is augmented by the fact that poorer farmers produce a greater quantity of products for self-consumption, which are excluded from price support programs. Because they are based on production, these types of programs advantage large farms over small ones and contribute to the creation of income inequality in farming. Second, the benefits that farmers receive are much smaller than the expenses incurred. The latter may include those for storage and the purchase of additional farm inputs (fertilizers, machines, and so forth) that are induced by participation in these programs. In this respect, suppliers of storage facilities and input providers—but not farmers—are those who may benefit the most. Finally, rather than achieving the desired objective of increasing farmers' incomes, price-support programs keep people on the farm, increase the quantity of farm production, and force farmers to face a centralized form of control on what and how much they can produce.

Friedman maintains that the negative consequences of price-support programs are multifaceted and are felt by consumers, the country, and also foreign producers. Consumers suffer the consequences of this form of state intervention by paying higher food prices and the taxes required to finance these initiatives. The countries are left with a larger bureaucracy and international problems. In fact, protectionist policies associated with price-support programs increase world prices that induce farmers (domestically and internationally) to increase production. As domestic overproduction is released into the international market, prices collapse, with detrimental effects on international producers that were encouraged by altered market signals to expand output. This process creates diplomatic difficulties for countries, such as the United States, that are viewed as engendering problems for other, less developed, countries (Friedman [1962] 1982, 182).

Paralleling Friedman's argument, in his *The Constitution of Liberty*, Hayek ([1960] 2011) insists on the distortions generated by price-support programs. Dismissing problems associated with rural to urban migration, the sociocultural importance of farmers' attachment to their land and way of life, and issues associated with food sovereignty, Hayek contends that the reduction of the size of the agricultural population is a must in all societies that aspire to continue on the road to modernity and development. This is particularly the case if the improvement of farmers' income levels is to be achieved (Hayek [1960] 2011, 482). He contends that price-support programs and protectionist policies promote the reluctance of farmers and peasants to leave farming. In fact, policies that prevent the outflow of workers from agriculture created problems of such a magnitude that solutions have been very difficult to find. Also agreeing with Friedman, he claims that the assertion that the agricultural population is unable to earn a reasonable income is inaccurate. It is only the least productive farmers that cannot earn an adequate income (Hayek [1960] 2011, 483). Accordingly, price-support programs must be abandoned in favor of the free fluctuation of agri-food commodity prices.

Remaining silent on the social consequences of the collapse of agricultural prices, he maintains that price adjustments must be allowed even if they were to fall much below existing levels. If prices are not allowed to adjust, the reduction of the agricultural population and technological innovation will not occur. Similarly, disregarding problems associated with food shortages, he argues that the elimination of marginal land and the reduction of the food supply are necessary parts of the adjustment process. Ultimately, he contends, adaptation means that farmers must become businesspersons, and if this process is not allowed to develop, the "alternative for the agricultural population would be to become more and more a sort of appendage to a national park, quaint folk preserved to people the scenery, and deliberately prevented from making the mental and technological adjustments that would enable them to be self-supporting."(Hayek [1960] 2011, 487). In essence, Hayek's contention is that state intervention in agriculture and protectionist policies either are motivated by romantic and nostalgic feelings about a bucolic past that no longer exists or are conditions that can be successful only in a command economy. Both these circumstances, he argues, have very little to do with economic rationality and should be avoided.

For Friedman and Hayek, the superiority of the free functioning of the market over any form of "intelligent design" is ultimately based on the impersonality of the market and the overcoming of the imperfect knowledge associated with any group of experts. Because the market cannot be affected by any individual decision, it is free from manipulations by special interests. Conversely, state intervention is always the subject of political designs that tend to generate distorted and often unjust outcomes. Additionally, state intervention is based on the opinions of experts who, regardless of their level of knowledge, cannot know all the factors that affect economic outcomes. This is not the case for the free functioning of the market. In the free market, the formation of prices allows the inclusion of all relevant phenomena. In essence, the impersonality of market outcomes is, in the neoliberal proposal, always superior to objectives that are decided at the political level. As in the case of state-sponsored protectionist policies, the desired goal of improving the economic conditions of farmers is not only unmet, but it is accompanied by such distortions as the persistence of unprofitable farms, underemployed labor, and overproduction.

The popular appeal of the argument about the impersonality of markets is at the origins of the success of Neoliberalism. Even critics of this ideology, such as Habermas (1975), recognize that as Fordism experienced its final crisis, the strength of the neoliberal proposal derived from calls for solutions that present themselves as independent of specific political views (Habermas 1975, 22). They are based on the classical idea of "exchange of equals" that defined early bourgeois discourses against seigniorial privileges and authority. Because the market is formed by the actions of equals that freely exchange goods and services with no constrictions and limitations, market outcomes are superior to other arrangements and embody the desirability of the functioning of a free society (Habermas 1975, 22). For Friedman, Hayek, and likeminded neoliberals, individualism and economic rationality are far superior to arrangements based on moral economy and substantive rationality. Dismissing the charge that all decisions are ultimately political, in this construct, solidarity is achieved through the recognition of individual freedom and the individual's ability to pursue the maximization of his/her interests while respecting those of others. It is the maintenance of the free exchange among equals that defines the rightness and desirability of outcomes.

In this construction, collaboration and consensus are derived exclusively from market exchanges; excluded are all other forms of cooperation, including those that defined the development of Japanese agricultural communities as previously described. As illustrated by Hayek ([1960] 2011, 491–493), the management and exploitation of natural resources should be based exclusively on the economic interests of their users and not on conservation- and community-based goals. It is through the rapid use of these resources that new resources are discovered. As existing resources become scarce, their cost will increase, and incentives to use alternative resources or technology will emerge, leading to the availability of more resources and technology. Attacking conservationist projects as irrational, Hayek contends that the history of the development of capitalism shows the inadequacy of conservationist propositions and views that call for a balanced use of natural resources. He writes, "Industrial development would have been greatly retarded if sixty or eighty years ago the warning of the conservationists about the threatening exhaustion of the supply of coal had been heeded; and the internal combustion engine would have never revolutionized transport if its use had been limited to the known supplies of oil (during the first few decades of the era of the automobile and the airplane the known resources of oil at the current rate of use would have been exhausted in ten years)" (Hayek [1960] 2011, 493).

Employing the work of American neoliberals,[6] Michel Foucault (2004) contends that Neoliberalism involves the processes of economization of society, politics, and the individual (Dean 2010; Rose 1996). The economization of society refers to processes whereby the organization of social relations is transferred from the state to the market. Market relations and profitability become the core conditions for desirable social arrangements. In this context, the distinction is erased between society regulated and governed by the actions of the state and the economy defined by the search for profit and the satisfaction of individual interests. Accordingly, market-based rationality becomes the entity that regulates the entire society. In the economization of politics, political institutions employ "economic rationality" and operate in a corporate-like manner. Simultaneously, corporations take up charges that once were assigned to the state and regulate matters (such as ethics and morality) that once were the exclusive prerogative of the state (Ronen 2008). The displacement of the state as the political regulatory authority allows corporations to assert greater power in defining rules of regulation, as what is good for profit becomes automatically good for society (Bonanno and Cavalcanti 2014) and control is shifted to those close to the problem (Busch 2014). The economization of the individual refers to processes whereby individual actors assume moral responsibility for their actions ("responsibilization") (Ronen 2008). Dismissing structural constraints and power relations, individuals are seen as endowed with the ability to define their actions. Moreover, solutions to problems are increasingly assigned to the individual sphere (individualization). As indicated by Bourdieu (1998), individualization weakens or abolishes "collective standards or solidarities." In this context, the struggle for the creation of a better agri-food system is placed in the actions of responsible individual consumers.

Historical Level

The neoliberal ideology illustrated above inspired the restructuring of Japanese agri-food. State intervention in support of commodity prices, family holdings, and rural and community development was drastically reduced and, in many instances, eliminated. Yet state intervention did not disappear; it was redirected toward the support of corporations and their initiatives.[7] As a result, while wealth redistribution policies were significantly curtailed, political and financial moves that favored a greater corporate presence in agri-food and the establishment of new forms of regulation characterize the twenty-first-century role of the Japanese state. Arguably, important defining aspects of this new role of the state are the introduction of pro-corporate legislation, the establishment of SEZs and SZRs in the areas affected by the 2011 disasters, and reduced state oversight in the sector. While resistance persists and actual outcomes do not often match original expectations, the neoliberalization of Japanese agri-food continues. In this context, policies that support the search for corporate profit, deregulation, and private initiative as solutions of existing problems define the current state of affairs. Farming, fishing, and their communities have been transformed from spaces of residence and production into loci in which economic revitalization translates into corporate investment and acquisition of financial assets. Moreover, the existence of farming and fishing as simultaneously economic activities and ways of life is increasingly challenged by designs and practices in which their commodification and financialization are promoted as the desired final objectives.

Despite emphatic pronouncements about being the solution to existing problems, Neoliberalism in agri-food engenders results that often contradict expectations. The lack of correlation between corporate profit and community socioeconomic development has emerged as one of the most evident of these outcomes. Corporate investment in Japanese agri-food has not created jobs that matched expectations and promises. To be sure, employment has been created. But these jobs are few in number and are often part-time, precarious, and staffed by marginal workers that, in some cases, even come from other communities. The increasing precariousness of labor continues unabated in rural Japan. As in other cases recorded globally, corporate hypermobility plays a fundamental role in the relationship between investment and community well-being. The fact that the liberalization of markets allows increased mobility of capital creates opportunities for corporations to select areas and labor pools in ways that satisfy their needs. In this context, local labor is confronted with competition from other, often distant, labor pools that pit equally deserving workers against one another. As issues arise, corporations can relocate investment with relative ease. It follows that communities either permit the poorly compensated exploitation of their labor and natural resources or become sites of corporate disinvestment in favor of more "convenient" locations. Under these conditions, opposition remains difficult, politically weak, and poorly organized. Yet it continues to be practiced and finds grounds for development in the incompatibility between the neoliberal proposal and the local way of life. These trends occur despite the involvement of the state, which has shifted its intervention from the task of supporting socioeconomic development to that of backing profit seeking.

To be sure, the task of increasing the economic competitiveness of Japanese farming and fishing is a difficult one. The number of large farms remains low, land consolidation has not proceeded at an adequate pace, and investment has been inadequate. Moreover, the high value of the yen has made agricultural exports less competitive in the world market. Accordingly, most Japanese farms and fishing operations can hardly compete in the current market, making the revitalization of Japanese agri-food an uphill battle. Yet this scenario is congruent with reality if the type of market competition envisioned by neoliberal theory is the selected option. Other possible "realities" could be practiced. These are those alternative agri-food production practices, such as civic agriculture, community farming (*teikei*), and organic farming, whose development is more compatible with local current conditions and resources. But they remain largely unpracticed and unsupported by mainstream policies. In effect, it is not news that the historical development of Japanese agri-food has produced a less than competitive sector. It is equally evident that the proposal of achieving economic growth through participation in open competition requires complex economic reforms and radical social changes. Arguably, these reforms and changes cannot take place without significantly disruptive and largely unwanted social consequences. In essence, these structural conditions make neoliberal restructuring and calls for supporting behaviors based on the economization of the social and individual spheres problematic.

Most of the literature and discussions about Japanese agri-food focuses on the productive dimension of this sector and its perceived inadequacies with respect to advanced models of production. Inadequate attention, however, is paid to the important cultural issues associated with the lives and production practices of farmers and fishermen. The narration of the cases and instances presented in the previous chapters provides an illustration of the relevance of these cultural dimensions. The neoliberal measures that govern agri-food and promote its productivist restructuring call for self-help and postures that make responsibilization a key component of this process. In contrast, local rural residents seek community solidarity through the established practices of creating cooperation and achieving consensus in decisionmaking. Rather than the logic of the market and the economization of politics, society, and the individual, members of Japanese farming and fishing communities employ a different form of rationality that is group centered and collectivist in nature. This type of behavior has historically characterized their existence and was pivotal in the postwar growth period. The essence of this cultural incompatibility rests on the individualistic and utilitarian essence of Neoliberalism and its lack of suitability for the cultural requirements of Japanese farming and fishing communities.

Largely missing are the structural components that would promote a change in cultural patterns. Despite its overt structural functionalist character, classical modernization theory stresses that changes in culturally based attitudes and behaviors are fundamental components of the transformation of traditional societies into modern ones. However, these changes must be promoted by interventions—often through educational programs promoted by the state—that create the conditions for the emergence of reformed cultural behaviors (Parsons 1971; Rostow 1960). Similarly, radical theories of society and social change converge on the fundamental importance of the existence of structural conditions that promote cultural change (Brewer 1980). In the case of farming and fishing communities in Japan, these structural conditions are largely lacking. The state-directed transfer of resources—that throughout the second portion of the twentieth century contributed to buffering the unwanted consequences of the evolution of agri-food—has come to a virtual halt in the twenty-first century. Investment in infrastructure, the provision of services, and requalification programs have been discontinued by a retreating state or left to self-help initiatives. Schemes that control and regulate the outmigration of young members of farming and fishing communities are either lacking or inefficient. In essence, while neoliberal culture is promoted, the structural conditions that would allow its diffusion, performance, and, therefore, acceptance are lacking or weak at best.

Crisis of System Stability

The lack of cultural compatibility between the individualism-based neoliberalism and the group-oriented, collectivist culture of rural Japan—along with the results that the introduction of Neoliberalism produced in farming and fishing—can be read in terms of a crisis of system stability. Similarly to the case of the end of the systemic compatibility of agriculture and fishing with the old postwar growth model illustrated earlier in this chapter, there is incompatibility between the role and behaviors sought for agri-food by the applications of Neoliberalism and the socioeconomic conditions of the sector and its people. Following Habermas (1975), it can be maintained that Neoliberalism in farming and fishing lacks social integration: that is, there is a lack of recognition of the validity of the model proposed among those touched by this proposal. Farmers and fishermen reject the pro-corporate market reforms that characterize the first two decades of this century, even though they live and cope with the transformations that took place in these years. Certainly, this opposition has been weak and often poorly organized. It has also been mitigated by the entrenched institutional loyalty so typical of rural cooperative and farmers' organizations. Yet the lack of support and the dissatisfaction that local rural residents express is clear. The neoliberal proposal clashes with the ways in which farming and fishing have been locally practiced and understood. Called to reorganize their behavior and outlook on their way of life, agriculturalists and fishermen find themselves without the desire or conditions to change and meet the new requirements. The trading of behaviors seeking consensus and cooperation for those based on utilitarian individualism does not meet expectations, and market mechanisms and their results appear unconvincing to residents. Additionally, while disagreement and opposition can be and are tolerated within social systems, the incompatibility of Neoliberalism with the structural and cultural conditions of rural Japan makes the practice of this type of behavior difficult to foresee for the future.

Also following Habermas, system integration appears similarly problematic. Farming and fishing remain secondary in the overall economic development of Japan. While they experienced change along with the entire economy, this secondary position has not been altered. Additionally, it is unlikely to be modified in the short and medium term, given not only the sizes of the manufacturing, finance, and service sectors and their contributions to the country's GDP and employment, but also their political influence and the special interests associated with them. Without diminishing their economic importance, the relevance of Japanese farming and fishing rests on their social dimensions. This is not only related to the social importance of the production and consumption of food. But it also refers to the social equilibria involving an aging but still relatively large rural population and the existence of entire rural communities whose persistence is important from several points of view. Additionally, these groups are directly or indirectly connected to the management of natural resources, the safeguard of natural and built environments, the preservation of culture, and a host of other socially relevant functions.

Because its social importance, the role that agri-food performs cannot be simply reduced to production, and, above all, it cannot be framed simply in terms of market relations. Accordingly, the social relevance of Japanese farming and fishing involves important incompatibilities with the productivist push of Neoliberalism and the corporatization of social relations that the latter proposes. Twenty years of neoliberal reforms and their acceleration after the 2011 disasters generated many changes but did not create a competitive, efficient, and productive sector. In effect, it is hard to imagine, even for the most fervent supporters of the neoliberal proposal, a Japanese agri-food system that is globally competitive and has costs of production that rival those from much more productively efficient regions of the world.

Moreover, as indicated above, the neoliberal proposal for Japanese agri-food has hardly contemplated alternatives to its goal of a productively efficient, corporate-based sector. This unilateralism clashes with a situation in which a significant portion of this sector consists of family units whose presence has a high social relevance and whose economic transformation is linked to the resolution of these social problems. As market mechanisms have obtained poor results, state-sponsored transfer of resources to these communities and workers has been halted, and alternative forms of development have not been implemented; limited possibilities for solving existing problems defines the current situation.

The New Frontier: The Crisis of Neoliberalism and a (Pseudo) Neo-Fordism Proposal

The ineffectiveness of Neoliberalism in Japanese agri-food, the crisis of social integration, and the crisis of system integration were instrumental in the development of a broader national dissatisfaction with the neoliberal proposal. The level of this dissatisfaction is captured by the results of the December 2012 political elections.[8] These elections sanctioned the appointment of Mr. Shinzo Abe of the LDP to the office of prime minister of Japan (see chapter 3). Abe campaigned on a platform promoting the introduction of a new form of economic and social policy that departed from the type of Neoliberalism that has been practiced in the country. In effect, Abenomics—as this posture is commonly known—proposes a neoliberal form of governing that centered on state intervention to advance the functioning of the market (see the Introduction). While it is too early to tell whether this program will be able to address the issues affecting the Japanese economy[9] and agri-food in particular, it is important to stress that this proposal was implemented by the very LDP that has strongly advocated Neoliberalism over the past few decades. It also represents a departure from the more laissez-faire market-oriented approach employed by Abe during his pervious tenure as prime minister in 2007. These policies were resisted in rural districts, and their lack of popularity represented a key factor in the LDP's poor performance in the following political elections and loss of its position as the country's ruling party (see chapter 3).

In contrast, the new Abenomics has received some popular support. Centered on the so-called Three Arrows, it is set to address the longstanding deflation, sluggish demand, and weak wealth production through steps that contemplate state intervention. These measures are intended to increase the supply of money and generate public investment (Prime Minister of Japan and His Cabinet 2014). Yet deregulation is also being proposed, and it is aimed at promoting investment and tax abatements, the introduction of advanced technological innovations, and incentives for the increased use of marginal labor segments (such as women and young workers, as well as the elderly). Considering these terms, Abenomics seems to be an example of Neoliberalism as described by its classic texts. Abe's victory in the 2014 elections provided the administration with a stronger mandate to continue this policy.

In the case of farming and fishing, Abenomics has also maintained a neoliberal posture. Downplaying the importance of the problems and characteristics of small family operations, their position in the global economy, the conditions of rural labor, and its appeals for stable and better remunerative employment, agri-food Abenomics calls for a productivist posture designed to strengthen the competitiveness of production units. The achievement of this goal is proposed through the implementation of state-led structural reforms that over a 10-year period beginning in 2013 should allow Japanese agri-food to become world competitive and to increase exports. Planned structural adjustments include the restructuring of price-support programs (such as the gradual elimination of rice-support programs but also the introduction of new subsidies for such crops as wheat, soybeans, and rice for feed). They also include the creation of direct payment programs for the maintenance of multifunctionality in agriculture; the increase in the number of farm operators[10] (including corporations, entrepreneurial farmers, and community-based farm organizations) to reach 50,000[11] by 2023; and the consolidation of farmland and increase in the size of farms through the creation of Farmland Accumulation Banks that would collect land from retired farmers and make it available to existing operators. Under these reforms, the authority of agricultural committees[12] would be diminished, and farmers would not be able to elect the members of these committees. The direct election of committee members by farmers was one of the democratizing dimensions that characterized the agricultural committees since their inception after World War II. The 50,000 farm operators that (according to the plan) would populate Japanese farming in 2023 will work 80 percent of all farmland. Costs of production will be lower and productivity higher. Additionally, the quantity and perhaps the rate of corporate investments will be also higher (Prime Minister of Japan and His Cabinet 2014).

A reform of agricultural committees is part of the proposal made by the Council for Regulatory Reform, an Abe advisory body. Accordingly, land trade will be removed from the control of these farmers' organizations and delegated to local mayors' offices. Through this move, the full liberalization of land trade would be accomplished (*Japan Agricultural Newspaper* 2014a). Moreover, the participation of nonagricultural corporations in farming and their direct ownership of farmland will constitute defining aspects of this recommended reform. Proposed changes in the functioning and role of cooperatives and the concomitant abolition of the *Zenchu*[13] will transform them from counterparts to the government into agencies of the government. The National Mutual Aid Association of Agricultural Cooperative or *Zenkyoren* will also be restructured and nationally centralized. All banking and insurance business will be removed from the local level, de facto weakening local agricultural cooperatives economically (*Japan Agricultural Newspaper* 2014b). Finally, reforms would allow nonagricultural corporations to access funds previously earmarked exclusively for farmers and fishermen (A-FIVE 2014).

As indicated above, it is premature to assess the actual outcomes of these reforms at this time. However, their direction proposes a trajectory that is neo-liberal at heart. Also in this case, faith in the power of the market is preferred to strategies that would take into consideration the overall position of agri-food in the Japanese economy and society and the sociostructural position of farmers and fishermen in the domestic and international socioeconomic contexts. In essence, rather than proposing a path of development that takes into account the reality of local agri-food, Abenomics suggests a top-down path that is inspired by an abstract neoliberal model. From this perspective, the crises of social integration and system integration are ignored in favor of a program that aims at enhancing the global competitiveness of a sector that significantly lacks the structures and the human dimensions to achieve this goal. In light of the questionable ability of these reforms to deliver a globally competitive sector and the more questionable assumption that the implementation of this neoliberal model would improve the economic and social conditions of stakeholders, the crisis of Japanese agri-food will, more likely, continue. It is time, therefore, to seriously consider alternative approaches that would dwell on the strengths of the local communities and culture and would oppose those powers that in Japan (and in the rest of the world) have dissociated food production from its historical mission of feeding people and transformed it into asset-generating and profit-making processes. The overall dissatisfaction with the application of Neoliberalism in Japan offers an opportunity for the mobilization of the political resources for such a move. Simultaneously, however, the clout of currently dominant socioeconomic forces creates a contested terrain, where the future directions of Japanese agri-food will be decided.

NOTES

1.   This is the thesis presented by Habermas (1975) in his classic text *The Legitimation Crisis.* Dwelling on the Functionalist system theories of Parsons and Luhmann, Habermas rejects the simplistic view that crises arise when "the structure of the social system allows for fewer possibilities for problem solving than are necessary to the continued existence of the system" (Habermas 1975, 2). He calls these instances "disturbances of the system integration." A crisis, in his view, includes the lack of social integration that consists of consensus on the legitimacy of the normative structure. Validity claims (that, if accepted, create legitimacy) are shared and evaluated by speaking and interacting subjects. This subjective understanding of the crisis is objectified when problems cannot be solved by employing instruments (steering mechanisms) that are contemplated by the organizational principles of society. In mature capitalism (*spät-capitalismus*), these organizational principles are defined by the intervention of the state to

direct and control the market and avoid its unwanted consequences (organized capitalism). A legitimation crisis emerges when "the legitimizing system does not succeed in maintaining the required level of mass loyalty while the imperative taken over from the economic system are carried through . . . [and] it is not possible by administrative means to establish effective normative structures to the extent required" (Habermas 1975, 46–47). For Habermas (1975, 2), "Crises in social systems [arise] through structurally inherent system-imperatives that are incompatible and cannot be hierarchically integrated." The same point, but in significantly different terms, is made by Michel Foucault (2004) through the concept of governamentality, whereby validity claims made by governing authorities are accepted in society, and this acceptance allows for the legitimate control of behavior.

2.   Friedrich A. Von Hayek joined the University of Chicago in 1952 and remained there until 1962, when he moved to the University of Freiburg in Germany. He retired in 1968. After his formal retirement, Hayek continued to work and was on the faculty at the University of California, Los Angeles, and at the University of Salzburg, Germany. He eventually returned to Freiburg, where he worked until his death in 1992 at the age of 92. Prior to his tenure at the University of Chicago, Hayek was professor at the London School of Economics (1931–1952). Friedman joined the University of Chicago in 1940 and remained there until 1977, when he moved to the Hoover Institution at Stanford University in California until his death at age 94 in 2006. Hayek and Freidman were not in the same department at the University of Chicago, but they collaborated in the promotion of Neoliberalism.

3.   Their theories have been explicitly heralded as guides for desirable political conduct by neoliberal political leaders, such as Ronald Reagan and Margaret Thatcher.

4.   Friedman's critique was primarily directed at Keynesian policies, which were dominant in the 1950s and early 1960s in the United States. In the case of Hayek, his argument was against all forms of collectivism. In essence, his polemic was aimed at all forms of "intelligent design," that is, all forms of governing that involved state planning. To be sure, Hayek allows some forms of state intervention (monetary policies, control of monopoly, and maintenance of defense and internal security), but strongly criticizes any other form of state control of the economy. The extent of this state intervention remains an unsolved problem in Hayek's theory and an item that was strongly criticized by his personal friend and intellectual opponent, John Maynard Keynes.

5.   In his *Individualism and Economic Order*, Hayek ([1948] 1980) specifically addresses the issues of individualism and its importance in Neoliberalism. For Hayek, individualism is both a theory of society and a political posture. "True individualism" needs to be distinguished from "pseudo individualism or Cartesian (rationalist) individualism." The latter refers, Hayek contends, to the mistaken idea that the rational mind of the individual can lead humans to the construction of a desirable society. True individualism is irrational and allows for the contention that society is the "unforeseen result of individual action" (Hayek [1948] 1980, 8). While Cartesian individualism leads to command societies, true individualism leads to free societies. In the same text, Hayek regards the equating of individualism with egoism as utterly false.

6.   Foucault uses the work of the social economist and Nobel Laureate Gary Becker (1930–2014) in particular to demonstrate the economization of the social and political realms that characterizes the neoliberal proposal. See Foucault (2004) and Becker ([1964] 1994).

7.   This posture is very much in line with Neoliberalism, which calls for state intervention to establish markets and through the functioning of these markets to address social needs (Crouch 2011; Mirowski 2013).

8.   Dissatisfaction with the results of the implementation of neoliberal measures, while major, should not be considered the only reason for the DPJ defeat in the elections.

9.   Data indicate some positive results from the application of the Abenomics measures. The average stock prices in the Japanese stock market increased 71 percent during the first four months of 2014, and corporate profits rose by 35 percent in 2013 compared to their levels in 2012. Much more modest gains were attained for workers and the economy in general. However, there has been an uptick in hiring, and the GDP increased by 2.6 percent in 2013. Wages have increased by 2.2 percent since the beginning of 2014, making this the highest rate of growth in the past 10 years. The employment rate for women between 25 and 44 years old reached its highest level in December 2013 at 70.9 percent. Consumption expenditures also increased in 2013 but by only 1.1 percent. This, however, represents the highest increase since 2008. In 2014, the number of bankruptcies reached its lowest level in 23 years. The yen has depreciated significantly, which translated into more favorable conditions for export industries. Simultaneously, predictions for future economic growth are gloomy and indicate that Japan will enter a period of recession (Prime Minister of Japan and His Cabinet 2014).

10.   These types of operators (*ninaite*) are viewed as efficient and competitive family farmers and corporations that, because of their productivity, deserve to be supported by agricultural policies.

11.   This proposed number is four times larger than the number of farmers in 2010.

12.   As indicated in chapter 2, agricultural committees were established after World War II as administrative entities with the objective of democratizing of farmland distribution. Agricultural committee members are elected from all farmers. Corporate supporters view this committee as an obstacle to corporate penetration of agriculture.

13.   The *Zenchu* is an independent administrative body of agricultural cooperatives that determine the policy of the cooperatives. Under the proposed reform, it would lose its ability to set policy.

REFERENCES

AUTHOR INTERVIEWS

Chapter 5

Interview. 2012a. *I Love Tome Farm. September 4, 2012.*

Interview. 2012b. *Tome City. September 5, 2012.*

Interview. 2006a. *Hokkaido Sanchoku Center. July 17, 2006.*

Interview. 2006b. *JA Kagoshima Izumi. February 15, 2006.*

Interview. 2006c. *Takaono Town, the Takaono Agricultural Committee, JA Izumi. February 15, 2006.*

Interview. 2006d. *Silver Human Resource Center of Takaono Town. February 15, 2006.*

Interview. 2006e. *East Izumi Polder Land Improvement Association. July 20, 2006.*

Interview. 2006f. *Goto City. July 18, 2006.*

Interview. 2005. *Hokkaido Sanchoku Center. July 18, 2005.*

Interview. 2004a. *Hokkaido Sanchoku Center. July 20, 2004.*

Interview. 2004b. *Mukawa Town, the Mukawa Agricultural Committee, JA Mukawa. July 21, 2004.*

Interview. 2004c. *JA Kagoshima Izumi. June 30, 2004.*

Chapter 6

Interview. 2013a. *Sendai Agricultural Cooperative. September 19, 2013.*

Interview. 2013b. *Michisaki Farm. September 18, 2013.*

Interview. 2013c. *Southern Gamo Neighborhood Association. September 18, 2013.*

Interview. 2013d. *Sendai City. September 19, 2013.*

Interview. 2013e. *Citizens' Council for Reconstruction of Sendai Eastern District. September 17, 2013.*

Interview. 2012a. *Sendai Agricultural Cooperative. October 15, 2012.*

Interview. 2012b. *Sendai City. October 15, 2012.*

Interview. 2012c. *Butai Farm. October 17, 2012.*

Interview. 2012d. *Miyagi Prefecture Citizens' Center for Support of Recovery and Reconstruction from the Great Eastern Japan Earthquake. October 16, 2012.*

Interview. 2012e. *Land Improvement District of Eastern Sendai. October 16, 2012.*

Chapter 7

Interview. 2013a. *Branch Office in Ishinomaki of Miyagi Prefecture Fisheries Cooperative. September 18, 2013.*

Interview. 2013b. *Momonoura Oyster Producers. September 18, 2013.*

Interview. 2012. *Miyagi Prefecture Citizens' Center for Support of Recovery and Reconstruction from the Great Eastern Japan Earthquake.* October 17, 2012.

PRIMARY AND SECONDARY SOURCES

Abe, Makoto. 1999. "Current Issues in Intermediate and Mountain Areas and Challenges of Regional Development." Pp. 188–206 in *Regional Development in Transition*, edited by M. Nakajima and R. Hashimoto. Kyoto: Nakanishiya (in Japanese).

AFFRC (Agriculture, Forestry and Fisheries Research Council). 2005. "Evolving Greenhouse Culture: From Large-Sized Greenhouses to Plant Factories." *Report of Research and Development on Agriculture, Forestry and Fisheries.* No. 14. Tokyo: AFFRC (in Japanese).

A-FIVE. 2014. "About Us." Retrieved at http://www.a-fivej.co.jp/corporate/outline on May 25, 2014 (in Japanese).

Aglietta, Michel. 1979. *A Theory of Capitalist Regulation.* London: New Left Books.

Agricultural Marketing Society of Japan, ed. 1999. *Studies on Modern Wholesale Markets.* Tokyo: Tsukuba Shobo (in Japanese).

———. 1996. *Agricultural Trade and Agribusiness.* Tokyo: Tsukuba Shobo (in Japanese).

Agricultural Policy Council. 1996. *Directions of Reform of Agricultural Cooperatives and Organization of Financial Business.* Retrieved at http://www.maff.go.jp/j/council/kanbo/pdf/nhoukoku.pdf on May 14, 2014 (in Japanese).

Akahata Newspaper. 2012. "IBM Japan's Evil Lockout Dismissals. Laborers Sue for Retraction." *Akahata Newspaper.* October 29 (in Japanese).

Albala-Bertrand, J. M. 2006. "Globalization and Localization: An Economic Approach." Pp. 147–167 in *Handbook of Disaster Research*, edited by Havidan Rodriguez, Enrico L. Quarantelli, and Russell L. Dynes. New York: Springer.

ALIC (Agriculture and Livestock Industries Corporation). 2011. "Trends in Vegetable Production and Shipping under the Price Stabilization System for Specified Vegetables: Tomatoes." *Vegetable Information.* Retrieved at http://vegetable.alic.go.jp/yasaijoho/senmon/1103/chosa01.html on June 21, 2013 (in Japanese).

Allinson, Gary D. 2004. *Japan's Postwar History.* Second edition. Ithaca, NY: Cornell University Press.

Allison, Ann. 2013. *Precarious Japan.* Durham, NC: Duke University Press.

Amemiya, Hiroko I. 2011. "From TEIKEI to AMAP." Pp. 314–337 in *Current Food and Agriculture*, edited by K. Ikegami and K. Harayama. Kyoto: Nakanishiya (in Japanese).

Antonio, Robert J., and Alessandro Bonanno. 2000. "A New Global Capitalism? From Americanism and Fordism to Americanization-Globalization." *American Studies* 41 (2/3): 33–77.

Asahi Newspaper. 2014. "Prime Minister's Policy: Creating Special Zones for Regional Revitalization Next Spring." *Asahi Newspaper.* December 19. Retrieved at http://www.asahi.com/articles/ASGDM3DMHGDMUTFK002.html on December 22, 2014 (in Japanese).

———. 2013. "1.2 Trillion Yen of the Reconstruction Budget Diverted Outside Damaged Areas." *Asahi Newspaper.* May 9 (in Japanese).

———. 2011. "Chairman of *Keidanren* Proposed to Settle Special Zone for Reconstruction in Tohoku Region Basing Zero Corporate Tax." *Asahi Newspaper.* April 11 (in Japanese).

Asher, David L. 1998. "What Became of the Japanese 'Miracle.'" Pp. 199–218 in *Dimensions of Contemporary Japan*, edited by E. R. Beauchamp. New York: Garland.

Bailey, David, Dan Coffey, and Phil Tomlinson, eds. 2007. *Crisis or Recovery in Japan: State and Industrial Economy.* Cheltenham and Northampton, MA: Edward Elgar.

Bailey, Paul J. 1996. *Postwar Japan: 1945 to the Present.* Oxford: Blackwell.

Bain, Carmen. 2010. "Governing the Global Value Chain: Globalgap and the Chilean Fresh Fruit Industry." *International Journal of Sociology of Agriculture and Food* 17 (1): 1–13.

Beck, Ulrich. 2009. *World at Risk.* Malden, MA: Polity Press.

Beck, Ulrich, Munenori Suzuki, and Midori Ito, eds. 2011. *Japanese Society Getting Risk: A Dialogue with Ulrich Beck.* Tokyo: Iwanami Shoten (in Japanese).

Becker, Gary. [1964] 1994. *Human Capital: A Theoretical and Empirical Analysis with Special Reference to Education.* Chicago: University of Chicago Press.

Birmingham, Lucy, and David McNeill. 2012. *Strong in the Rain: Surviving Japan's Earthquake, Tsunami, and Fukushima Nuclear Disaster.* New York: Palgrave.

Block, Fred, and Margaret R. Somers. 2014. *The Power of Market Fundamentalism. Karl Polanyi's Critique.* Cambridge, MA: Harvard University Press.

Bonanno, Alessandro. 2014a. "The Legitimation Crisis of Neoliberal Globalization: Instances from Agriculture and Food." Pp.13–31 in *The Neoliberal Regime in the Agri-Food Sector: Crisis, Resilience and Restructuring,* edited by Steven Woolf and Alessandro Bonanno. Milton Park, UK: Routledge.

———. 2014b. "Agriculture and Food in the 2010s." Pp. 3–15 in *Rural America in a Globalizing World,* edited by Conner Bailey, Leif Jensen, and Elizabeth Ransom. Morgantown: West Virginia University Press.

———. 2013. "Globalization." Pp. 21–41 in *The Handbook of Rural Development,* edited by Gary P. Green. Northampton, MA: Edward Elgar.

———. 1987. *Small Farms: Persistence with Legitimation.* Boulder, CO: Westview Press.

Bonanno, Alessandro, and Lawrence Busch, eds. 2015. *Handbook of International Political Economy of Agriculture and Food.* Cheltenham, UK: Edward Elgar.

Bonanno, Alessandro, Lawrence Busch, William H. Friedland, Lourdes Gouveia, and Enzo Mingione, eds. 1994. *From Columbus to ConAgra: The Globalization of Agriculture and Food.* Lawrence: University Press of Kansas.

Bonanno, Alessandro, and Josefa Salete Barbosa Cavalcanti, eds. 2014. *Labor Relations in Globalized Food.* Bingley, UK: Emerald.

———. 2011. *Globalization and the Time-Space Reorganization.* Bingley, UK: Emerald Publishing.

Bonanno, Alessandro, and Douglas H. Constance. 2008. *Stories of Globalization: Transnational Corporations, Resistance, and the State.* University Park: Pennsylvania State University Press.

Bourdieu, Pierre. 1998. "The Essence of Neoliberalism." *Le Monde Diplomatique.* December. Retrieved at http://mondediplo.com/1998/12/08bourdieu on November 4, 2007.

Boyd, William, and Michael Watts. 1997. "Agro-Industrial Just-in-Time: The Chicken Industry and Postwar American Capitalism." Pp. 192–225 in *Globalising Food: Agrarian Questions and Global Restructuring,* edited by David Goodman and Michael Watts. London: Routledge.

Brewer, Anthony. 1980. *Marxist Theories of Imperialism: A Critical Survey.* London: Routledge and Kegan Paul.

Brown, Wendy. 2015. *Undoing the Demos. Neoliberalism Stealth Revolution.* New York: Zone Books.

Burbach, Roger, and Patricia Flynn. 1980. *Agribusiness in the Americas.* New York: Monthly Review Press.

Burch, David, and Geoffrey Lawrence, eds. 2007. *Supermarkets and Agri-Food Supply Chains: Transformations in Production and Consumption.* Northampton, MA: Edward Elgar.

Busch, Lawrence. 2014. "How Neoliberal Myths Endanger Democracy and Open New Avenues for Democratic Action." Pp. 32–51 in *The Neoliberal Regime in the Agri-Food*

Sector: Crisis, Resilience and Restructuring, edited by Steven A. Wolf and Alessandro Bonanno. New York: Routledge.

Busch, Lawrence, and Carmen Bain. 2004. "New! Improved? The Transformation of Global Agrifood System." *Rural Sociology* 69 (3): 321–346.

Butai Agri Innovation. 2013. "About Us." Retrieved at http://www.butai-agri-innovation .co.jp/test/company.html on November 5, 2013 (in Japanese).

Butai Farm. 2013. "About Us." Retrieved at http://www.butaifarm.co.jp/company.html on November 5, 2013 (in Japanese).

Button, Gregory. 2010. *Disaster Culture: Knowledge and Uncertainty in the Wake of Human and Environmental Catastrophe*. Walnut Creek, CA: Left Coast Press.

Cabinet Secretariat. 2011. "On the Formation of the Reconstruction Design Council in Response to the Great East Japan Earthquake." Cabinet Decision. Retrieved at http:// www.cas.go.jp/jp/fukkou/pdf/kousou1/siryou1.pdf on May 27, 2013 (in Japanese).

Carolan, Michael. 2013. *Reclaiming Food Security*. New York: Routledge.

Chiba, Tsukasa. 2001. "The Establishment of WTO Regime and Liberalization of the Agricultural Sector: From GATT to WTO." Pp. 45–67 in *Globalization and International Agricultural Markets*, edited by Issin Nakano and Sugiyama Michio. Tokyo: Tsukuba Shobo (in Japanese).

Constance, Douglas H., Marie-Christine Renard, and Marta G. Rivera-Ferre, eds. 2015. *Alternative Agrifood Movements*. Bingley, UK: Emerald.

Consumer Cooperative Seikatsu Club. 2013. "Linking Again Consumers with Producers." *Seikatsu to Jichi* 529:8, 14–17.

Crouch, Colin. 2011. *The Strange Non-Death of Neoliberalism*. Cambridge: Polity Press.

Daily Tohoku. 2012. "3 Organizations of Agriculture, Forestry and Fishery Collaborate in Recommendation for Anti-TPP." *Daily Tohoku*. November 27 (in Japanese).

Dean, Mitchell M. 2010. *Governmentality: Power and Rule in Modern Society*. London: Sage.

Demura, Masaharu. 2012. "Missing Viewpoints about Special Zones for Fisheries Reconstruction." Pp. 1–6 in *Towards Reconstruction after the Great East Japan Earthquake*, edited by Norinchukin Research Institute. Tokyo: Norinchukin Research Institute. Retrieved at http://www.nochuri.co.jp/genba/pdf/otr120918.pdf on May, 14, 2014 (in Japanese).

———. 2011. "Damages in the Fishing Industry by the Great Eastern Japan Earthquake and Challenges to Reconstruction." *Norinkinyu*. August 2011 (in Japanese).

———. 2008. "Impact on the Fishery of Fuel Prices." *Norinchukin Research Institute Research and Information* 8:4–5 (in Japanese).

Dole Food Company. 2013a. "About Us." Retrieved at http://www.dole.com/Company -Info/About-Dole on June 17, 2013.

———. 2013b. "About Philosophy." Retrieved at http://www.dole.com/Company%20Info /Philosophy on June 17, 2013.

———. 2013c. "Dole Timeline." Retrieved at http://www.dole.com/Company%20Info /Timeline on June 17, 2013.

Dole Japan. 2013a. "History of Dole." Retrieved at http://www.dole.co.jp/company_info /history/his_a001.html on June 17, 2013 (in Japanese).

———. 2013b. "Dole's Domestic Vegetables." Retrieved at http://www.dole.co.jp/ilove -yasai/farm/index.html on June 17, 2013 (in Japanese).

———. 2004. "News Release: New Brand 'I LOVE' Launched." Retrieved at http://www .dole.co.jp/company_info/news/2004/news_ilove.html on June 17, 2013 (in Japanese).

Dower, John W. 1999. *Embracing Defeat: Japan in the Wake of World War II*. New York: W. W. Norton.

———. 1993. "Peace and Democracy in Two Systems: External Policy and Internal Conflict." Pp. 3–33 in *Postwar Japan as History*, edited by A. Gordon. Oxford: University of California Press.

Dumenil, Gerard, and Dominique Levy. 2011. *The Crisis of Neoliberalism*. Cambridge, MA: Harvard University Press.

Eargle, Lisa A., and Ashraf Esmail, eds. 2012. *Black Beaches and Bayous: The BP Deepwater Horizon Oil Spill Disaster*. New York: University Press of America.

Endo, Shokichi. 1966. *Postwar Japanese Economy and Society*. Tokyo: Chikuma Shobo (in Japanese).

Endo, Takeo. 2014. "Plant Factories Are the Symbol of Reconstruction." *Zen no Tomo* (July): 2–5 (in Japanese).

Energy and Capital. 2013. "Solar Investing 2013." Retrieved at http://www.energyandcapital.com/articles/solar-investing-2013/2977 on May 27, 2013.

FDMA (Fire and Disaster Management Agency). 2013. *Report on the Great East Japan Earthquake*. Tokyo: FDMA (in Japanese).

Fisheries Agency. 2012. *Damages in Fisheries*. Tokyo: Fisheries Agency. Retrieved at http://www.jfa.maff.go.jp/j/kikaku/wpaper/h23_h/trend/1/t1_1_1_2.html on March 8, 2014 (in Japanese).

———. 2011a. *Master Plan for Fishery Reconstruction*. Tokyo: Fisheries Agency. June 2011 (in Japanese).

———. 2011b. *Summary of Master Plan for Fishery Reconstruction and Updated Data*. Tokyo: Fisheries Agency. December (in Japanese).

Food System Research Association of Japan. 2012. *The Great East Japan Earthquake and Food Systems: From Recovery to Reconstruction*. Tokyo: Norin Tokei Shuppan (in Japanese).

Foucault, Michel. 2004. *The Birth of Biopolitics*. New York: Picador.

Freudenburg, William, Robert Gramling, Shirley Laska, and Kei Erikson. 2009. *Catastrophe in the Making: The Engineering of Katrina and the Disasters of Tomorrow*. Washington, DC: Island Press.

Friedman, David. 1988. *The Misunderstood Miracle: Industrial Development and Political Change in Japan*. Ithaca, NY: Cornell University Press.

Friedman, Milton. [1962] 1982. *Capitalism and Freedom*. Chicago: University of Chicago Press.

Friedmann, Harriet. 2005. "Eating in the Gardens of Gaia: Envisioning Polycultural Communities." Pp. 26–48 in *Fighting for the Farm: Rural America Transformed*, edited by Jane Adams. Philadelphia: University of Pennsylvania Press.

———. 2003. "From Colonialism to Green Capitalism: Social Movements and the Emergence of Food Regimes." Pp. 227–264 in *Research in Rural Sociology and Development*, edited by Frederick H. Buttel and Philip D. McMichael. New York: Elsevier.

———. 1994. "International Relations of Food." Pp. 174–204 in *Food*, edited by Barbara Harris-White and R. Hoffenberg. Oxford: Basil Blackwell.

Fujii, Yoichi. 2007. "Internationalization of Japanese Agricultural Policy and New Phase of Farmland Ownership and Use," Pp. 181–207 in *Globalization and Agriculture in the World*, edited by I. Nakano and T. Okada. Tokyo: Otsuki Shoten (in Japanese).

Fukuda, Tokuzo. 1924. *The Principles of Reconstruction Economy and Some Related Problems*. Tokyo: Dobunkan (in Japanese).

Fukushima, Kazue. 2013. "Damage to, and Reconstruction of, Agriculture and Rural Communities in the Eastern Area of Sendai City." Pp. 183–196 in *Reconstruction after the Earthquake and Municipality: Towards Humanitarian Reconstruction*, edited by Okada Tomohiro and Japan Institute of Local Government. Tokyo: Jichitai Mondai Kenkyu Sha (in Japanese).

Furukawa, Miho. 2014. "Shock Doctrine in Tohoku Region: Disaster Areas in Pilot Programs." *SEKAI* 855 (April): 126–135 (in Japanese).

Furusawa, Koyu. 1994. "Tei-kei: Partnership between Farmers and Consumers." *ILEIA Newsletter* 3:10–11.

———. 1989. "Life Rooted in the Rice Plant." *Resurgence* 137:20–23.

Garside, W. R. 2014. *Japan's Great Stagnation*. Cheltenham, UK, and Northampton, MA: Edward Elgar.

Gerth, Hans Heinrich, and C. Wright Mills, eds. [1948] 1998. *Max Weber: Essays in Sociology, Capitalism and Rural Society in Germany*. New York: Routledge.

Gill, Tom, Bridgette Steger, and David H. Slater, eds. 2013. *Japan Copes with Calamity: Ethnographies of the Earthquake, Tsunami and Nuclear Disaster of March 2011*. New York: Peter Lang.

Glover, David, and Ken Kusterer. 1990. *Small Farmers, Big Business: Contract Farming and Rural Development*. New York: Palgrave Macmillan.

Goto, Takuya. 2013. *Geography on Agribusiness*. Tokyo: Kokon-Shoin (in Japanese).

Goto City. 2006. *Promotion Plan for Goto's Agriculture*. Goto City (in Japanese).

Gunewardena, Nandini, and Mark Schuller, eds. 2008. *Capitalizing on Catastrophe: Neoliberal Strategies in Disaster Reconstruction*. New York: Alta Mira Press.

Habermas, Jürgen. 1975. *The Legitimation Crisis*. Translated by Thomas McCarthy. Boston: Beacon Press.

Hamada, Koichi, Anil K. Kayshap, and David E. Weinstein. 2011. *Japan's Bubble, Deflation and Long-Term Stagnation*. Cambridge, MA: MIT Press.

Hamada, Takeshi. 2013a. *Fisheries and Earthquake Disaster*. Tokyo: Misuzu Shobo (in Japanese).

———. 2013b. "Trends of Reconstruction of Disaster Areas: The Future of Special Zones for the Reconstruction of Fisheries." *Fisheries Promotion* (Tokyo Fisheries Promotion Foundation) 47 (1): 1–39 (in Japanese).

———. 2012. "Damage and Reconstruction in Fisheries by the Great Eastern Japan Earthquake." Pp. 245–284 in *Breath of Reconstruction: Reconstruction of Human and Revitalization of Agriculture, Forestry and Fisheries*. Tokyo: Nobunkyo (in Japanese).

Hannigan, John. 2012. *Disasters without Borders: The International Politics of Natural Disasters*. Malden, MA: Polity Press.

Harada, Sumitaka. 2011. "The Reform of Farmland Institutions and Its Direction." Pp. 37–67 in *Regeneration of Local Agriculture and Farmland Systems*, edited by S. Harada. Tokyo: Nobunkyo (in Japanese).

Harvey, David. 2005a. *Brief History of Neoliberalism*. Oxford: Oxford University Press.

———. 2005b. *Spaces of Neoliberalization: Towards a Theory of Uneven Geographical Development*. Stuttgart: Franz Steiner Verlag.

———. 1989. *The Condition of Postmodernity*. Oxford: Basil Blackwell.

Hasegawa, Kenji. 2003. "Aquaculture." P. 153 in *Distribution and Marketing of Food and Agricultural Products*, edited by A. Takizawa, S. Kai, M. Hosokawa, and O. Hayakawa. Tokyo: Tsukuba Shobo (in Japanese).

Hasegawa, Koichi. 2014. "The Fukushima Nuclear Accident and Japan's Civil Society: Context, Reactions, and Policy Impacts." *International Sociology* 29 (4): 283–301.

Hashimoto, Tsutomu. 2014. "Discourses on Neoliberalism in Japan." *Eurasia Border Review* 5 (2): 99–119.

Hattori, Shigeyuki. 2013. *Consequences of Neoliberalism*. Tokyo: Iwanami Shoten (in Japanese).

Hayami, Yujiro. 1988. *Japanese Agriculture under Siege: The Political Economy of Agricultural Policies*. Hampshire, UK: Palgrave Macmillan.

Hayek, F. A. [1960] 2011. *The Constitution of Liberty*. Chicago: University of Chicago Press.

———. [1948] 1980. *Individualism and Economic Order*. Chicago: University of Chicago Press.

Heffernan, William D., and Douglas H. Constance. 1994. "Transnational Corporations and the Globalization of the Food System." Pp. 29–51 in *From Columbus to ConAgra: The Globalization of Agriculture and Food*, edited by Alessandro Bonanno, Lawrence

Busch, William H. Friedland, Lourdes Gouveia, and Enzo Mingione. Lawrence: University Press of Kansas.

Helleiner, Eric. 2010. "A Bretton Woods Moment? The 2007–2008 Crisis and the Future of Global Finance." *International Affairs* 86 (3): 619–636.

Hindmarsh, Richard, ed. 2013. *Nuclear Disaster at Fukushima Daiichi: Social, Political and Environmental Issues.* New York: Routledge.

Hisano, Shuji.2002. *Agribusiness and Transgenic Crops: A Political Economy Approach.* Tokyo: Nihon Keizai Hyoron Sha (in Japanese).

Hokimoto, Ken. 2009. "The Present Situation and Problems of the FCA in Japan." *Journal of National Fisheries University* 58 (1): 53–58.

Holroyd, Carin, and Ken Coates. 2011. *Japan in the Age of Globalization.* New York: Routledge.

Hosaka, Masayasu. 1986. *Strife against the US–Japan Security Treaty in 1960.* Kodansha (in Japanese).

Hosokawa, Masashi. 2012. "How Will Wholesale Markets Be Changed? The Search for Strategies for the Ninth Improvement Program." *Agriculture and Economy* 78 (12): 5–16 (in Japanese).

Hyogo Prefecture. 2011. *Recovery after the Southern Hyogo Prefecture Earthquake in 1995.* Hyogo Prefecture. Retrieved at http://web.pref.hyogo.jp/wd33/documents/fukkyu -fukko2012-12.pdf on February 1, 2013 (in Japanese).

Iba, Haruhiko, and Kiyohiko Sakamoto. 2014. "Beyond Farming: Cases of Revitalization of Rural Communities through Social Services Provision and Community Farming Enterprises." Pp. 129–149 in *The Neoliberal Regime in Agri-Food: Crisis, Resilience and Restructuring,* edited by Steven A. Wolf and Alessandro Bonanno. New York: Routledge.

IBM Japan. 2013a. "About IBM Corporation." Retrieved at http://www-06.ibm.com/ibm /jp/about/corpo.html on July 3, 2013 (in Japanese).

———. 2013b. "History of IBM." Retrieved at http://www-06.ibm.com/ibm/jp/about /enkaku.html on July 3, 2013 (in Japanese).

———. 2013c. "Financial Performance." Retrieved at http://www-06.ibm.com/ibm/jp /about/financial/gyouseki.html on July 3, 2013 (in Japanese).

———. 2013d. "Smarter Planet." Retrieved at http://www-06.ibm.com/innovation/jp /smarterplanet/?lnk=ftf-smpl-jpja on July 5, 2013 (in Japanese).

Ichihara, Saki F. 2006. "Organic Agriculture Movement at a Crossroad: A Comparative Study of Denmark and Japan." Working paper, Department of Economics, Politics and Public Administration. Aalborg: Aalborg University.

Ichinose, Yuichiro. 2011. "Damage to Agriculture by the Great East Japan Earthquake and Challenges to Reconstruction." *Norin Kinyu* 2011 (8): 42–54 (in Japanese).

Ikeda, Satoshi. 2004. "Japan and the Changing Regime of Accumulation: A World-System Study of Japan's Trajectory from Miracle to Debacle." *Journal of World-Systems Research* 10 (2): 363–394.

Ikegami, Koichi. 2010. "Changes in the Purpose of Organic Farming and the Roles of Newly Involved Farmers in Japan." *Asian Rural Sociology* 42:500–508.

Ino, Ryuichi. 1971. "Postwar Japanese Capitalism Development and Agriculture." Pp. 37–86 in *State Monopoly Capitalism and Agriculture,* edited by R. Ino, S. Teruoka, and K. Tomishige. Tokyo: Otsuki Shoten (in Japanese).

Inoue, Kazue. 2010. *Review Report of Goto City Agricultural Committee.* Internal report, City of Goto Agricultural Committee. (in Japanese).

Iris Oyama. 2013. "About Us." Retrieved at http://www.irisohyama.co.jp/company/index .html#company09 on December 5, 2013 (in Japanese).

Ishida, Nobutaka. 2008. "Achievements and Challenges of Agricultural Cooperatives' Mergers: Taking Advantage of Extended Management Size." *Norinkinyu* (June): 6–12 (in Japanese).

Ishinomaki City. 2014a. *About Reconstruction of Ishinomaki City.* Ishinomaki, Japan: Ishinomaki City (in Japanese).

———. 2014b. "Population and Area of Ishinomaki City." Retrieved at http://www.city .ishinomaki.lg.jp/cont/10102000/0040/2204/2204.html on February 20, 2014 (in Japanese).

Isobe, Tsukuru. 1999. "Regional Development of Coastal Areas with a Focus on Fishing Villages." Pp. 207–220 in *Regional Development in Transition,* edited by M. Nakajima and R. Hashimoto. Kyoto: Nakanishiya (in Japanese).

Isoda, Hiroshi. 2001. *The U.S. Grain Industry and Agri-Food Businesses.* Tokyo: Nihon Keizai Hyoron Sha (in Japanese).

Iwamura, Takaharu. 2008. "What Will 'the Heisei Land Reform' Bring?" *Nomura Research Institute Public Management Review* 65:1–5 (in Japanese).

Iwasa, Kazuyuki. 2005. *Agricultural Development and Agribusiness in Malaysia: Light and Shadow of Export-Oriented Development.* Kyoto: Horitsu Bunka Sha (in Japanese).

———. 2004. "The Globalization of the Sea Food Market." Pp. 193–220 in *Food and Agribusiness under Globalization,* edited by S. Otsuka and T. Matsubara. Tokyo: Yuhikaku Publishing (in Japanese).

Izumi City. 2004. *Local Magazine of Izumi* 2 (in Japanese).

Izumi Farm. 2006. *Application Form for Approval of Farming Improvement Plan.* Izumi Farm (in Japanese).

———. 2002. *Articles of Incorporation.* Izumi Farm (in Japanese).

JA Goto. 2006. *Meeting Report on Broccoli Contract Farming in 2005.* Goto, Japan: JA Goto (in Japanese).

JAJA (Japan Agricultural Journalists' Association), ed. 2004. *What is the Goal of the Special Zones for Structural Reform?* Tokyo: Norin Tokei Kyokai.

Jansen, Kees, and Vellema Sietze. 2004. *Agribusiness and Society: Corporate Response to Environmentalism, Market Opportunities and Public Regulations.* London: Zed Books.

Japan Agricultural Newspaper. 2014a. "Additional Deregulations Are Discussed for Special Zones for National Strategies." *Japan Agricultural Newspaper.* May 13 (in Japanese).

———. 2014b. "Facing the Crisis of Agricultural Cooperatives' Disorganization. Council for Regulatory Reform Presented a Proposal for Agricultural Research." *Japan Agricultural Newspaper.* May 15 (in Japanese).

Japan Association of Corporate Executives. 2011. *2nd Urgent Appeal: Toward Reconstruction after the Great East Japan Earthquake Disaster.* Tokyo: Japan Association of Corporate Executives. April 6 (in Japanese).

Japan Council against Atomic and Hydrogen Bombs. 2005. *Towards the World without Nuclear Weapons: 60th Anniversary of Atomic Bombs and Movement against Nuclear and Hydrogen Bombs.* Tokyo: Japan Council against Atomic and Hydrogen Bombs (in Japanese).

Japan Economic Research Institute. 2011. *Emergency Proposal: Making the Great East Japan Earthquake Disaster a New Rebirth for Fisheries.* Research report. Tokyo: Japan Economic Research Institute (in Japanese).

———. 2007. *Hurried Strategic and Drastic Reform of the Fisheries Industry to Maintain Fish Diet.* Tokyo: Japan Economic Research Institute (in Japanese).

Japan Meteorological Agency. 2011. "Portal Site on the Great East Japan Earthquake." Retrieved at http://www.jma.go.jp/jma/menu/jishin-portal.html on May 8, 2013 (in Japanese).

Japan Press Weekly. 2012a. "170,000 Anti-nuclear Power Demonstrators Rally in Central Tokyo." *Japan Press Weekly.* July 11.

———. 2012b. "Consulting Firm Selects Corporate Recipients of Government Subsidy for Post-disaster Recovery" *Japan Press Weekly.* October 28.

Japanese Association for Rural Studies, ed. 2008. *New Developments of Green Tourism in Rural Japan: Urban-Rural Interaction as a Strategy to Revitalize Farming Areas.* Tokyo: Nobunkyo (in Japanese).

Johnson, Chalmers, ed. 1982. *MITI and the Japanese Miracle: The Growth of the Industrial Policy, 1925–1975.* Stanford, CA: Stanford University Press.

Jones Eric C., and Arthur D. Murphy, eds. 2009. *The Political Economy of Hazards and Disasters.* Lanham, MD: AltaMira Press.

Jordan, Sangeeta, and Shuji Hisano. 2011. "A Comparison of the Conventionalisation Process in the Organic Sector in Japan and Australia." *Agricultural Marketing Journal of Japan* 20:15–26 (in Japanese).

J-Power. 2013. "About J-Power." Retrieved at http://www.jpower.co.jp/company_info /about/aisatu/index.html on June 24, 2013 (in Japanese).

Jussaume, Raymond Jr. 1994a. "The Japanese Food Distribution System." Pp. 29–37 in *Understanding the Japanese Food and Agrimarket*, edited by A. Desmond O'Rourke. Binghamton, NY: Haworth Press.

———. 1994b. "An Introduction to the Japanese Juice Industry: Trading Firms, the State, and New Liberalization Policies." Pp. 160–183 in *From Columbus to ConAgra: The Globalization of Agriculture and Food*, edited by Alessandro Bonanno, Lawrence Busch, William H. Friedland, Lourdes Gouveia, and Enzo Mingione. Lawrence: University Press of Kansas.

———. 1991. *Japanese Part-Time Farming: Evolution and Impacts.* Ames: Iowa State University Press.

———. 1990. "Quality of Life Perceptions of Japanese Part-Time Farmers." *Journal of Rural Studies* 6 (3): 259–268.

Jussaume, Raymond A. Jr., and Lorie Higgins. 1998. "Attitudes towards Food Safety and the Environment: A Comparison of Consumers in Japan and the U.S." *Rural Sociology* 63 (3): 394–411.

Jussaume, Raymond A. Jr., and D. H. Judson. 1992. "Public Perceptions about Food Safety in the United States and Japan." *Rural Sociology* 57 (2): 235–249.

Jussaume, Raymond A. Jr., Shuji Hisano, and Yoshimitsu Taniguchi. 2000. "Food Safety in Modern Japan." *Japanstudien* 12:211–228.

Kagatsume, Masaru. 2007. "Economic Globalization and Agriculture: Opportunities in the East Asian Economic Partnership Agreements." Chairman's address to the 2006 Annual Meeting of the Agricultural Economics Society of Japan. *Journal of Rural Economics* 79 (2): 46–48 (in Japanese).

Kagome. 2013a. "Kagome's History: From 1960s to 1979." Retrieved at http://www.kagome .co.jp/company/about/history/1960.html on June 21, 2013 (in Japanese).

———. 2013b. "Kagome: Group Companies." Retrieved at http://www.kagome.co.jp/company/about/group.html on June 21, 2013 (in Japanese).

———. 2013c. "Kagome: About Company." Retrieved at http://www.kagome.co.jp/company/about/info/index.html on June 21, 2013 (in Japanese).

———. 2013d. "Operation on the Field." Retrieved at http://www.kagome.co.jp/hinshitsu /guide/guide01.html on June 22, 2013 (in Japanese).

———. 2013e. "Direction of Farming." Retrieved at http://www.kagome.co.jp/hinshitsu /guide/guide05.html on June 24, 2013 (in Japanese).

———. 2013f. *Securities Report 2012.* Nagoya, Japan: Kagome (in Japanese).

Kagoshima Prefecture. 2013. "The Minimum Wage in Kagoshima Prefecture." Retrieved at http://www.pref.kagoshima.jp/af04/sangyo-rodo/rodo/tokei/saitin.html on December 8, 2013 (in Japanese).

Kahoku Shinpo Newspaper. 2012. "Young Power in Tomato Production. Mr. Mamoru Kikuchi in Wakabayashi District, Sendai City." *Kahoku Shinpo Newspaper.* February 14 (in Japanese).

Kai, Satoshi. 2012. "Potentials and Conditions for Large Scale Vegetable Production Using Contractual Schemes to Employed Labor." *Vegetable Information* 99:28–39.

Kakaku.com. 2014. "Prices of Oysters from Hiroshima." Retrieved at http://kakaku.com /search_results/%89%B2%E5y+%8DL%93%87/?category=0028_0006_0002 on August 15, 2014 (in Japanese).

Kako, Toshiyuki. 2006. "Progress of Globalization and Changes in Local Agriculture." *Journal of Rural Problems* 41 (4): 6–15 (in Japanese).

Kamemoto, Kazuhiko. 2005. "Damages and Reconstruction after the Mid Niigata Prefecture Earthquake in 2004" *Issue Brief* 467:1–9 (in Japanese).

Kase, Yoshiaki. 2008. "Conversion into, and Promotion System of, 'Global Capitalism' and Restructuring Structure of Global Agricultural Issues." Pp. 1–38 in *Global Capitalism and Agriculture*, edited by Rural Issues Association of Japan. Tokyo: Tsukuba Shobo (in Japanese).

———. 1993. "Japanese Food Industries and Agri-Food Trade." Pp. 73–130 in *Issues for a Country Dependent on Imported Foodstuffs to Consider: Implications of Recent Structural Changes in the Trade of Farm Products*, edited by K. Horiguchi, T. Toyoda, Y. Yaguchi, and Y. Kase. Tokyo: Nosangyoson Bunka Kyokai (in Japanese).

Katsumata, Shizuo. 1986. *Revolt (Ikki)*. Tokyo: Iwanami Shoten (in Japanese).

Kawai, Kazushige. 2011. *The Sea Crashes*. Tokyo: Kouyou Shuppan (in Japanese).

Kawai, Tomoyasu. 1994. *Japanese Fishery*. Tokyo: Iwanami Shoten (in Japanese).

Kawamura, Yoshio. 2012. "Social Responsibility of Rural Sociologists in Japan under the Globalizing Economy." *Journal of Rural Studies* 18 (2): 1–11 (in Japanese).

Keidanren. 2012. "Proposal for the Acceleration of the Reconstruction after the Earthquake Disaster." July 9. Retrieved at https://www.keidanren.or.jp/policy/2012/047 _honbun.html on August 19, 2015 (in Japanese).

Kikkoman. 2013. "Brand Story." Retrieved at http://www.kikkoman.co.jp/corporate/about /story/delmonte.html on June 21, 2013 (in Japanese).

Kim, Anderson. 1987. "Japan's Agricultural Policy in International Perspective." *Journal of the Japanese and International Economies* 1 (2): 131–146.

Kimura, Aya Hirata. 2013. "Standards as Hybrid Forum: Comparison of the Post-Fukushima Radiation Standards by a Consumer Cooperative, the Private Sector, and the Japanese Government." *International Journal of Sociology of Agriculture and Food* 20 (1): 11–29.

———. 2010. "Between Technocracy and Democracy: An Experimental Approach to Certification of Food Products by Japanese Consumer Cooperative Women." *Journal of Rural Studies* 26 (2): 130–140.

Kimura, Aya Hirata, and Yohei Katano. 2014. "Farming after the Fukushima Accident: A Feminist Political Ecology Analysis of Organic Agriculture." *Journal of Rural Studies* 34 (1): 108–116.

Kingston, Jeff, ed. 2012. *Natural Disaster and Nuclear Crisis in Japan*. New York: Routledge.

Kishikawa, Zenko, and Kyeong Sim Park, eds. 2010. *Agribusiness*. Tokyo: Gakubun Sha (in Japanese).

Klein, Naomi. 2007. *The Shock Doctrine: The Rise of Disaster Capitalism*. New York: Picador.

Kneen, Brewster. 1995. *Invisible Giant: Cargill and Its Transnational Strategies*. London: Pluto Press.

Komai, Toru, Joseph B. Dial, Morihiro Yamauchi, and Koichi Kaku. 1999. *Agribusiness*. Tokyo: Yokendo (in Japanese).

Koshio, Kaihei. 2014. "Who Needs Plant Factories?" *SEKAI* 855:207–215 (in Japanese).

Krugman, Paul. 2013a. "As Jobs Disappear, Labor Likely to Need Safety Net." *Houston Chronicle*. June 8: B5.

———. 2013b. "Austerity Doctrine Benefits Only the Wealthy." *Houston Chronicle*. April 26: B7.

———. 2012a. *End This Depression Now.* New York: Melrose Road Partner.

———. 2012b. "Robots, Robber Barons and Labor." *Houston Chronicle.* December 11:B11.

Lawrence, Felicity. 2004. *Not on the Label.* London: Penguin.

Lechavalier, Sébastien, ed. 2014. *The Great Transformation of Japanese Capitalism.* London and New York: Routledge.

Lindhout, Gerard. 2010. "Japan Reconstituting Plant Factory Concept." Retrieved at http://www.freshplaza.com/news_detail.asp?id=61481 on May 25, 2013.

Luhmann, Niklas. 2013. *Introduction to Systems Theory.* Cambridge: Polity Press. Translated by Peter Gilgen.

Lundahl, Mats. 2013. *The Political Economy of Disaster: Destitution, Plunder and Earthquake in Haiti.* New York: Routledge.

Lupel, Adam. 2005. "Tasks of a Global Civil Society: Held, Habermas and Democratic Legitimacy beyond the Nation-State." *Globalizations* 2 (1): 117–133.

MAFF (Ministry of Agriculture, Forestry and Fisheries). 2015. "Statistics on Agriculture and Trade in Foreign Countries." Retrieved at http://www.maff.go.jp/j/kokusai/kokusei /kaigai_nogyo/pdf/area.pdf on January 7, 2015 (in Japanese).

———. 2013a. *Basic Data Book of Agriculture, Forestry and Fishery in Japan.* Retrieved at http://www.maff.go.jp/j/tokei/sihyo/index.html on March 27, 2013 (in Japanese).

———. 2013b. Website. Retrieved at http://www.maff.go.jp/j/tokei/ on February 20, 2013 (in Japanese).

———. 2013c. "Statistics on Vegetables." Retrieved at http://www.e-stat.go.jp/SG1/estat /List.do?lid=000001102731 on July 22, 2013 (in Japanese).

———. 2012a. *2011 Data Book on Wholesalers in Japan.* Retrieved at http://www.maff.go .jp/j/shokusan/sijyo/info/pdf/02genjyou.pdf on March 27, 2013 (in Japanese).

———. 2012b. *Recovery and Reconstruction of Agriculture and Fishery from the Great East Japan Earthquake.* Tokyo: MAFF (in Japanese).

———. 2012c. "Press Release on the Process and Schedule of Recovery of Farmland Damaged by the Tsunami." Retrieved at http://www.maff.go.jp/j/press/keiei/saigai/111125 .html on April 20, 2012 (in Japanese).

———. 2012d. *Questionnaire for Request of Tariff Review in 2012.* Tokyo: MAFF (in Japanese).

———. 2012e. *Efforts toward the Reduction of Food Losses.* Tokyo: MAFF (in Japanese).

———. 2012f. *The System of Agricultural Production Corporations.* Tokyo: MAFF (in Japanese).

———. 2012g. *Research Report on the Map of the Radioactive Material Concentration in Farmland Soil.* Tokyo: MAFF (in Japanese).

———. 2011a. "Summary of Results of 2010 World Census of Agriculture and Forestry in Japan." Retrieved at http://www.maff.go.jp/j/tokei/census/afc/about/pdf/kakutei_ zentai.pdf on February 20, 2013 (in Japanese).

———. 2011b. *2010 Annual Report on Food, Agriculture and Rural Areas in Japan.* Retrieved at http://www.maff.go.jp/j/wpaper/w_maff/h22/pdf/z_2_3_2.pdf on March 26, 2013 (in Japanese).

———. 2011c. "Press Release on the Great East Japan Earthquake." Retrieved at http:// www.maff.go.jp/j/press/keiei/saigai/111125.html on May 9, 2013 (in Japanese).

———. 2011d. *Estimated Area Inundated by Tsunami of the Great East Japan Earthquake.* Tokyo: MAFF (in Japanese).

———. 2010a. *2009 Annual Report on Food, Agriculture and Rural Areas in Japan.* Retrieved at http://www.maff.go.jp/j/wpaper/w_maff/h21_h/trend/part1/chap3/c3 _05.html on March 26, 2013 (in Japanese).

———. 2010b. "2008 Summary of Results of 2008 Census of Fishery in Japan." Retrieved at http://www.maff.go.jp/j/tokei/census/fc/2008/pdf/gyogyou_census08_kakutei.pdf on March 27, 2013 (in Japanese).

————. 2010c. *Agricultural Census*. Tokyo: MAFF (in Japanese).

Magdoff, Fred, John Bellamy Foster, and Frederick H. Buttel, eds. 2000. *Hungry for Profit: The Agribusiness Threat to Farmers, Food, and the Environment*. New York: Monthly Review Press.

Makino, Atsushi. 2010. *Rethinking Damage to the Wildlife: Cultural Approaches in Rural Life*. Tokyo: Nobunkyo (in Japanese).

Martinez, Francisco, Gilberto Aboites, and Douglas H. Constance. 2013. "Neoliberal Restructuring, Neoregulation, and the Mexican Poultry Industry." *Agriculture and Human Values* 30 (4): 495–510.

Maruhama, Eriko. 2011. *The Dawn of Signing Activities against Atomic and Hydrogen Bombs*. Tokyo: Gaifu (in Japanese).

Mashima, Yoshitaka. 2011. "Food Crisis, Food Sovereignty and La Via Campesina." Pp. 125–160 in *Grand Design for Food Sovereignty: Japan Resisting Market Liberalization and Global New Trend*, edited by Takeshi Murata. Tokyo: Nosan Gyoson Bunka Kyokai (in Japanese).

Masugata, Toshiko. 2014. "Local Food and Agriculture." Pp. 169–188 in *Sociology of Food and Agriculture: From the Point of View of Life in the Region*, edited by Toshiko Masugata, Taniguchi Yoshimitsu, and Masashi Tachikawa. Kyoto: Minerva Shobo (in Japanese).

Masui, Yoshio, and Seishu Jo. 2003. "Market, Distribution and Price of Sea Foods." Pp. 139–152 in *Distribution and Market of Food and Agricultural Products*, edited by A. Takizawa, S. Kai, M. Hosokawa, and O. Hayakawa. Tokyo: Tsukuba Shobo.

Matsubara, Jiro. 1971. *Pollution and Local Society: Sociology of Life and Residents' Movement*. Tokyo: Nihon Keizai Shinbun Sha (in Japanese).

Matsushita Institute of Government and Management. 2014. "What's the Matsushita Institute of Government and Management?" Retrieved at http://www.mskj.or.jp/how/index.html on February 25, 2014 (in Japanese).

Maya-Ambia, Carlos J. 2012. "Globalization of Uncertainties: Lessons from Fukushima." Pp. 223–236 in *Globalization: Approaches to Diversity*, edited by Hector Cuadra-Montiel. Retrieved at http://www.intechopen.com/books/globalization-approaches-to-diversity/globalization-of-uncertainties-lessons-from-fukushima on August 30, 2014.

McMichael, Philip. 2013. *Agrarian Change and Peasant Studies*. Black Point, Canada: Fernwood Books.

————. 2007. *Development and Social Change*. Thousand Oaks, CA: Pine Forge Press.

METI (Ministry of Economy, Trade and Industry). 2000. "Enactment of Law Concerning the Adjustment of Retail Business Operations in Large-Scale Retail Sectors." Retrieved at http://www.meti.go.jp/policy/economy/distribution/daikibo/downloadfiles/rittihou.pdf on September 2, 2013 (in Japanese).

MFJ (Ministry of Finance of Japan). 2014. *How Large is Japan's Public Debt?* Retrieved at http://www.mof.go.jp/gallery/201407.htm on September 16, 2014 (in Japanese).

————. 2011. *Trade Statistics*. MFJ (in Japanese).

MHLW (Ministry of Health, Labor and Wealth). 2012a. *White Book on Health, Labor, and Wealth*. Retrieved at http://www.mhlw.go.jp/wp/hakusyo/kousei/12/ on January 1, 2014 (in Japanese).

————. 2012b. *New Criteria of Radioactive Materials in Food*. Tokyo: MHLW (in Japanese).

————. 2010. "Overview of National Livelihood Survey." Retrieved at http://www.mhlw.go.jp/toukei/saikin/hw/k-tyosa/k-tyosa10/ on January 1, 2015 (in Japanese).

MIC (Ministry of Internal Affairs and Communications). 2013. *The List of Governmental-Ordinance-Designated Cities*. Retrieved at http://www.soumu.go.jp/main_sosiki/jichi_gyousei/bunken/shitei_toshi-ichiran.html on December 5, 2013 (in Japanese).

———. 2008. *Report on Results of Past Census of Agriculture and Forestry in Japan.* Retrieved at http://www.e-stat.go.jp/SG1/estat/List.do?bid=000001012037&cycode=0/ on March 26, 2013 (in Japanese).

Michisaki Farm. 2013. *Application Form for Appointment of Enterprise in Special Zone for Reconstruction.* Gamo, Japan: Michisaki Farm (in Japanese).

Mikuni, Hidemi. 2000. *Development Process of Food Distribution Problems.* Tokyo: Tsukubashobo (in Japanese).

Miller, Lee M., Robert J. Antonio, and Alessandro Bonanno. 2011. "Hazards of Neoliberalism: Delayed Electric Power Restoration after Hurricane Ike." *British Journal of Sociology* 62 (3): 504–522.

Mirowski, Philip. 2013. *Never Let a Serious Crisis Go to Waste.* London. Verso.

Misawa, Takeo. 1969. "An Analysis of Part-Time Farming in the Postwar Period." Pp. 250–269 in *Agriculture and Economic Growth: The Japanese Experience*, edited by K. Ohkawa, B. F. Johnston, and H. Kaneda. Tokyo: University of Tokyo Press.

Mishima, Tokuzo. 2001a. *Deregulation and Agri-Food Market.* Tokyo: Nihon Keizai Hyoron Sha (in Japanese).

———. 2001b. "Development of Deregulation Policy and Agriculture and Agricultural Products." Pp. 33–69 in *Reorganization of the Japanese Agriculture and Market Issues*, edited by H. Mikuni and Y. Kurima. Tokyo: Tsukuba Shobo (in Japanese).

Mitsubishi Research Institute. 2011. *Proposal for Disaster Reconstruction.* April 8. Tokyo: Mitsubishi Research Institute (in Japanese).

Miyagi Prefecture. 2013. "Map of Shipping Restriction and Voluntary Restraints of Agricultural Products." Retrieved at http://www.r-info-miyagi.jp/r-info/restrictionmap/ on September 5, 2013 (in Japanese).

———. 2012. *Reconstruction after the Great East Japan Earthquake: Agriculture.* Sendai, Japan: Miyagi Prefecture (in Japanese).

Miyagi Prefecture Disaster Reconstruction Council. 2011. *The Organization of the Prefecture of Miyagi Disaster Reconstruction Council.* Sendai, Japan: Miyagi Prefecture (in Japanese).

Miyamoto, Kenichi. 1998. "Urban-Rural Coexistence and Interaction in the Era of Decentralization." Pp. 265–270 in *Regional Management and Endogenous Development*, edited by K. Miyamoto and H. Endo. Tokyo: Nobunkyo (in Japanese).

Mooney, Patrick H. 1988. *My Own Boss: Class, Rationality and the Family Farm.* Boulder, CO: Westview Press.

MOP (Momonoura Oyster Producers). 2014. "Footprint of MOP." Homepage of MOP. Retrieved at http://www.momonoura-kakillc.co.jp/story2011.html on August 14, 2014 (in Japanese).

Mori, Kahee. 2007. *Studies on Farmers' Revolts in Nambu Clan.* Tokyo: Hosei University Press (in Japanese).

Moriya, Fumio. 1971. *Postwar Japanese Capitalism.* Tokyo: Aoki Shoten (in Japanese).

Mukawa Town. 2004. *Agricultural Guide in Mukawa Town.* Mukawa, Japan: Mukawa Town (in Japanese).

———. 2002a. *Self-Reliance Plan of Mukawa Town as an Underpopulated Area.* Mukawa, Japan: Mukawa Town (in Japanese).

———. 2002b. *Memo of Meeting with Nittan Farm.* Mukawa, Japan: Mukawa Town (in Japanese).

Mukawa Town Agricultural Committee. 2004a. *Questionnaire on Buying and Selling of Farmland.* Mukawa, Japan: Mukawa Town Agricultural Committee (in Japanese).

———. 2004b. *News of Agricultural Committee.* Mukawa, Japan: Mukawa Town Agricultural Committee (in Japanese).

———. 2002. *Results of Intention Survey on Farming.* Mukawa, Japan: Mukawa Town Agricultural Committee (in Japanese).

———. 1998. *News of Agricultural Committee*. Mukawa, Japan: Mukawa Town Agricultural Committee (in Japanese).

———. 1995. *News of Agricultural Committee*. Mukawa, Japan: Mukawa Town Agricultural Committee (in Japanese).

———. 1992. *News of Agricultural Committee*. Mukawa, Japan: Mukawa Town Agricultural Committee (in Japanese).

Mulgan, Aurelia G. 2006. *Japan's Agricultural Policy Regime*. London: Routledge.

Murata, Takeshi. 2003. "Free Trade under the WTO Regime and Conversion of Agricultural Policies in Developed Countries." *Journal of Agriculture and Agricultural Cooperatives Research Institute* 29 (August): 1–14 (in Japanese).

Muroya, Arihiro. 2007. "Status Quo and Challenges in Corporate Involvement in Agriculture." *Journal of Agriculture and Forestry Finance (Norinkinyu)* 26 (2): 13–26 (in Japanese).

Nakajima, Makoto, and Kensaku Kanda, eds. 2001. *Perspective of the Agri-Food Market in the 21st Century*. Tokyo: Tsukuba Shobo (in Japanese).

Nakamura, Koji. 2002. "Trends and Challenges in Production of Domestic Tomatoes for Processing." *Nourin Kinyu* (Norinchukin Research Institute) August: 42–56 (in Japanese).

Nakano, Isshin, ed. 1998. *Agribusiness*. Tokyo: Yuhikaku (in Japanese).

Nakano, Isshin, and Sugiyama Michio, eds. 2001. *Globalization and International Agricultural Markets*. Tokyo: Tsukuba Shobo (in Japanese).

National Geographic. 2013. "Seconds from Disaster—Kobe Earthquake. National Geographic Video." Retrieved at http://videopediaworld.com/video/22564/Seconds-from-disaster-Kobe-Earthquake on May 22, 2013.

Niigata Prefecture. 2009. *Final Report on the Damage by Mid-Niigata Prefecture Earthquake in 2004*. Retrieved at http://www.pref.niigata.lg.jp/HTML_Article/174saisyuhou.pdf on May 7, 2013 (in Japanese).

Nikkei BP. 2011. "Reconstruction of Japan: Former Governor of Hyogo Prefecture Talks about 'Creative Reconstruction' in Kobe and the Future of Tohoku Region." Retrieved at http://www.nikkeibp.co.jp/article/reb/20110607/272974/ on June 10, 2013 (in Japanese).

———. 2008. "IBM Japan Dismissed 1,300 Employees." Retrieved at http://itpro.nikkeibp.co.jp/article/NEWS/20081210/321094/ on July 5, 2013 (in Japanese).

Nikkei Business. 2011. "Reasons Why Food Is Not Provided on the Table: Affected Food Processing Factories." *Nikkei Business*. April 18 (in Japanese).

Nikkei Newspaper. 2014. "Oysters in the Special Zone for Reconstruction Sold Nationwide." *Nikkei Newspaper*. August 11 (in Japanese).

———. 2013a. "IBM America's New 'Vein.'" *Nikkei Newspaper*. June 21 (in Japanese).

———. 2013b. "High Precision GPS Use in Industries. Preventing Car Accidents. Automatic Operation of Agricultural Machinery." *Nikkei Newspaper*. May 14 (in Japanese).

———. 2013c. "Will 'Petit Solar' Work on Farmland? Locally Produced and Locally Consumed Energy." *Nikkei Newspaper*. May 6 (in Japanese).

———. 2013d. "Reconciliation for Compensation for Nuclear Power Plant Accident in Deadlock. *Nikkei Newspaper*. May 4 (in Japanese).

———. 2013e. "Iris Oyama Establishes A New Corporation with an Agricultural Production Corporation to Seek Revolution in Agriculture." *Nikkei Newspaper*. April 25 (in Japanese).

———. 2013f. "Special Zone Systems. Increasing Competitiveness and Inviting Investments." *Nikkei Newspaper*. April 16 (in Japanese).

———. 2013g. "Itochu Corporation Established New Corporation after Acquisition of Dole's Businesses." *Nikkei Newspaper*. April 2 (in Japanese).

———. 2013h. "Solar Panel Supported by Pillars Possibly to Be Settled on Farmland. By the MAFF." *Nikkei Newspaper*. April 2 (in Japanese).

———. 2013i. "Labor Shortage as Failure of Reconstruction. Less than 0% of Progress 2 Years after the Disaster." *Nikkei Newspaper*. March 12 (in Japanese).

———. 2013j. "Indicated Path toward Zero Nuclear Power Plants by the Members of LDP and Experts." *Nikkei Newspaper*. March 9 (in Japanese).

———. 2013k. "25 Trillion Yen for Reconstruction Budget. Government Adds 6 Trillion Yen." *Nikkei Newspaper*. January 28 (in Japanese).

———. 2012a. "3rd Year of Reconstruction at Its Halfway [Point]. Favorable for Transportation Networks, Serious Delay for Decontamination." *Nikkei Newspaper*. December 28 (in Japanese).

———. 2012b. "Nomination Dismissal Started. Challenges [That] IBM Japan [Is] Facing." *Nikkei Newspaper*. November 26 (in Japanese).

———. 2012c. "Strategy for Zero Nuclear Power Plants Operating in 2030s. Decided in the Government Meeting." *Nikkei Newspaper*. September 14 (in Japanese).

———. 2012d. "Complete Nationalizing [of] TEPCO. 1 Trillion Yen of Investment by Nuclear Damage Liability Facilitation Fund." *Nikkei Newspaper*. July 31 (in Japanese).

———. 2012e. "The Accident in Fukushima. Radioactive Materials Was One-Sixth Amount of Chernobyl. 900,000 Tera Bq. Two Times More than Expected." *Nikkei Newspaper*. May 25 (in Japanese).

———. 2012f. "All Domestic Nuclear Power Plants Stopped for the First Time in Over 42 Years. Three Reactors of Tomari Plant under Control." *Nikkei Newspaper*. May 4 (in Japanese).

———. 2012g. "One Year after the Great East Japan Earthquake." *Nikkei Newspaper*. March 11 (in Japanese).

———. 2012h. "Still 340,000 of Evacuees, Cross-Prefectures 70,000 in Damaged Three Prefectures." *Nikkei Newspaper*. March 11 (in Japanese).

———. 2011a. "Special Zone for Reconstruction. Zero Corporate Tax. Five Years for Newly Established Corporations." *Nikkei Newspaper*. October 8 (in Japanese).

———. 2011b. "Construction of Eco-town in Affected Area by 20 Corporations' Alliance Including IBM Japan and Kagome." *Nikkei Newspaper*. September 1 (in Japanese).

———. 2011c. "Special Zone for Fishery without Restriction on Entry of Corporations. The Governor of Miyagi Prefecture." *Nikkei Newspaper*. May 31 (in Japanese).

———. 2011d. "Fukushima Daiichi Nuclear Power Plant. The Level 7 as the Worst. Emitting Quantity of Radioactive Materials." *Nikkei Newspaper*. April 12 (in Japanese).

Nippon Del Monte. 2013. "Corporation History." Retrieved at http://www.delmonte.co.jp /company/c_enkaku.html on June 21, 2013 (in Japanese).

Nomura Research Institute. 2011. *Proposal for Emergency Plan for Disaster Reconstruction*. Eleven proposals from March 30 to May 19. Tokyo: Nomura Research Institute (in Japanese).

Northern Tohoku Regional Development Office. 2009. *Recovery and Promotion of Industries in Kurihara Region*. Osaki, Japan: Northern Tohoku Regional Development Office.

Noumin Newspaper. 2013. "Nomado as Base of Reconstruction in Fukushima." *Noumin Newspaper*. January 7 (in Japanese).

Ogino, Takatoshi. 2002. *Mainstream of Japanese Agricultural Cooperative Reform: Can Agricultural Cooperatives Support Food and Agriculture in Japan?* Tokyo: Nihon Keizai Hyouronsha (in Japanese).

Ohkawa, Kazushi, Bruce F. Johnston, and Hiromitsu Kaneda, eds. 1970. *Agriculture and Economic Growth: The Japanese Experience*. Princeton, NJ: Princeton University Press.

Okada, Tomohiro. 2012a. *Regeneration of Regions after Earthquake Disaster: Recovery of Human Beings or "Structural Reform" under the Shock Doctrine?* Tokyo: Shin Nihon Press (in Japanese).

———. 2012b. "Expanding Reconstruction Gaps and Basic Viewpoints on Revitalization of the Local Society and Local Economy: Criticism of the Shock Doctrine Type Creative Reconstruction and Alternatives." Pp. 17–59 in *Breath of Reconstruction: Reconstruction of Humans and Revitalization of Agriculture, Forestry and Fisheries*. Tokyo: Nobunkyo (in Japanese).

———. 2007. "Globalization and Crisis of Rural Society." Pp. 209–230 in *Globalization and Agriculture in the World*, edited by I. Nakano and T. Okada. Tokyo: Otsuki Shoten (in Japanese).

———. 1998. "Conversion of Japanese Agri-Food Policy and Agribusinesses." Pp. 195–209 in *Agribusinesses*, edited by I. Nakano. Tokyo: Yuhikaku (in Japanese).

Okada, Tomohiro, and Japan Institute of Local Government, eds. 2013. *Reconstruction after the Earthquake and Municipality: Towards Humanitarian Reconstruction*. Tokyo: Jichitai Mondai Kenkyu Sha (in Japanese).

Okuma, Michiru. 2011. "The Transition and the Prospect of Regional Agriculture and Agricultural Policies under the Influence of Globalization." *Journal of Rural Problems* 46 (4): 26–37 (in Japanese).

Ooki, Shigeru. 2013. "Radioactive Pollution in Fresh Food among Retailers (Including Consumer Cooperatives)." *Journal of Rural Economics* 85 (3): 151–163 (in Japanese).

Orito, Etona. 2013. "Les Teikei: les Precurseurs au Japon de l'Agriculture Biologique; Face a la Catastrophe Nucleaire de Mars 2011." *Geographie et Cultures* 86:83–99.

Otsuka, Shigeru. 2005. *Satiated Japan Towards Asia: Behind the Scenes of a Large Food Importer*. Tokyo: Ieno Hikari Kyokai (in Japanese).

Otsuka, Shigeru, and Toyohiko Matsubara, eds. 2004. *Contemporary Food and Agribusinesses*. Tokyo: Yuhikaku (in Japanese).

Oyama, Toshio. 2004. "Diversified Marketing Systems for Organic Products and Trade in Japan." Paper presented at the Asian Productivity Organization Seminar on Organic Farming for Sustainable Agriculture, September 20–25, 2004, Taichung, Taiwan, ROC.

Parker, Gavin. 2005. "Sustainable Food? Teikei, Co-operatives and Food Citizenship in Japan and UK." Working paper in real estate and planning.

Parsons, Talcott. 1971. *The System of Modern Societies*. New York: Prentice Hall.

———. [1937] 1968. *The Structure of Social Action*. Volumes I and II. New York: The Free Press.

Prefecture of Iwate. 2011. *Basic Plans for Reconstruction*. Iwate, Japan: Prefecture of Iwate (in Japanese).

PRIMAFF (Policy Research Institute, Ministry of Agriculture, Forestry and Fisheries). 2012. *Suggestions about Recovery from the Great East Japan Earthquake Based on Analyses of Past Recovery Cases: Reorganization of Agriculture and Fisheries and toward the Reconstruction of Communities*. Retrieved at http://www.maff.go.jp/primaff/koho/seika/project/pdf/zirei.pdf on February 1, 2013 (in Japanese).

Prime Minister of Japan and His Cabinet. 2014. "Abenomics's Three Arrows." Retrieved at http://www.kantei.go.jp/jp/headline/seichosenryaku/sanbonnoya.html on May 24, 2014 (in Japanese).

Rai, Shunsuke. 2012. *Reform of Agribusiness in Indonesia: Export-Oriented Agricultural Development and Farmers*. Tokyo: Nihon Keizai Hyouronsha (in Japanese).

Raulet, Gérard. 2011. "Legitimacy and Globalization." *Philosophy and Social Criticism* 37 (3): 313–327.

Reconstruction Agency. 2013a. *Certified Programs for the Promotion of Reconstruction*. Tokyo: Reconstruction Agency (in Japanese).

———. 2013b. *Status Quo and Efforts of Reconstruction*. Tokyo: Reconstruction Agency (in Japanese).

———. 2012. "Basic Guidelines for Special Zone for Reconstruction." Retrieved at http://www.reconstruction.go.jp/topics/001094.html on May 13, 2013 (in Japanese).

Reconstruction Design Council in Response to the Great East Japan Earthquake. 2014. "Official Web-Site of the Reconstruction Design Council in Response to the Great East Japan Earthquake." Retrieved at http://www.jica.go.jp/english/our_work/thematic _issues/water/earthquake/related01.html on March 10, 2014.

———. 2011. *Towards Reconstruction: Hope beyond the Disaster.* Tokyo: Reconstruction Design Council of the Great Eastern Japan Earthquake (in Japanese).

Roberts, Michael. 2014. "Abenomics: A Keynesian Neoliberal." Retrieved at https:// thenextrecession.wordpress.com/2013/06/11/abenomics-a-keynesian-neoliberal/ on May 8, 2014.

Robinson, William. 2004. *A Theory of Global Capitalism.* Baltimore, MD: The Johns Hopkins University Press.

Rodriguez, Havidan, Enrico L. Quarantelli, and Russell Dynes, eds. 2007. *Handbook of Disaster Research.* New York: Springer.

Ronen, Shamir. 2008. "The Age of Responsibilization: On Market-Embedded Morality." *Economy and Society* 37 (1): 19.

Rose, Nikolas. 1996. *Inventing Our Selves: Psychology, Power and Personhood.* Cambridge: Cambridge University Press.

Rostow, Walter W. 1960. *The Stages of Economic Growth: A Non-Communist Manifesto.* Cambridge: Cambridge University Press.

Ruddle, Kenneth. 1984. "The Continuing of Traditional Management Practices: The Case of Japanese Coastal Fisheries." Pp. 159–179 in *The Traditional Management of Coastal Systems in Asia and the Pacific,* edited by K. Ruddle and R. E. Johannes. Paris: UNESCO.

Sadakiyo, Eiko. 2012. "Agricultural Sector in Acceleration of Corporations' Involvement." *Sumitomo Mitsui Trust Bank Monthly Review.* July: 1–7 (in Japanese).

Safina, Carl. 2011. *A Sea in Flames: The Deepwater Horizon Oil Blowout.* New York: Crown.

Saizeriya. 2013a. "Corporate Information." Retrieved at http://www.saizeriya.co.jp /corporate/information/outline/ on December 5, 2013 (in Japanese).

———. 2013b. "Tomato Farm in Sendai." Retrieved at http://www.saizeriya.co.jp /corporate/effort/factory/index.html on December 5, 2013 (in Japanese).

Sakai, Keiichi. 2012. "Damages of Fisheries in the Prefecture of Miyagi and Efforts to Reconstruct." *Nippon Suisan Gakkaishi* 78 (2): 285–287 (in Japanese).

Sakamoto, Kiyohiko, Yong-Ju Choi, and Larry L. Burmeister. 2007. "Framing Multifunctionality: Agricultural Policy Paradigm Change in South Korea and Japan?" *International Journal of Sociology of Food and Agriculture* 15 (1): 24–45.

Sakazume, Hiroshi. 1999. *Fresh Fruits and Vegetable Distribution in Contemporary Society: Structures and Logic of Distribution Restructuring by Large-Sized Retailers.* Tokyo: Tsukuba Shobo (in Japanese).

Samuels, Richard. 2013. *3.11: Disaster and Change in Japan.* Ithaca, NY: Cornell University Press.

Sankei Newspaper. 2013. "Prime Ministry Abe Withdrawing the Final Report on the Nuclear Power Plant Accident." *Sankei Newspaper.* March 13 (in Japanese).

Sassen, Saskia. 1998. *Globalization and Its Discontents.* New York: New Press.

Scott, James C. 1979. *The Moral Economy of the Peasant: Rebellion and Subsistence in Southeast Asia.* New Haven, CT: Yale University Press.

Sekine, Kae. 2013. "New Vegetable Production Project in Special Zones for Reconstruction of the Great Eastern Japan Earthquake: A Case Study of Agricultural Producer Michisaki." *Vegetable Information* 117:30–40 (in Japanese).

———. 2012. "Development of Large Scale Horticulture Managed by Corporations and Local Agriculture: A Case Study on Paprika Production by I LOVE Farm Tome." *Vegetable Information* 106:28–35 (in Japanese).

———. 2008. "Multinational Agribusiness Involvement in, and Withdrawal from, Regional Agriculture: A Case Study of Dole Japan's Fresh Vegetable Business." *Journal of the Rural Issues* 63:1–12 (in Japanese).

———. 2006. "A New Form of Multinational Agribusiness Involvement in Japanese Agriculture: A Case Study on Dole Japan's Fresh Vegetable Business." *Journal of Political Economy and Economic History* 193:16–30 (in Japanese).

Sekine, Kae, Jean-Pierre Boutonnet, and Shuji Hisano. 2008. "Emerging 'Standard Complex' and Corporate Social Responsibility of Agro-Food Businesses: A Case Study of Dole Food Company." *Kyoto Economic Review* 77 (1): 67–77.

Sekine, Kae, and Shuji Hisano. 2009. "Agribusiness Involvement in Local Agriculture as a 'White Knight'? A Case Study of Dole Japan's Fresh Vegetable Business." *International Journal of Sociology of Agriculture and Food* 16 (2): 70–89.

Sekishita, Minoru. 1987. *Trade Friction between Japan and the U.S. and Food Trade.* Tokyo: Dobunkan Shuppan (in Japanese).

Sendai City. 2013a. *Data Sendai 2013.* Sendai, Japan: Sendai City (in Japanese).

———. 2013b. "History of Sendai City." Retrieved at http://www.city.sendai.jp/shisei /ayumi.html on September 6, 2013 (in Japanese).

———. 2013c. *Efforts at Recovery and Reconstruction of Agriculture in Sendai City.* Sendai, Japan: Sendai City (in Japanese).

———. 2013d. "Support for Emergency Installation of Greenhouses." Retrieved at http:// www.city.sendai.jp/business/d/1208713_1434.html on September 6, 2013 (in Japanese).

———. 2013e. *List of Certified Farmers and Farming Corporations in the Special Zone for Reconstruction.* Sendai, Japan: Sendai City (in Japanese).

———. 2012a. "Shipping Restriction of Shiitake Mushrooms Produced in Sendai City." Retrieved at http://www.city.sendai.jp/hoshano/1203255_2762.html on September 5, 2013 (in Japanese).

———. 2012b. *Construction of an Agri-Food Frontier in the Eastern District.* Sendai, Japan: Sendai City (in Japanese).

———. 2007. *The Basic Plan for Sendai Agriculture.* Sendai, Japan: Sendai City (in Japanese).

Sendai Suisan. 2013. "Profiles of Sendai Suisan's Group Corporations." Retrieved at http:// www.sendaisuisan.co.jp/grp_profile/index.html on July 12, 2013 (in Japanese).

———. 2012. "Advancing Projects Connecting Miyagi and Mie Prefectures." *Goshinsen* 68 (1): 2–5 (in Japanese).

Shimada, Katsumi, Toshiharu Shimowatari, Katsumi Oda, and Miyuki Shimizu. 2006. *Food and Trading Companies.* Tokyo: Nihon Keizai Hyouronsha (in Japanese).

Shimamoto, Tomio. 2011. "Postwar Farmland System and Its Revision and Effects." Pp. 8–36 in *Regeneration of Local Agriculture and Farmland Systems,* edited by S. Harada. Tokyo: Nobunkyo (in Japanese).

Shimizu, Junichi, Bannai Hisashi, and Shigeno Ryuichi, eds. 2013. *From Recovery to Construction of Locally Circulating Society: Sustainable Development of Agriculture and Rural Society.* Tokyo: Norin Tokei Shuppan (in Japanese).

Shimizu, Miyuki. 1995. *History of the Anti-pollution Movement in the Modernization of Japan.* Tokyo: Nihon Keizai Hyoron Sha (in Japanese).

Shimizu, Shuji. 2011. *Can We Still Commit Our Future to Nuclear Power Plants? The Accident in Fukushima.* Tokyo: Jichitai Kenkyu Sha (in Japanese).

SME (Organization for Small and Medium Enterprises and Regional Innovation, Japan). 2012. *Research Report: Current Situation and Challenges of Fish Processing in Affected Areas.* Tokyo: Organization for Small and Medium Enterprises and Regional Innovation, Japan. Retrieved at http://www.smrj.go.jp/keiei/dbps_data/_material_/b _0_keiei/chosa/pdf/fukkousuisankakou.pdf on August 14, 2014 (in Japanese).

Statistics Bureau, Ministry of Internal Affairs and Communications. 2015. "Labor Force Survey." Retrieved at http://www.stat.go.jp/index.htm on January 1, 2015 (in Japanese).

Stedman Jones, Daniel. 2012. *Masters of the Universe*. Princeton, NJ: Princeton University Press.

Stiglitz, Joseph E. 2013. *The Price of Inequality*. New York: W. W. Norton.

———. 2003. *The Roaring Nineties*. New York: W. W. Norton.

Sumida, Tomoo. 2013. "Elasticized Commission Rates in Central Wholesale Markets." Agricultural Management Support Center. Retrieved at http://nougyou-shien.jp/kenkyu/kaiin-itaku.html#top on July 12, 2013 (in Japanese).

Tabata, Tamotsu. 2008. "Japanese Agriculture and Its Locality: Trends after 2000." Pp. 129–169 in *Global Capitalism and Agriculture*, edited by Rural Issues Association of Japan. Tokyo: Tsukuba Shobo (in Japanese).

———. 1990. "Land Issues and Agricultural Policies in Modern Japan." Pp. 197–220 in *International Agricultural Adjustment and Agricultural Protection*, edited by I. Nakano, T. Otahara, and M. Goto. Tokyo: Nosanson Bunka Kyokai (in Japanese).

Tada, Kenichiro. 1999. "Municipal Mergers and Resident Autonomy in Underpopulated Areas." Pp. 103–118 in *Regional Development in Transition*, edited by M. Nakajima and R. Hashimoto. Kyoto: Nakanishiya (in Japanese).

Takaono Town. 2004. *Report on Agricultural Production Corporations*. Takaono, Japan: Takaono Town (in Japanese).

Takaono Town Agricultural Committee. 2002. *The Granting of the Rights of Users*. Takaono, Japan: Takaono Town Agricultural Committee (in Japanese).

Takeda, Kyoji. 2014. "Rural Social Policies and Reactions from Rural Society under Neoliberalism." Pp. 33–54 in *Regions, Agriculture and Agricultural Cooperatives under Neoliberalism*, edited by K. Kanda. Tokyo: Tsukuba Shobo (in Japanese).

Takizawa, Akiyoshi, and Masashi Hosokawa, eds. 2000. *Distribution Reorganization and Agri-Food Market*. Tokyo: Tsukuba Shobo (in Japanese).

Takizawa, Akiyoshi, Satoshi Kai, Masashi Hosokawa, and Osamu Hayakawa, eds. 2003. *Distribution and Markets for Food and Agricultural Products*. Tokyo: Tsukuba Shobo (in Japanese).

Tanaka, Keiko. 2008. "Seven Samurai to Protect 'Our' Food: The Reform of Food Safety Regulatory System in Japan after the BSE Crisis of 2001." *Agriculture and Human Values* 25 (4): 567–580.

Taniguchi, Kenji. 2006. "Agricultural Products Trade in Eastern Asia and Globalization: The Possibility of Regional Agriculture Development through Export of High-Quality Agricultural Products." *Journal of Rural Problems* 41 (4): 16–26 (in Japanese).

Taniguchi, Nobukazu. 2008. "Regional Agriculture under Economic Globalization: Examining Various Possibilities." *Journal of Rural Economics* 80 (2): 49–54 (in Japanese).

Taniwaki, Osamu. 2011. "Background and Status Quo of Stock Companies' Involvement in Agriculture." Pp. 201–217 in *Regeneration of Local Agriculture and Farmland Systems*, edited by S. Harada. Tokyo: Nobunkyo (in Japanese).

Tashiro, Yoichi. 2012. "Trans-Pacific Partnership Agreement and the Great Eastern Japan Earthquake: Opposition to Disaster Capitalism." *Agriculture and Agricultural Cooperatives Studies* 48:2–14 (in Japanese).

———. 2011. *Opposition Movement to Trans Pacific Partnership Agreement towards Reconstruction of Agriculture*. Tokyo: Tsukuba Shobo (in Japanese).

———. 2005. *The Figure of "Bottom Line of Postwar Agricultural Policies": A Criticism of the New Basic Plan*. Tokyo: Tsukuba Shobo (in Japanese).

———. 2003. *An Introduction to Agricultural Issues*. Tokyo: Otsuki Shoten (in Japanese).

Teruoka, Shuzo, ed. 2008. *Agriculture in the Modernization of Japan (1850–2000)*. New Delhi: Manohar.

Teshima, Masaki. 1966. *Japanese State Monopoly Capitalism*. Tokyo: Yuhikaku (in Japanese).

Tierney, Kathleen J. 2006. "Businesses and Disasters: Vulnerability, Impacts, and Recovery." Pp. 405–412 in *The Handbook of Disaster Research*, edited by Havidan Rodriguez, Enrico L. Quarantelli, and Russell L. Dynes. New York: Springer.

Toho Area Research Institute. 2011. "Damage to the Fishing Industry by the Great Eastern Japan Earthquake: From the 2011 Fisheries White Paper." *Future of Fukushima (Fukushima no Shinro)* 352:20–21. Fukushima: Toho Area Research Institute (in Japanese).

Tohoku Regional Agricultural Administration Office, Sendai City, Sendai Agricultural Cooperative and Land Improvement District of Eastern Sendai. 2011a. *Toward the Future of the Region: Eastern Area of Sendai City*. Sendai, Japan: Agricultural Administration Office (in Japanese).

———. 2011b. *Questions and Answers at the First Briefing Session*. Sendai, Japan: Agricultural Administration Office (in Japanese).

Tokyo Newspaper. 2011. "The Enactment of the Basic Law of Reconstruction. Reconstruction Agency and Special Zones for Reconstruction Will Be Established." *Tokyo Newspaper*. June 21 (in Japanese).

Tome City. 2008. *Tome City's Basic Plan for Food, Agriculture and Rural Community: Vision of Tome City's Agriculture Promotion*. Tome, Japan: Agricultural Office.

Toyoda, Takashi. 2001. *International Development in the Age of Agribusiness: Trade of Agro-Food Products and Multinational Corporations*. Tokyo: Nobunkyo (in Japanese).

Tsuchiya, Keizo. 1969. "Economics of Mechanization in Small-Scale Agriculture." Pp. 155–171 in *Agriculture and Economic Growth: Japan's Experience*, edited by K. Ohkawa, B. F. Johnston, and H. Kaneda. Tokyo: University of Tokyo Press.

Tsunashima, Fujio. 2014. "Issues in the Establishment Process of 'the Special Zones for Reconstruction of Fisheries' in the Prefecture of Miyagi and Challenges for the Future: Significance of Fishing Rights and the Area Fishery Adjustment Committee." *Journal of the North Japan Fisheries Economics* 42:61–71 (in Japanese).

———. 2012. "Special Zones for Fisheries Reconstruction and Fishing Rights." *Northern Japan Fisheries* 40:49–51 (in Japanese).

Tsunashima, Fujio, and Seiji Ogawa. 2013. "The Formation Process of Special Zones for Reconstruction for Fisheries in the Prefecture of Miyagi and Its Problems." Paper presented at the forty-second Congress of the North Japan Fisheries Economics Society, November 9–10 (in Japanese).

Tsuru, Rieko. 2014. "Women in Rural Society: Empowerment and Value Creation." Pp. 233–252 in *Sociology of Food and Agriculture: From the Point of View of Life and Region*, edited by Toshiko Masugata, Taniguchi Yoshimitsu, and Masashi Tachikawa. Kyoto: Minerva Shobo (in Japanese).

Tsurumi, Yoshiyuki. 1982. *The Banana and the Japanese: Between Philippines Plantations and the Japanese Table*. Tokyo: Iwanami-Shoten (in Japanese).

Tsutaya, Eiichi. 2000a. *Ecological Agriculture: Strategies for Regeneration of Food and Agriculture*. Tokyo: Ieno Hikari Kyokai (in Japanese).

———. 2000b. "Status Quo of Corporate Involvement in Agriculture and Agricultural Corporations: Questioning Agricultural Cooperatives' Existence." *Journal of Agriculture and Forestry Finance* 53 (5): 32–49 (in Japanese).

Uchida, Takio. 2011. "Process of Recovery and Reconstruction in the Mid-Niigata Prefecture Earthquake in 2004." *Norin-Kinyu*. August: 66–74 (in Japanese).

Underhill, G., and X. Zhang. 2008. "Setting the Rules: Private Power, Political Underpinnings, and Legitimacy in Global Monetary and Financial Governance." *International Affairs* 84 (3): 535–554.

Usami, Shigeru. 1990. "Postwar Transformation of Owner-Farmers and Operators' Problems." Pp. 221–248 in *International Agricultural Adjustment and Agricultural Protection*, edited by I. Nakano, T. Otahara, and M. Goto. Tokyo: Nosanson Bunka Kyokai (in Japanese).

Uzawa, Hirofumi. 1996. *What Is "Narita": A Tragedy in Postwar Japan.* Tokyo: Iwanami Shoten (in Japanese).

Vogel, Ezra Feivel. 1979. *Japan as Number One: Lessons for America.* Cambridge, MA: Harvard University Press.

Waswo, Ann, and Yoshiaki Nishida. 2002. *Farmers and Village Life in Twentieth-Century Japan.* London: Routledge.

West Izumi Land Improvement District. 1972. *History of West Land Improvement District.* West Izumi, Japan: West Izumi Land Improvement District (in Japanese).

Wittman, Hanna, Annette Aurèlie Desmarais, and Nettie Wiebe. 2010. *Food Sovereignty: Reconnecting Food, Nature and Community.* Oakland, CA: Food First.

Wolf, Steven A., and Alessandro Bonanno. 2014. *The Neoliberal Regime in the Agri-Food Sector: Crisis, Resilience, and Restructuring.* New York: Routledge.

Wright, Wynne, and Gerad Middendorf. 2007. *The Fight over Food.* University Park: Pennsylvania State University Press.

Xu, Beina. 2013. "Abenomics and the Japanese Economy." Retrieved at http://www.cfr.org /japan/abenomics-japanese-economy/p30383?cid=rss-analysisbriefbackgroundersexp -abenomics_and_the_japanese_eco-040413 on May 8, 2014.

Yamada, Akira, H. Endo, and T. Hobo. 1998. "The Present State of Regional Policy and New Perspectives on Public Policy." Pp. 265–270 in *Regional Management and Endogenous Development,* edited by K. Miyamoto and H. Endo. Tokyo: Nobunkyo (in Japanese).

Yamada, Jun. 2013. "4.2% Unemployment Rate. Is It Really Improved after Three Months? What Are the Mechanisms that Make the Rate Differ from the Reality?" *Yahoo News.* March 1. Retrieved at http://bylines.news.yahoo.co.jp/yamadajun/20130301-00023692/ on January 1, 2015 (in Japanese).

Yamao, Masahiro. 2011. "Globalizing Fishery and Marine Product Trade in Eastern Asia." Pp. 131–157 in *Current Food and Agriculture,* edited by K. Ikegami and K. Harayama. Kyoto: Nakanishiya (in Japanese).

Yamao, Masahiro, and Takashi Torrii. 2000. "Sea Food Imports in Japan: Transition of Demand and New Supply System." Pp. 225–247 in *Food Market Issues under Reorganization: Cases of Fresh Foods,* edited by H. Mikuni. Tokyo: Tsukuba Shobo (in Japanese).

Yasuda, Shigeru. 1986. *Organic Farming in Japan.* Tokyo: Diamond Press (in Japanese).

Yokoyama, Hidenobu. 2011. "Reconstruction of Neglected People's Rights to Life and Personality. Is Neoliberal Totalitarianism? Critique of Creative Reconstruction in Agriculture, Forestry and Fisheries." Pp. 49–55 in *Cause for Reconstruction: Criticism of Neoliberal Reconstruction Trampling Victims' Dignity.* Tokyo: Nobunkyo (in Japanese).

——. 2008. "Trends of WTO Agricultural Negotiations and Basic Features of 'Agricultural Policy Reform.'" Pp. 39–79 in *Global Capitalism and Agriculture,* edited by Rural Issues Association of Japan. Tokyo: Tsukuba Shobo (in Japanese).

——. 2000. "Reorganization of Price and Income Policies for Wheat and Soybeans." Pp. 203–228 in *Changes of Agricultural Policies and Price and Income Policies,* edited by T. Murata and T. Mishima. Tokyo: Tsukuba Shobo (in Japanese).

Yorimitsu, Ryozo, ed. 2011. *Deer and Forests in Japan.* Tokyo: Tsukiji Shokan (in Japanese).

Yoshikawa, Hiroshi. 2009. "Japanese Economy: Domestic Demand-Led Recovery and Potential for Sustainable Development." Special lecture delivered at RIETI Seminar, Tokyo, July 3. Retrieved at http://www.rieti.go.jp/jp/events/09070301/yoshikawa.html on August 1, 2015 (in Japanese).

Yoshioka, Hitoshi. 2011. *Social History of Nuclear Energy in Japan.* New edition. Tokyo: Asahi Shinbun (in Japanese).

You, Gyunghee, Ginu Lee, and ShigeoYoshida. 2011. "Neoliberalism and Agricultural Cooperatives." *Report of Japan-Cooperative General Research Institute* 18 (Summer): 30–37 (in Japanese).

Yukitomo, Wataru. 2013. "Reopening the Debate on 'Stock Company's Property in Farm-land.'" Retrieved at http://www.google.co.jp/url?sa=t&rct=j&q=&esrc=s&source=web&cd=2&ved=0CCMQFjAB&url=http%3A%2F%2Fwww.nochuri.co.jp%2Ftopics%2Fpdf%2F20130628new.pdf&ei=zCyiVID2KMWnNriUgbAH&usg=AFQjCNEYod3VSuxbrYxLylmsEJwoturdZg on December 29, 2014 (in Japanese).

Zhang, Juan, Gaowa Bao, and Toshio Nomiyama. 2011. "A Study on the Status and Evaluation of Processed Tomato Contract Cultivation: Based on the Contract Price." *Agricultural Marketing Journal of Japan* 20 (2): 22–27.

INDEX

Abe, Shinzo: neoliberal policies, 6, 11, 102, 177, 178, 188–189, 202–203; nuclear power industry and, 79, 82, 92n13

Abe administration, SZR program and, 81

Abenomics, 11, 90–91n1, 178, 185n2, 189, 202–204; positive results from, 206n9

Aeon, 64, 139, 140, 145, 150n11, 152n25

Agricultural Basic Law of 1961, 48–49, 52, 60, 97, 190. *See also* New Agricultural Basic Law

Agricultural committees, 131n7, 206n12; neoliberal policies and, 177, 203

Agricultural cooperatives. *See* Farming cooperatives

Agricultural Land Act: Creative Reconstruction and, 73; deregulation of, 98; Dole Japan and bypass of intent of, 121, 129; family farms and, 46, 66, 190; land ownership and, 110, 112; restructuring, 61, 62, 80, 81

Agricultural Marketing Society of Japan, 30

Agricultural output, value of, 68n21

Agricultural Production Corporations, 60

Agriculture Management Entities, 59, 68n23

Agri-food: concept of, 1–2; evolution under Neoliberalism, 2, 11. *See also* Japanese agri-food

Agri Produce (Dole Japan), 110

Agro-ecology, 58

Aichi Prefecture, Dole Japan and broccoli market in, 114–115

Akinori, 144

Alternative energy in Japan, 82–83

Alternative forms of agri-food, 36

Alternative reconstruction plans, Iwate fishery, 164–165

American IT, agri-food market and, 93

Anticorporate violence, 183

Antinuclear movement, Fukushima-Daiichi disaster and, 25–26, 76

Aquaculture, 64, 88, 154, 169n11

Area Fishery Adjustment Committee, 28, 162, 163, 177, 184

Artificial negativity, 17, 37n1

Association for the Promotion of Industry (Tome), 128

Atsuma (Hokkaido), 116

Banana market, 94, 105n3

Basic Act on Reconstruction, 79, 155–156, 157

Basic Plan for Sendai Agriculture (report), 134

Basic Plan of Reconstruction, Iwate, 165

Basic Policies of Reconstruction of the Prefecture of Miyagi, 158

Beck, Ulrich, 24–25, 91n6

Becker, Gary, 205n6

Block, Fred, 24

Bourdieu, Pierre, 197

Bretton Woods, collapse of, 40, 50

Broccoli production, 105n6; Dole Japan and, 108, 114–115, 118, 121, 123, 124–125

Broilers (chickens), corporate industrial strategies for, 32–33

Butai Agri Innovation, 139, 151n12, 151n13

Butai Farm, 138–140, 145, 146, 150n8, 150n10, 151n12

Canon, 85

Capitalism and Freedom (Friedman), 193

Castle & Cook, 94, 105n3

Central Wholesale Market, 56–57

Central Wholesale Market Law of 1923, 56

Certified agricultural producers, 131n4; Izumi Farm as, 122, 124; Nittan Farm as, 116; resistance and delaying corporate, 183; Tome Farm as, 127

Challenge Plan for the 21st Century (reconstruction plan), 147–148

Chernobyl nuclear accident, 75, 91n5

Chiba, Tsukasa, 18

Civil society, response to disasters, 25–26

Climate change, consequences of disasters and, 24

CPSIA information can be obtained
at www.ICGtesting.com
Printed in the USA
LVOW13s2355131017
552413LV00026B/1515/P